The Way It Was

Thank you for your loyalty and love
to the Technion and Israel.

Amos Horev

A.H.

November 2024

The Way It Was

An Autobiography

Unique Israeli leader and visionary

By Amos Horev

Hebrew edition editor: Efrat Mass

Translation: Eetta Prince Gibson

English edition editor: David A. Guberman

Peter E. Randall Publisher
Portsmouth, New Hampshire
2024

©2024 Amos Horev

All rights reserved.

ISBN: 978-1-942155-73-7

Library of Congress Control Number: 2024908187

English edition publisher:

Peter E. Randall Publisher

5 Greenleaf Woods Drive, Suite 102

Portsmouth, NH 03801

Printed in the United States of America

English translation: Eetta Prince Gibson

English edition editor: David A. Guberman

©2020 Carmel Publishing; Hebrew edition

ISBN Hebrew edition: 978-965-7778-34-0

Hebrew editor: Efrat Mass

Cover design: Yanay Segal

Front cover photographer: Robert Osborn

To my Shanka; to our children, Yehiam and Nira; and to the entire Horev clan.

Contents

List of Photographs

The Ballad of the Beds

The Ballad of the Beds

In a room, in Ma'ale Hachamisha, four guys
and four beds.
Four go out to battle—three return
And one is missing.
One death and four beds
One made and three rumpled.
They go out again—and return, and now two deaths
Two made and two buried.
And two more are added to fill the ranks
And now—
In our room are four guys and four beds
Until the next battle . . .
Go into action
And it all repeats itself
In a strange sequence
And every bed results in a death.

Eitan Yarkoni wrote these words after the battle of the Kastel in April 1948 to break the Arab siege of Jerusalem and published them in his book, *The Palmach Way—Diaries and Memories,* which he handed out to his friends. And he also wrote:

> *At night, at night we went to collect the hidden weapons, and in the morning we recovered the bodies of the ten fallen soldiers and buried them. The next day, the bereaved parents arrived, and they*

1

asked to hear every possible detail about what happened to their loved ones. We sat with them, our heads bowed, and we did not know how or what to tell them.

And as it turned out, the parents who had lost that which is most precious to them were the ones who encouraged us to go on and to be "strong." "Take care of yourselves," one of the parents said as they left.

"How can we take care of ourselves?" Shmulik whispered to me. "We won't stick our heads out to return fire? We won't get up and charge the enemy?"

That evening I sat alone in the empty room and looked at Tzafrir and Kashavala's beds, and suddenly, as if in a daze, I grabbed a scrap of paper and a pencil and wrote "The Ballad of the Beds."

It was there, during those difficult times when nothing could be taken for granted and results couldn't be predicted, that I built the foundations for the ideas and values that have stayed with me throughout my life. Today, now that I am ninety-nine years old, decades after the struggles in which I took part and some of which I had initiated, I look at life with wonder and awe. I am at peace with the opportunity to provide an honest view of history for a new generation, a generation for whom the existence of the state is a given and for whom security is not laced with existential questions and a sense that we may not succeed. And maybe, just maybe, I will contribute something to the next generation's deep commitment, so that they will not be complacent or arrogant, and so that they will feel a sense of mission to preserve everything we began.

My life has been intertwined with the lives of many of my contemporaries, which is not unusual. The success belongs to all of us—a generation fortunate enough to have been born at an extraordinary intersection in time: the beginning of the formation of an ideological, creative, and security-focused critical mass, the height of which was the establishment of that which we should never-take-for-granted—the Jewish State, the State of Israel—which was followed by the establishment and design of its institutions, which we also seemed to create as if out of nothing. On my eightieth birthday, my friend Tsera (Lieutenant-General Zvi Tsur—the sixth IDF chief of staff) said:

> *If I review the story of your life, I see clearly that it is actually a roadmap of the State of Israel. We find the challenges, missions, values and our most important objectives at every stop along the way:* Haganah, Palmach, the IDF, Rafael, and the Technion. *I almost forgot the stories of "Burma Road" in which you put all your talents to use. Our generation, undeniably, made history and contributed so much to the fulfillment of the Zionist dream . . .*

All my years I have been busy doing, and I never devoted time or value to looking back, to taking stock. I allowed myself to talk about myself only among my family and close friends. We are made of the same stuff, and among ourselves there is so much that we can take for granted and that does not require so many words or explanations.

Today I am in a place from which I can take a broad view of the past, viewing myself, that period in time, and my contemporaries. I chose to delve beyond the "taken for granted" and lay out my life story—the story of a generation. With trepidation, in measured steps, I began writing this book. Slowly, from out of the details, the image that is greater than my own personal story began to become clearer. An unpolished, unpoetic image of the generation of 1948 and its roots, what it meant to establish a state under the conditions in those times, and an inside glance at the process of the formation of the Israel Defense Forces, based on the experiences of fighters and survivors.

I look at what was imprinted on me in my youth as if they are the stories of the rings of a tree trunk. A tree's secrets are hidden in its trunk. The trunk is made of the rings created by the span of its life. In this book, I imagine myself looking at those rings that make up my life story, and each ring is a part of who I am. I have chosen to return to the rings in the center—to tell about the four anchors that shaped who I am, to which I owe all that I have accomplished in my life:

My father's house, a house that believed in science, technology, and education.

My childhood in Jerusalem during the 1920s and '30s of the past century, "a small city of Jewish and Arab neighborhoods," two kindergartens, and one Gymnasia.

Affiliation to the palmach, the militant youth movement of the labor, training and fighting in the toughest years of the struggle to establish the state. After the Palmach and keeping to its spirit, continuing on to leadership and achievements in the IDF, from its establishment through to the Yom Kippur War. The technological world that I was fortunate enough to enter during my childhood thanks to my father, and a higher education at the best institutions. I have had the privilege of serving in positions that gave me the opportunity to harness technology at its best in service to security and civic institutions.

And the fourth anchor, Shanka, my wife, the love of my life from the first day that I met her and through all of the years that we have been together, as she would say, always there for each other. Over the chapters of our tumultuous life we created a family, beginning with our children—Yehiam and Nira—that expanded to include their partners, grandchildren, and great-grandchildren. Our together ended when she passed away, leaving me without my second half, learning a new chapter in life about the pain of loneliness and about the slow withdrawal from public activity and losing the ability to make a difference.

Amos Horev, November 2019

CHAPTER 1

I Carry within Me the Seal of Jerusalem, Where I was Born and Raised

I was born in and into Jerusalem in 1924. In those days, Jerusalem felt like an international city and it had everything: Jews, both religious and secular, Muslims, Christians; some in separate neighborhoods and some in mixed neighborhoods; some within the walls of the old city and some outside the walls in new neighborhoods that had just been built. Just over half the residents were Jewish, and the total number of residents didn't exceed sixty-nine thousand. The center of the British Mandate in the Land of Israel, the most important Arab institutions for the management of Muslim affairs in the Land of Israel, including the Supreme Arab Committee and the offices of the Mufti of Jerusalem, and the national institutions of the Jewish state-in-the-making were all found there.

Growing up in Jerusalem was not the same as growing up in Tel Aviv, the Hebrew city from which you needed to go as far as Jaffa to discover that Arabs lived there, too. Anyone who grew up in Jerusalem absorbed, unknowingly, the roots of the problematics of the establishment of a Jewish state in a Muslim-Arab region ruled by a foreign government. Any time you walked by the Schneller neighborhood, for example, you risked being stoned. I remember the houses across from that neighborhood, where Arabs and Germans lived. Traces of those days can still be seen in the names of German cities that were etched into the walls of the houses in the Schneller neighborhood.

During the first year of my life, my parents were a part of a team of "attendants," as my father referred to them, at the residence of the first British high commissioner, Lord Herbert Samuel. My father was the main mechanic for the house. When I was born, the high commissioner's wife arrived at our house with gifts and held me in her arms. Even back then I didn't follow the proper etiquette, and I threw up on her.

When I was young, a student in secondary school, our class was taken to experience hospitality at the commissioner's residence. Senegalese servants with their red sashes served us small sandwiches on silver platters. We also met with other, non-Jewish schools in sports competitions.

Most of the people who lived in the Bukharan neighborhood where we lived were poor, and only their children's generation fulfilled their hopes for formal education. This was the atmosphere. The kitchen and the bathroom were in the yard. Today, when every home has a faucet, it's difficult to imagine life without running water in the house, just like it was in the nineteenth century. My mother would send me to the well at the Moussaieff's residence with a bucket, and I learned to pump the "plunger," because you could start drawing the water only after you did that. We would shower once a week in some sort of a tub. We heated the water tank with sawdust soaked in fuel oil. And yet, despite it all, I have no hard feelings; rather, I remember my joy, a child whose childhood was filled with so many different experiences.

There were only a few kindergartens, and I went to the kindergarten run by Hasya Sukenik. Later, they changed their last name to Yadin. The preschool was in the Zichron Moshe neighborhood, the first modern Hebrew kindergarten outside the walls of the Old City, located in the center of Jerusalem, between Nevi'im Street and Shabbat Square in Mea She'arim.

As a teenager, Yigael Yadin taught me how to trace a picture out of a book using tracing paper, and that image is still in my mind to this very day. When we grew up a little, I was on a radio show that broadcast plays he had written. We were four friends from Hasya

The kindergarten

Sukenik's kindergarten, and together we all found our way into the youth movement and the Palmach: Uzi Narkiss, Elad Peled, Matti Peled—and me. We all finished our military service as major generals in the IDF General Staff.

By the time I attended the Tachkemoni School, people were already trying to instill Yiddishkeit in me. And I, who grew up in a secular home both in terms of its daily routines and our parents' worldviews, did not meet my teachers' expectations, usually because I was so mischievous. The teacher, whose nickname was "Lulu" and would later become a member of Knesset, would bring me up to the podium to hit me with a ruler before the lesson even started, as a preventative measure, so I wouldn't start fooling around. When the teacher tried to convince my mother that I should become a cantor, my mother quickly transferred me to a school for workers' children on Abyssinian Street where the teaching and education were more in line with her socialistic views. Not even a year had gone by when we found out that studying at school was a low priority compared to raising rabbits and working with the livestock. My parents, for whom education was the most important thing, transferred me to the Hebrew Gymnasia as soon as the school year was over, and that was where I completed my studies. All the teachers were men, apart from two women, both English teachers. Among the teachers were Ben Zion Gettler, A. A. Kabak, Ledzinski, Avizohar, and Carmon Kalai. Shloosh, Bartana, and Mohilever, the principals, were deeply rooted in the essence of Jerusalem. Teacher Gettler would invite us to his home to talk about anything in the curriculum that had not been forbidden by the British Mandate, mostly about Zionist values and the youth movements. Teacher Kalai, on the other hand, would tell us, in the middle of a lesson, about his time as a teacher in Iraq. We were twenty-four students in the math and sciences track, our teachers were our role models, and we were always watching and absorbing their way of life.

CHAPTER 2

The Influence of My Father's Home

As I was preparing to write my life story, I reviewed an interview that Ezra Greenboim conducted with my father in 1987, and his words are brought here and in the final chapter of this book, as though we are listening to him tell about the home that had such a profound influence on me and about his own character, which shaped my future life:

> When I married Tova I told her: "Listen, we're going to make a deal. I take care of money, you will never be wanting for anything, and you make sure we have a home, that the children get an education, etc. etc." And that's how we lived all our lives. I didn't interfere in raising the children or in their education. I did not attend a single parent-teacher meeting at any school, she was always the one who went. When there was a siege on Jerusalem my wife took care of everything. She would leave the house with a handbag with all the documents and deeds relating to the house, the money we had, and our Boxer dog. And Tova would go and buy bread, she would buy whatever there was to buy. There wasn't much to buy in the market. (Ezra Greenboim, "An interview with Amos Horev" [Yigal Allon Publishing, May–July 1987])

My mother, Tova (Genya, in Polish) Itzkowitz was born in 1903 and raised in Warsaw, Poland, and she received a secular education even though there were many religious philosophers and rabbis in her family. She was a graduate of the Hebrew Seminar for Teachers and Kindergarten teachers, which was headed by Shmuel Leib Gordon, the noted Hebrew educator, writer, and editor. Her knowledge of Hebrew

My mother, Tova (in Polish Genya) Itzkowitz

was excellent. In Warsaw, she worked as a kindergarten teacher and knew educator Janusz Korczak. In 1922, at the age of nineteen, she arrived in Israel, about two years after my father. They apparently met while he was working for the British army in Camp Sarafand (known today as Tzrifin) in the central part of Israel. She taught my father Hebrew. We don't know anything about their courtship or how they felt about each other. Our lives proceeded precisely as my father had mapped out—my mother at home with the children and my father spending most if not all of his time at work, or, more accurately, his calling, as he understood it to provide for his family and to simultaneously help the Haganah organization with the skills he was so good at: the repair, design, and manufacture of weapons.

My parents—Tova and Elek

At the same time, he would solve technological problems in the civil economy, since knowledge on this subject in Israel in the '20s was very minimal.

That's how my father was, he and the technological world were one, and when my father would talk about how he brought my mother to the hospital to give birth to me, there was a technological aspect even to this event:

> *I didn't take the sidecar. I didn't like it because the motorcycle was too slow when it was attached. But, in the meantime my son was being born, so I attached the sidecar, and took my wife with the big motorcycle, that American X, and we went to Hadassah Hospital. Just imagine, at night, and there were potholes on the roads, not like today. I had already set up an electrical light on the motorcycle. There was a magneto, I put together some sort of contraption and built a battery out of boxes made of celluloid.*

When my father tells about the time I was a year old, technology once again finds its way to the center of the story:

When we arrived in Afula (in the Jezreel Valley in the north where my father moved with my mother and me at the request of a man from the "Hashomer" organization to establish the first weapons manufacturing factory) *and it turned out there was nothing there yet . . . I built a radio with six light bulbs. This was in 1924 and everything stood on the kitchen table. The batteries stood on the floor, under the table, and Amos was instructed: you may not enter the kitchen and you may not touch anything.*

But my father did make sure that I had an actual toy—an electric train—and he also bought me two games from which I could build a simple radio.

When we were little children, my mother was the center of life for me and my sister, BatSheva, who was born five years after me and named after my father's mother. She was ill twice during her childhood. The first time she was hospitalized at the Mandatory hospital for contagious diseases in the Russian Compound in central Jerusalem, which was run by nuns. Later she suffered from a heart condition that lasted for a year and a half. My mother was with her at the hospital the entire time. I was about eleven, and my job was to bring my mother books from the national library, which she read to BatSheva.

My father almost never came to visit. He worked. Thanks to dedicated treatment and will power, my sister made a full recovery, and she even served in the Palmach.

My mother was a good-looking woman, short of stature. They, my father and mother, were very different from each other. I remember my mother as a very intelligent woman, loving and effusive. My father also expressed his feelings, but differently, through a handshake or at most a hug. I was surrounded by love from both my parents. I had a happy childhood. I was given freedom. But I was also angry at my father for being overly strict. I was never, not once, angry at my mother. She was a full-time mother. She didn't work and was always there for us.

We had deep and meaningful conversations with my mother, but not with my father. I talked about the dilemmas of adolescence or things that troubled me only with my mother. I didn't consult with my father even when I joined the Palmach. I had a very strong connection with him, but I never involved him.

I remember the following scene: Hagai Street in the Geula neighborhood, winter. We are listening to the radio together, on a porch facing the sun. A round table. My mother cooked Polish food, and soup was served at the end. She was a wonderful cook. We loved what she made, and she made an effort to always make what we liked. She wanted me to eat meat, but I hated meat. There was a frame around the table, and once, when she was cleaning it, my mother found the meat I had hidden during meals . . .

Financially, relative to the conditions in those days, my father provided what we needed. By 1936–7, we already had an electric refrigerator in our apartment in Tel Arza. It is important to remember that even in the '50s, when I was living with my wife, Shoshana, in Moshav Neta'im, we didn't have an electric refrigerator. We didn't have the money.

For my bar mitzvah I got a puppy, a boxer. I named her Aviva, and later I changed her name to Vicky. After that, I named all my dogs Vicky, except for the last one, which was a male. I took a dog training course led by Dr. Rudolphina Menzel, who had trained police dogs in Vienna, made Aliyah, and brought the first boxers. I took it seriously, and I even participated in dog competitions.

When my sister and I were older, my mother had time for public activities, and she volunteered to teach Hebrew to new Jewish immigrants. She never made so much as a penny from the day they got married. My father never talked about what happened before he and my mother met and got married.

It took time before my parents—who, as I mentioned, were so different from one another—found a way to live together in understanding and harmony. From the time I was a very young boy, I remember the fights between them. Later, I suppose, they found a way to live together. My mother developed heart disease after she gave birth to me under the terrible conditions of those days, and she also suffered from glaucoma and eventually went blind. For a long time she managed to hide that from us. It was only when she was seventy that it became apparent that she could not see. I remember how she used to make us tea without seeing. She listened to recorded books. She never stopped listening to books. She knew English, Yiddish, Polish, and Russian. In 1975, when she was seventy-two, she was hospitalized at Hadassah Hospital because of her heart disease, and she died there. She was a very strong woman. We buried her on the Mount of Olives.

The house I grew up in was filled with books in many languages and a variety of topics—technology, history, and fine literature. There was an entire collection of classics, translated into Hebrew by the Shtiebel publishing house. In our home, we had the entire *Encyclopedia Britannica* and many newspapers—*Davar* (a daily newspaper published by the Histadrut workers' organization), the *Jerusalem Post*, and others. Reading was a regular part of life in our home, and I used to go to the Ever Library on Jaffa Street to bring back books that we would all read. With the English I learned at the Rehavia Gymnasia, I could read Jack London and Upton Sinclair. At school, I was also good at drawing. The drawing teacher called my parents in and recommended that they send me to study drawing—in Paris, no less. Of course, I didn't go. I may have known how to draw, but I wasn't really an artist. My daughter Nira is an artist. Love of music, on the other hand, was inculcated into me from childhood. At the age of twelve, I heard the celebrated violinist Bronislaw Huberman and the conductor Arturo Toscanini at the Edison Theater in Jerusalem. I still have the record player and my collection of classical records from those days. I chose to study classical Arabic, and among other things I read the *Al-Ahram* newspaper. There was a time when I knew spoken Arabic as well, and I even majored in Arabic in high school.

That's the way it was, that was my house. A home that stood for science, technology, and as broad an education as possible. The urge to know and learn in any way possible could be felt in every corner of our house and in our lifestyle. When I was a little older and could understand something of my father's technological world, we became significantly closer.

My father taught me how to work, to use machines and tools from his workshop, which was in the basement of the house. He educated me on the principles of precision and thoroughness. I always wanted to hear him. But he was a tough man as far as quality went. A strict man who would not compromise excellence. He also never compromised with me. For example, he asked me to create a cube. He gave me a chunk of metal and a file and demanded that I file it into a cube and to make sure that it was precise. He didn't give up. He was also very strict when he taught me how to weld or fuse things together, to hold a screwdriver, or to carve with a carving tool. We didn't fight, but this was over-strictness—after all, I was just a boy. There was tension between us. He didn't punish me, but his pedantic behavior annoyed me.

Later in my life, my father really wanted me to come work with him, to join the factory he had built. He was an inventor, not a businessman, and over the years I helped him in many ways, and so it was only natural that he would ask and expect me to continue on with him, working together. I could not agree to this, because I am so very different from him in personality, management style, and leadership. I couldn't meet all his expectations; but still, I took much of who he was with me for the rest of my life. His work, always striving for excellence, stayed with me throughout everything I ever faced in my life. Over time, when I read things my father said about life, especially here in Israel, I feel that I strongly identify with his approach, as if we had not been separated by an entire generation:

I came to Israel because I thought and believed and still believe that it is the only place in the world where I can stand tall and say: this is my country and here I am, and I don't care what you think of me . . . I didn't want to be called "filthy Jew." Here I feel at home, I feel every corner and every stone . . . and I have the right to be here. I'm not doing anybody any favors, and nobody is doing me any favors.

Within this house, with this man, I embarked on my own independent path.

During childhood and my teenage years, I had friends who influenced me. I was close to Avrasha Tamir, my cousin and later a major general, who was a year older than I. When he was seven or eight, he wrote his first story, "The Ascent to Everest," and he let me read it. I was amazed. We laughed together. We used to read books together, like "The Forty Days of Musa Dagh" by Franz Werfel and Henryk Sienkiewicz's books—"The Deluge," "In Desert and Wilderness," and "Quo Vadis"—translations of classics. We acted out the descriptions of the warriors; we were the heroes. We were very mischievous, real menaces. My dad made me a slingshot, an open leather pouch into which you place the stone and two leather strips that essentially extend the arm by about thirty-nine inches, and twisting the slingshot creates a centrifugal force that propels the stone very far. I was quite an expert, which is how we broke the windows of the synagogue in the Bukharan neighborhood, and the neighborhood kids started chasing us all the way to the rubble hill. We climbed the rubble mountain, and a stone fight ensued, and we really felt that we were defending ourselves.

I was six or seven when Avrasha dragged me to the Scouts, my first youth movement. We went hiking. Once we came back very late, and my mother had gone out looking for me in the dark. It is important to remember that in the late 1920s Jerusalem did not have street lights. The streets were lit with portable kerosene lamps, and a special worker operated them. He would use a pulley to get each of the lamps down, and after lighting it he would put it back up.

The Scouts group eventually became the Mahanot HaOlim youth movement. The counselors of the youth movement were Uri Yoffe; Gitta'le Sevorai from Kibbutz Maoz Haim, who married Zerubbabel Arbel; Nahum Sarig; and Israel Libertovsky (later a noted scientist and president of the Weizmann Institute of Science).

As a seven-year-old, I remember crawling into "the dripping cave," named after the water droplets at the entrance. And there, in the place where the Israel Museum stands today, near the Valley of the Cross, in candlelight, Libertovsky read us Kipling. The Scouts' shack was near the Mamila Pool. There was a big hole in the ground that filled up with water in the winter. We called it the Volga. We built rafts and sailed on them. Like many Jerusalemites, we were afraid to swim. The exceptions in our Jerusalem group, Yohay Ben-Nun and Izzi Rahav, actually knew how to swim very well, and later formed the Palmach's navy seals. During my years at the Rehavia Gymnasium, so named for its location in the Rehavia neighborhood, I was influenced by students and friends who came from different and varied backgrounds. There were representatives of the Jerusalem bourgeoisie, children of officials from the British Mandate, some who came from rich homes, and also workers from Jerusalem, representatives from the Sanhedria, Tel Arza, Kerem Avraham, and Geula neighborhoods—everyone was there. And I was neither from the working class nor from the rich, so does that mean I was middle class? Later on, gymnasia students became members of the future underground forces. Among them were those who inspired us: Yigal and Yossi Yadin, Ben-Zion Rabinowitz, and the Katchalskis—Ephraim Katzir (who became president of Israel) and Aharon Katzir (a scientific pioneer who was one of twenty-six people murdered in a terrorist attack at Ben Gurion Airport in 1972).

CHAPTER 3

It is Not Surprising that by the Time I Was Fourteen I was Already a Member of the Haganah

From the time I was born and through my childhood and teenage years, the conflict between the Jewish and Arab communities was bubbling both below and above the surface. I was exposed to the heart of this conflict gradually and with growing intensity, and so my path was paved to join the elite soldiers who were responsible for keeping the pre-state Jewish community safe and for the war for the establishment of the Jewish state—the Palmach.

I was five years old when, in August 1929, very severe hostilities broke out between Jews and Arabs. Jews and Arabs were murdered. This week is known in the history of our country as The Disturbances of August 1929.

In the years 1936-1939, when I was twelve to fifteen years old and already aware and mature enough to consolidate my positions and ways, an organized rebellion and terror broke out by the Arabs of the country—mainly against British rule, but also against Jews. Starting at seven in the evening a total curfew was imposed, and news poured in about the dead and wounded among the Jews, the Arabs, and the British.

When I turned thirteen and a bar mitzvah boy, I received a real pistol from my father as a gift, a revolver with a small amount of ammunition. It was a natural move in a house like ours. In honor of my grandmother and my mother's wish, I also went to the synagogue to put on tefillin, and we held a traditional bar mitzvah ceremony.

On Saturdays, my father took me to the amphitheater on Mount Scopus, and we practiced with a Finnish submachine gun, the weapon used by the "Haganah".

I knew about my father's activities in the Haganah. He told me about them. We had a large hiding place for weapons in the house. My dad was one of the builders of these hiding places. Next to the entrance to the house, on the upper-left side, there was an electric board with fuses. You would pull out one of the fuses, stick a key in, and the electric board would open. He assumed that if the British came to conduct a search, they wouldn't mess with electricity. In the back, there was a space of 60 x 40 x 24 inches, with private guns and weapons that belonged to the Haganah. The same was true for the basement. My father built a weapons hiding place behind the main radiator. He was very resourceful. I remember that friends like Manya Shochat, Kabutchke, from the Hashomer Organization and others would come to my father so he could fix their weapons.

It's not surprising that by the time I was fourteen, I was already a member of the Haganah. I swore an oath over a gun, and my childhood friends, Uzi Narkiss and Matti Peled (both later major generals), were with me. In my first position, I served in communications where I transmitted dispatches. My father knew. Maybe my mother knew, but she was not part of it. Later, I did include her. In 1941, when I reached the age of seventeen, I was with Yehiam Weitz, who was six years older, who influenced me and a whole group of young Jerusalemites. He recruited us, about twenty friends, into this organization that had just been established as part of the Haganah and was called Young Hish—"young Haganah corps" or "Hetz." We went together, friends since preschool, all high-school students. Among us were Miki Haft and Jack Tzvia, a future intelligence services and Mossad man. Under Yehiam's command, we began our training in Kiryat Anavim, the first kibbutz established in the Judean Hills outside Jerusalem, on land purchased from the neighboring Arab village of Abu Ghosh, and at Ma'ale HaHamisha, a kibbutz in the Judean Hills established as part of the "Tower and Stockade" campaign and named in honor of five men ambushed and killed nearby by Arab gunmen. Some of the weapons belonged to the Hebrew settlement police force. I remember our first training sessions with a Lewis gun (a First World War-era light machinegun). Yehiam Weitz, as the unit commander, examined each of us in turn. Yehiam was very close to me, and we, Shoshana and I, named our son after him. I remember him as a charismatic man, who spoke Hebrew very well and could sing beautifully. In June 1946, during his studies for his MA in chemistry, he took a day off to participate in the military operation known as "the Night of the Bridges" in which he was killed.

At the age of seventeen, together with Yossi Yadin, we established the Gordonia youth movement in Jerusalem. Our activity area was by the Menorah Club, founded by Jewish veterans of the British army from World War I. At the entrance were two cannons. I was a member of the movement until I graduated from high school. I was a true Gordonian. We believed in A. D. Gordon's approach to work as religion. To this very day, the foundations of my approach to the world are rooted in the remnants of the youth movement days, including a strong tendency to distance myself from a naïve view of the world.

What did we discuss? A. D. Gordon, socialism, Marx and Engels. We read *The Pedagogical Poem* by Soviet educational theorist Anton Makarenko and *The Republic of ShKID*, a children's novel written in the 1920s about Russian street boys by Belykh and Panteleyev. In those days, we learned most of our values in the youth movement. Gordonia, Mahanot HaOlim, HaNoar Ha'Oved, Bnei Akiva, these were the places in which ideology was discussed. We sat at night at the clubhouse and talked about fulfillment and settling the land. Sometimes there was a discussion leader. We sang Russian songs that had been translated into Hebrew, which were the popular songs at the time, and we danced. It was a completely different world. My group was supposed to settle in Gordonia—for training we went out to Neve

Eitan, a kibbutz in the Beit She'an Valley established during the "Wall and Tower" ("Homa v mgdal") campaign. We called it Kibbutz Pinhas Lubianiker (after the Zionist leader and politician who later changed his name to Lavon). And then they informed me that there were too many people going into the Palmach and I didn't make the cut. I met with Lavon, who was already an important leader, and I was just another young guy taking his first steps, and I was not afraid to tell my truth. I said thank you, I will not go for training; I will simply join the Palmach.

All-out war—World War II—had broken out in September of 1939 and lasted about six years. Our cooperation with the British increased, mostly during the period when the forces of Nazi Germany made their way through northern Africa, towards lands under British rule, and there was actually serious concern about the possibility of an invasion into the Land of Israel. These developments in and out of Israel created the conditions for the establishment of the Palmach— an acronym for *Plogot Mahatz* (Strike Forces)—on May 15, 1941. The Palmach was supposed to use guerilla warfare tactics to prepare the ground to resist a possible Nazi attack. Yitzhak Sadeh was appointed commander of this new unit and reported directly to the Haganah's general staff; Yigal Allon took over the command after Yitzhak Sadeh.

I threw myself into this chapter of history with all my heart, body, and soul, through nine years of battles, until the end of the War of Independence and the establishment of the State of Israel. Seven of those years were spent in the Palmach, and two more years as part of the IDF that was formed when the state was founded.

CHAPTER 4

We Strapped on a Backpack and Went Off to the Palmach Together

At the beginning of 1941, while I was training with the Hetz, Israel Libertovski of the civil engineering department in the Technion (Israel Institute of Technology) and head of the student association showed up in Jerusalem. He was an austere man, who rode a motorcycle, which was a rare commodity in those days, and had a special passion for completing his mission. We used to call him the "Darwish," a nickname taken from the description of a Muslim clergyman who lives an ascetic lifestyle devoted to religion. Libertovski was an activist and participated in missions against British rule.

This special man showed up with the intention of recruiting us into the Palmach. He spoke about driving the British out, establishing the Jewish state, and the World War. He enlisted about twenty of us high school students. That is how my journey in the Palmach started. My first mission was to distribute flyers that Libertovsky gave me, entering at night Allenby Camp, where the British officers lived, and sliding the flyers under their doors.

While studying at the Rehavia Gymnasium, we also started training at Beit Ha'Arava, a kibbutz founded in 1939 by youth movement members who had fled Nazi Germany. (Due to its isolated location, the kibbutz was abandoned in 1948 during Israel's War of Independence.) There was face-to-face combat training with Yehiam Weitz, weapons and machinegun training, learning to sneak into nearby Jericho in small units, and trips to Ein Feshkha (now a nature reserve on the northwestern shore of the Dead Sea). I was so completely engrossed in the training and the group that had banded

In the Rehavia Gymnasium—at the time of my first missions in the Palmach.

together, I had almost no free time for my studies. One day my mother said to me, "Amos'ke, listen, do what you want, but I ask one thing, give me that slip of paper called a high school diploma. I would like to see that diploma." I devoted about two months to this mission and gave my mother the high school diploma that she had so hoped for. To this day I thank her for that and carry this memory with me of when I decided to take a break from my other commitments in those crazy times and get myself a formal education.

When I look back at what my friends and I went through at that time, where we started and closed that part of our young lives, we can see that there were three different chapters, each leading up to the next. We, the group of youngsters who enlisted in the Palmach during its early days, changed. We expanded and honed our capabilities and military experience. The transitions were gradual, and we almost didn't notice them. As far as we were concerned, for us it was a sequence of doing, fighting, and learning until we were almost entirely spent.

There was no "timeout" to observe what was happening to us, to consider what we had been through and how much we had changed. We weren't the type who celebrated the significant events, like the United Nations' decision to end the British Mandate and establish two independent nations in the Land of Israel—a Jewish state and an Arab state (the Partition Plan) or the events surrounding the declaration of the State of Israel.

The first chapter begins when we enlisted in the Palmach in 1941 and ends with the United Nations' decision to divide the land between the Arab settlement and the Jewish settlement, a decision taken on November 29, 1947. In this chapter, the youth movement gradually became a powerful force. This was a period of exploration and consolidation of abilities and goals.

The second chapter is essentially the first phase of the War of Independence, in which the Israeli Arabs went to war against the Partition Plan and it became gradually clear to us that we were facing a proper war. This war continued for about five and a half months—from November 29, 1947, until the declaration of the Jewish State on May 14, 1948. At the beginning, activities were carried out by unorganized armed Arabs and militias, one division in the Jerusalem area led by Abd al-Qadir al-Husseini and another on the coastal plain under the command of Hasan Salama. They were equipped with small arms and armored vehicles, originally British or Jewish, that had fallen into their hands. Then, still before the end of the British Mandate and the formal declaration of Israel's independence, the "Arab Liberation Army," which included irregular volunteer forces from neighboring Arab countries, also joined the battle. All the while, the British turned a blind eye.

At the beginning, when the United Nations was deciding about the Partition Plan, the Palmach was the only well-trained, fully-enlisted Jewish force available immediately to repel attacks as they happened, and it no longer resembled the previous forces. During the following months and up to the declaration of the Jewish state, additional forces joined the battle against the Arabs.

The third chapter, which is essentially the second phase, is deeply rooted in the War of Independence, when regular military forces from Arab countries joined the conflict. That was the day after the declaration of the Jewish state, and the fighting lasted eleven months, until March 1949. At this point, two weeks after the declaration of the State of Israel, the IDF was formed. We were very upset when Prime Minister Ben-Gurion decided to dismantle the Palmach and to combine its three brigades—Yiftach, Harel, and the Negev brigades—into the IDF. The three brigades continued to exist and fight until the end of the war, alongside additional brigades that were formed as part of the IDF.

CHAPTER 5

From a Youth Movement to a Fighting Force in the Palmach

We were one of the Palmach's first platoons. In the spring of 1941, we marched from Jerusalem to Modi'in to meet two other platoons and the founder of the Palmach, Yitzhak Sadeh. There were eighty of us, seventeen-year-olds with nineteen-year-old commanders, and we knew how to use live weapons. We heard Sadeh speak about us being the future of the future state. In this meeting, which had some elements of a formal ceremony, I felt that I was part of an organized system and that this was serious business. We talked, maybe we even sang. The Palmach anthem hadn't been composed yet. In another meeting, I heard Moshe Sneh, the Haganah chief of staff, and he impressed us all. Imagine, we sat for an entire hour and listened to a speech. And he knew how to speak. Then I met with Yigal Allon, and the Palmach chapter of my life really began, and it lasted until the end of the War of Independence. These were the first people to whom I owe my deep commitment to the Palmach, and I stayed committed even when there were many questions in the air and many others left.

At the beginning, when I was distributing flyers against the Mandate regime in the heart of the British camp, I was exposed, for the first time, to a mission intended to take someone's life. Yitzhak Sadeh instructed me personally—and I was only seventeen and a half years old, a student at the Rehavia Gymnasium—to take out a British official on behalf of the Haganah. I was part of an underground force, and we didn't exactly obey the Geneva Convention. The plan was to execute the mission on King George Street in downtown Jerusalem, where later the Knesset would stand, and then retreat towards the

Bezalel School and museum. I was told that I would be given a non-standard Haganah revolver, a Mosin-Nagant, and that I must find two others to go with me. My dad dealt with Haganah stuff, but I didn't want to involve him in this. I didn't sleep for a few nights. The hardest part was finding partners, and I breathed more easily when the mission was ultimately canceled.

Initial training began when we were sixteen and seventeen years old, and we all still lived with our parents. Our platoon went to Kibbutz Beit HaArava to train with weapons that had been stored in hidden weapons storage spaces. We went home in the evening. This area, just northwest of the Dead Sea, was chosen because it was far from the watchful eyes of the British. The Dead Sea water level was about thirty meters higher than it is today. The water reached the cliff. We held shooting practices around Nahal Kidron, which flows to the Dead Sea south of Ein Feshkha.

At this time, we didn't know about the concept of safety during training. Yaakov Hefetz and I hid behind an embankment by a freshwater aqueduct, holding the targets over our heads. Once, a bullet cut through the high voltage line of the potash factory and it fell into the water duct. The machinegun instructor was Eliyahu "Olesh" Zieliński-Gillon, who later became chief medical officer. The Haganah had three inch mortars made by our secret military industry and three types of light machineguns (Polish "Rekem," French "Chateau," and British "Bren.") Avraham Adan was given a Bren machinegun, and the nickname stuck because he knew how to use it so well. He was in my platoon, we called him "Brenchik"; he was an amazing athlete. I liked him very much. We also trained in face-to-face combat with "long stick, short stick." Our next instructor was a famous lawyer, Michael Piron, the future head of the IAI Israel aerospace industry. We took our training very seriously, so much so that Michael would hit my fingers—and I would hit his head until it bled.

Then we were one year older, and it was time for more serious training. At the end of 1941, we moved to Givat Haim (near

Hadera), where we lived in cabins that had been previously used as chickencoops. Etched into my brain are images, mostly of many hours of uprooting weeds with a hoe and the times the girls from Jerusalem and other places joined us for training. I also remember sitting around the bonfire, where we were taught "Hafinjan", a song written by our fellow Palmach member, Haim Hefer.

In 1942, when the German army under the command of General Rommel was advancing in North Africa and facing British General Montgomery at El-Alamein, there was no certainty that the Germans would not break their way through and make it to the Land of Israel, only 345 miles away. With that in the background, cooperation with the British, which initially had been covert, expanded and became public knowledge. That is how I was sent to an explosives course at Mishmar HaEmek, in the western Jezreel Valley in the north of the country. It was my first military course, and it was followed by a few others—not many compared to the scope of command and responsibility that my friends and I had in the days before the establishment of a proper army. With me were Haim Gouri, Benny Marshak, and Shneior Lifson. We were aware of the danger of a British retreat towards Iraq and Syria if the Germans invaded the Land of Israel, and we knew about the British plan for us to stay behind enemy lines, and the job we would be tasked with—attacking the German army by blowing up bridges and communications systems. I didn't know about the Masada plan—"The Plan of the Last Fortress"—whose goal was to create a line of defense in the mountainous areas of northern Israel. That line was supposed to position a fighting force in secure areas in the Carmel, the Gilboa, and the Shomron Mountains whose job would be to tail the Germans and hinder their progress. But it was clear to the leadership that, if the Nazis came, we would all be killed. Despite this, they did not prepare the people for the upcoming danger. In Tel Aviv there were celebrations. Others were silent. Maybe there were those who knew about the Holocaust. We knew something terrible was happening, but we didn't even imagine its scope. Those among our friends who did know about it were those who had been recruited for missions to save Jews in Nazi-occupied Europe, and they were part of the German division.

The British taught us to use explosives, disarm mines, and shoot. The commander was Colonel Hammond. Major Taylor taught us to use handguns, and a sergeant taught us communications. We ate military "Spam" or "Bully Beef" in the combat meals. In the IDF it was known as "Luf." I remember when we had to stand in formation in the court next to Mishmar HaEmek. Because of the war, the British army had to train a large number of people, and the most efficient way was to teach ten combat drills to a class so that the soldier could react automatically, just as he would in the drills. We were taken to the sports court of Kibbutz Mishmar HaEmek, where we learned battle drill.

We, however, had a completely different approach. In the Palmach, we taught and trained soldiers to think. We believed in practicing a response to the battle situation in which the soldier might find himself in the future. With the establishment of the IDF, this difference in opinion was the basis of conflict between the British military graduates and the Palmach graduates.

In addition to the explosives course, the British also trained Palmach members for other positions, which would be necessary if they failed against the Nazis:

A course for young Palmach members who spoke German taught them to dress as Germans and use German weapons, sing German songs, and even learn the "Heil Hitler" salute. There was also a course for Mista'arvim, Arabic speakers who would be sent as spies into Arab countries. Among them were Josh Palmon and Yeruham Cohen, who commanded the Mista'arvim platoon. There was also a Balkan platoon, whose soldiers were parachuted behind enemy lines. These trainings stayed with us and for most of us they were an important part in our continued roles as combat fighters.

At the end of 1942, the British defeated Rommel and no longer needed the Palmach—and with that, the cooperation ended. We were back to our own units. The British did not ask what we planned to do next.

There was a special atmosphere among those who went through training with the British, which Avraham Adan (Bren) describes in his 1984 book *Up to the Ink Flag—Autobiography* (chapter 3):

> . . . *we were waiting for the arrival of Valley Train, which would bring back all the people who had been far away. Clusters and circles formed in which people mingled and just hung out together. We told jokes and scary stories, along with tales of what did and did not happen, we sang the German platoon's song—in German, and the Arab platoon's songs—in Arabic. At one point the people from the Arab platoon faced Mecca, knelt down on their knees, touched their foreheads to the ground and started praying in Arabic. The people from the German platoon responded by screaming out orders and army codes in German. Even the older soldiers, from the non-commissioned officers' army course, joined in and told scary stories and jokes about the days of cooperation with the British during their invasion of Lebanon and Syria and about their exploits in Beirut and Damascus. We, "the paratroopers," (a nickname for new recruits) were enthralled. I was sorry when the train pulled in and took us away.*

After the end of the "British Era," we stayed on at Mishmar Ha'Emek for a noncommissioned officers' course commanded by Batz, whose full name was Ben-Zion Rabinowitz. He was a strong, tall man, a graduate of the civil engineering course at the Technion. I was the youngest participant, and it was my second military course. We learned, and later taught others, the main parts of the military doctrine of von Clausewitz: the general principles of war, shared by the squad, the platoon, the company, and the large formations. We learned, among other things, topography for day and night navigation, and how a unit moves. We learned to instruct and train, and how to write orders. The course was run in a way that encouraged us to think, ask, and argue. I remember using the hand motion Talmud scholars use, the one that starts with lifting a finger and moving it in a circular motion. That's how I was taught to become a thinking soldier. This training helped us to move on, without much difficulty, from smaller to larger units. "Yosefale" (Yitzhak) Tabenkin, one of the founders of the kibbutz movement and the Histadrut, decided on the nature of the course, and so he played an important role in shaping the next generation of commanders.

There was an essential difference between the training of noncommissioned officers in the Haganah and the Palmach. In the Haganah, the course on the principles of war was not mandatory for everyone; in the Palmach it was. And so, a fundamental argument broke out between the graduates of the British army and the Palmachniks. We said, we train a soldier to think from the time he is a private. We didn't teach them models of battle drills, we taught them how to think, and that proved to be valuable given the conditions in which we had to fight.

Why Stay in the Palmach?

In 1942, when the Palmach consisted of no more than five to six hundred people, headquarters decided that we should move to the Upper Galilee to join the First Company. After the NCO course, I didn't go back to Givat Haim and moved to Kfar Giladi as a squad commander in our company—the Sixth Company.

The company was based on the Jerusalemites, together with some students and other individuals who came from different places. Its first commander was Shimon Avidan, and after him Israel Libertovski, who had recruited us. The tough time in Kfar Giladi continued until I left for the platoon commanders course in 1943.

In the cold winter, we looked for a place to sleep, and we found an attic in the cowshed, which was built out of basalt rocks. We cleared piles of hay and straw and viper snakes slithered out. We cleaned it up and lived there. In addition, we had infantry training with guns that were in hidden weapon storage spaces in Kfar Giladi. There was a girls' squad, most of them from Jerusalem, who wanted to train with us in javelin throwing. Before the war, the girls demanded full equality in all physical tasks. Later, we realized there could never be full equality because of the physical differences between the sexes, and that we could not put a full load on the women. For example, I was certain the girls could not carry the weight of a mortar with its bipod, yet there was almost total equality between the sexes in training and marching. During the actual war, many of the women filled very sensitive positions such as being in touch with the families and taking care of the casualties, and they were also medics, signal operators, and drivers.

Etched into my memory from this time are the hard work, the frustration, and having to cope with those who abandoned us— we called it going AWOL—and joined the British army or simply disappeared one day never to be seen again. Despite all that, those of us who remained continued to train and hone our military skills.

Hard Work and Not Much Food

I remember what it was like to work on a farm. We did the hard jobs— and fought to get more professional positions. We were told, okay, we will give you professional work, but then as "electricians" we dug ditches, as "mechanics" we dug ditches, and as "sanitizers" we cleaned the sewage line. There was always some kind of digging. I cleaned toilets. I had an agreement with the woman in charge to let me work the way I wanted to, as a contractor. I cleaned, I wasn't ashamed, and afterwards I washed my hands really well and went off to read. We worked with field crops on land that belonged to Kfar Giladi, next to

Kfar Blum. I remember loading cow manure on a wagon hitched to two mules, coming down on my own from Kfar Giladi, scattering the fertilizer, and plowing with a two-prong plow.

Spring, snow on Mount Hermon, a wonderful view, and clouds in the sky. Once I was driving the wagon, galloping down the hill like Ben Hur, and I took a sharp left turn and went flying. The wagon came after me, as did all of the load. The moral of the story: slow down before a sharp turn, because if you don't, you'll be covered in manure. At least the mules were OK. Once I was sent to clear rocks out of four dunams (about one acre) by Kfar Hunin (today Margaliot) near Manara along the north border with Lebanon. I skipped out, and on a sunny, winter day there is nothing better than that. I just laid down and read a book instead of working.

I remember that relationships with the people living on the kibbutz were tense. In the dining hall, Kayla, Israel Giladi's widow, after whom the kibbutz was named, would serve carob honey in a tiny plastic bowl. That was all that we got. Tea was the only hot thing we ever got. When Yonatan Giladi, from Kibbutz Ramat Rachel, asked for more, Kayla said he would not get any more than the portion in the tiny bowl, and he called her a "bitch." A fight broke out immediately, like in a saloon in the Wild West. Yonatan stood there with Grisha and someone else from the Palmach, and Grisha poured a kettle of boiling tea on that guy, right on the most sensitive part of his body. Guards had to walk Grisha out so that he wouldn't be beaten up.

It was already the second half of winter by the time we received our first coats; until then, we wrapped ourselves up in bags whose color dripped off when it rained. We walked around in shorts, and the color dripped onto our legs. We were really hungry, we were only teenage boys, and food was scarce. So, every once in a while, we would swipe some eggs and cold cuts from the storage room.

We suffered from diarrhea more than once after eating clotted cream we stole from the cowshed. And another story from those days:

two biology students, including Olesh Zielinski, who would later become a head medical officer and the other a professor in Chicago, were growing marsh mosquitoes in a water hole for animals, which they had turned into a science laboratory. Most of the platoon— including me—were bitten by the marsh mosquitoes and contracted malaria. Because of the war there wasn't any quinine. We received a medication called Atebrin instead. When I got better, they sent me to recuperate in Shefayim, a kibbutz on the Mediterranean coast in the central part of the Israel.

In his memoir, *Up to the Ink Flag* (chapter 3), Bren recalls:

Most of us were imbued with the motivation of "the chosen ones."

We were chosen for the Palmach, and now each of us felt committed to proving that he was an excellent worker, better than the average kibbutz member. The result was high work productivity. The rows of corn stretched for kilometers. When we started working on a row, we would pick the corn without lifting our heads, almost running through the row. Anyone who did not want to join the competitive work style encountered our peer pressure. We wouldn't let them "shame the firm."

I remember the first song I sang in Kfar Giladi, written by Leah Goldberg: "Every night, the moon is watching," and we also sang Russian songs, among them, "I will send my first bullet to the enemy." Later, we sang songs by Haim Hefer.

For training, we would go up to Manara, which had not yet been established (the Jewish National Fund had bought the land sometime before); that was where the firing ranges were. In addition, we participated in absorbing the new immigrants who, escaping Europe, arrived by crossing the borders from Syria and Lebanon, under the noses of the British, as part of a campaign of illegal immigration called Aliyah Bet.

Frustration, Disagreement, and
AWOL—Palmach Deserters

At the beginning we were a platoon of "individuals"—people who arrived at the platoon on their own. An enriching interaction between people, every person had their own approach to life. The cross-fertilization was mostly on the intellectual side. Benjamin Tammuz, Ezra Zohar, Red Head Zion (Zion Eldad), Lulik Gershonowitz, Dan Ram, Denziger the sculptor, Matti Peled. Some of them acted like they were "Canaanites"—a cultural-ideological movement that tried to create a new culture based on the relationship between the different nations living in the Land of Israel during the second millennium BCE and between the Hebrew people in the Land of Israel in the twentieth century. Only Benjamin Tammuz, one of the leaders of the writers' movement, was actually a "Canaanite."

There were also those who preferred to think of us as a "Fighting People" and preached violence. ("A Fighting People" was a short-lived initiative during the second half of 1943 that sought to establish a body that would violently act against the British Mandate.) Among them, Matti Peled was one of the most extreme. We didn't fight with them, but we argued quite a bit. Yitzhak Rabin did not participate in the arguments. Finally, the leaders of "The Fighting People" group were dispersed among different units, so there wouldn't be any group of people together who opposed the Haganah's policy. At this time, when a harsh war was waging throughout the world and inside the Land of Israel, some people didn't really understand why a fighting force trained by the Palmach was necessary; to some people, the work and training seemed pointless. Questions such as what are we doing here were asked. Outside a world war is raging—and we are playing!? What is our worth compared to a soldier in the British army or compared to our friends who deal with the illegal immigration, or even compared to those who blow up British police stations? But, deep down, among those of us who stayed in the Palmach, there was a feeling that each of us personally carried on his shoulders the responsibility for the future of the Israeli people. There was a feeling that we were not just cogs in a big machine that we didn't understand. Each of us was responsible not only for himself but also for what others did. Because if we were not aware of our unique importance as individuals and as a group, it would be hard to stand up to public pressure and to the lack of public recognition for what we were doing.

Ideological energy and a search for the right path bubbled under the surface—and with them, the option of going AWOL, which at the time, for those of us who remained, was the same as deserting.

It was always done quietly. Israel Libertovski left for the British army. He deserted because his opinions were controversial—and his activism was even more controversial. Others, like Shimon Avidan, who was a company commander for a very short period and, after Avidan, Zion the Redhead, switched to other positions in the Palmach. In this way, the ranks of the old timers in the company dwindled, and only a few were left who knew each other and who remembered the history of the Jerusalem group.

Special training groups, boys and girls from youth movements, were called up to join us. The groups from training, unlike the "loners" groups, had a common political, settlement-related denominator, which is why they stood out in terms of their social and ideological cohesion.

I can recall an event that demonstrates the atmosphere prevalent in those times. It happened when Olesh Gillon returned from Kibbutz Ayelet HaShahar, where we had led a commanders' training course, and waited for the bus, which came by once a day, to take us back to Kibbutz Kfar Giladi. In the meanwhile, we enjoyed the pleasant winter day, laid down in the trench, and waited to hitch a ride. A military truck showed up. We lifted our hands up, the driver stopped. A tzabar, a native Israeli, a Hebrew speaker. We asked where he was going. "To Tripoli [in Lebanon]," he replied. We got onto the crate that was in the truck and I told Olesh, "Let's go to Tripoli, what do we care?" We got to Marjaayoun in southern Lebanon. But then we started thinking about what we would do next. They would obviously kick us out of the Palmach. We banged on the roof of the driver's cabin, the driver stopped, we got out of the truck and started walking back to Kfar Giladi. Olesh had a hard time walking, because of the "mighty tighties" as we called our underwear, which were made out of canvas. I carried him on my back part of the way, and so, at midnight, we arrived at Kfar Giladi. That was the spirit those days. One day Olesh got up and disappeared. He also went to the British army.

Where did people desert to? Some, as mentioned before, to the Jewish brigade in the British army, a step that was supported by the national institutions. Moshe Sharett—then head of the Jewish Agency's Political Department and later Israel's second prime minister—encouraged enlisting in the brigade. Ezra Gruenbaum, a member of the Palmach, told me that he was there when they grabbed two young guys by the neck, Yoske Simbol and Motke Zagi, and removed them from the "Heihal" theater in Petah Tikva because they were shirking their responsibilities—they didn't join the British army. They were both members of the Palmach, and after a while they were killed in a battle for the road to Jerusalem. There were members who left and went back to their studies at the university. Leaving the company and going back to school caused serious unrest. I remember the feeling of sharp disappointment. We asked difficult questions, why them and not others? Who decided? Has the Palmach served its purpose? Because of the arguments and the desertions, high-ranking commanders, like Nahum Sarig, Yitzhak Sadeh, and Yigal Allon, came to speak to us. Gradually and over time, reserve forces were created out of those who left to go and study, and they played an important role in the upcoming existential tests we were about to face.

Training and More Training—Building Our Strength behind the Backs of the British

Despite the frustration, the arguments about our goals, the disappointments, and having to say goodbye to close friends with whom we joined the Palmach almost as children, we didn't stop training, as if the cracks hadn't already started to form just under the surface.

Bren describes the military framework as having been dominant:

Every evening there was a shaving and shining inspection. Barracks inspection every other Saturday. A lot of applied sports, a lot of topography, and a lot of treks. After the "individual-soldier" training we moved on to team and squad training. This, too, was high level training. The knowledge I acquired was so thorough, that I relied on it in the future—not only during the War of Independence, but for many years in the IDF. (Adan 1984, chapter 3)

The platoon commander was Dan Ram from Hanita, until he and Matti Megged, a soldier in the platoon, were stopped at the British "check-post"—an inspection checkpoint in Rosh Pina—and were arrested for being members of the underground. That was when Yitzhak Rabin came to replace Dan Ram.

Yitzhak was a very handsome man, a red-headed tzabar. He was two years older than I. A different type of character, very closed. It took time until we were able to get a laugh out of him, but we finally did it. As a platoon commander, he was excellent. He trained us well. His sister Rachel was in Tel Hai, in a training group that was intended to go up to Manara. On Saturday evenings, the platoon would go down to Tel Hai to dance, and we were curious to see Yitzhak blushing when he met with his sister on the grass. At that time, we received knitted socks, I don't know who the women who knitted them were. When they were washed in boiling water on the kibbutz, the socks shrunk. Yitzhak loved those socks and the shirt with the one pocket and the high, orange Australian army boots.

At that time, I took a course about operating heavy weaponry as part of an auxiliary platoon. The course took place in Jo'ara near Ein HaShofet, a kibbutz in the north near Haifa, and lasted about three months. There were two guys with me in the tent, Nehemiah Shane from Kibbutz Ein Harod, and Shlimke Miller from Kibbutz Givat HaShlosha, who was killed in Fajja. They were both outstanding men. The staff of instructors included an instructor who had served in the Czechoslovakian army—we called him Chech—and two more officers with knowledge in that area of warfare. We learned to operate the heaviest weapons that we had at the time: three-inch mortars, heavy Hotchkiss machineguns from France, and an Austrian machinegun. We learned the principles of tactical support and ballistics as a basis for gunnery. All this knowledge enabled us, with no great difficulty, to operate artillery with the equipment that we added during the war. When I returned from Jo'ara as a heavy weaponry instructor, the Kfar Giladi platoon became an auxiliary platoon that operated heavy weaponry, and the burden of instruction fell to me. We could only have training sessions far away from the inquisitive eyes of the British. Later, when we were on Tel Yosef (a kibbutz in the Jezreel Valley), where Rabin was the platoon commander and I was his deputy, I gave a live-fire demonstration of three-inch mortars to a Haganah commanders' training course in the woods of Kibbutz Beit Oren on Mount Carmel. There were two roads in the woods, one from the bottom, from Atlit, and the other from the Druze village of Isfiya. We positioned guards who would alert us if the British were coming. The mortar shells were delivered on trucks with hidden compartments. I aimed and fired the shells, except for one which I kept for instructional purposes at Tel Yosef. Once the drill was over, Yitzhak put the remaining shell in his bag, and we returned to the kibbutz on a bus. He was court-martialed for that. Maybe someone ratted him out. I thought to myself, what would have happened if the British had searched the bus!

While I was Yitzhak Rabin's deputy, we would often train with weapons and go on treks. The biggest trek took place at the end of 1942, when we went to a spring in Ein Feshkha on the northwestern shore of the Dead Sea, and from there we walked through the Judean and Negev deserts to Ein Gedi, Masada, Mount Sodom, Kurnub, Nevatim, and Revivim, and then were driven back to Kfar Giladi on a truck. Seven days on foot, in the winter, after the rains, when there was still water in the cisterns in the desert. We were about fifty people, with no weapons other than one pistol that was hidden in a water canteen, and maybe one hand grenade left over from World War I. During the trek, we held a ceremony in which we took our oath of allegiance to the Palmach, the Haganah, and the Jewish people.

We received food in tin containers from the kibbutz kitchen. When we arrived at the foot of Masada, we opened the containers and discovered to our dismay that the eggs had gone bad and the cheese had rotted. We threw it all out and were left with no food. We were starving.

When we ran out of food on the march—the goat on the stretcher

We saw a Bedouin shepherd, and Yitzhak bought a goat from him for five pounds. We tied the goat with a rope and started walking towards Sodom. We decided that after Masada we would continue on to Wadi Ombrak, today Ein Bokek, butcher the goat, and have a good meal.

After a few kilometers, the goat almost dropped dead. We built a stretcher, and we carried the unconscious goat on the way to Nahal Bokek. On the way, the stretcher flipped over twice, and the goat nearly took its last breath. When we arrived near Mount Sodom, we butchered the goat and divided up the meat. We cooked the goat in five tin containers all night. The guards were hungry, but their hearts would not permit them to steal meat, so they drank the liquids that accumulated, and added some water every once in a while. In the morning, of course, the meat was as hard as the sole of a shoe, but we all nibbled at it with gusto. I remember Yohay Ben-Nun sitting at the foot of Mt. Sodom and acting like Charlie Chaplin, eating the sole of a shoe while pulling out the nails.

In a book dedicated to the memory of Yohay, who won the Medal of Valor during the War of Independence and later commanded the navy, is a description of part of our march (*Caught Up in the Times, Yohay Ben-Nun / a Portrait,* edited by Saya Ben-Nun and Dita Garry [Israel Navy Veterans Association, Ministry of Defense, 2003], page 26):

> . . . *and then we had to pass the potash factory that was owned by a British company. We traveled in a truck covered with canvas intended to hide us, but we were discovered, and the British refused to let us pass through the camp. This meant that we had to go around Mount Sodom, on foot, when we were completely exhausted and had no energy left. We sat in a small grove of Tamarisk trees, eight kilometers north of Sodom, the company was in very low spirits. Yehiam Weitz and Amos Horev went to the British to find out what else could be done. We sat, Yitzhak Rabin and myself, with the bitter and depressed platoon. I sang the* Song of Songs *to them*

with all of the trope, and that helped to slightly improve morale in
the corps for which things had gone so wrong.

We parked in a training area. There were no tents, only blankets.
We were brought weapons and ammunition for training and food
from Sodom. Moshe Lengowski, the potash-plant security man,
hunted a large boar, and brought it to us. The boar lasted us for two
days. Everyone ate and no one asked questions. There's food—eat
it. Freshwater came in from across the border, in a pipe that led to
Sodom. The soles of our shoes were all worn down, and we had them
fixed at the shoemaker's at the plant. There, to the west of Mount
Sodom, we trained with live fire for two days.

Yohay Ben-Nun tells about the rest of the march:

The race west had begun. There was a race between the Palmach
companies as to who could cross the desert along Revivim the fastest.
We ran across that distance like madmen. People passed out down
there, in the Arava, we stood them up on their feet, we watered
them with green still water we found, and we kept going. And we
did indeed succeed in setting a record. This was a company that
was prepared for anything. Those who know Haim Gouri's poem,
this was the company that appears in the "Convoy of the 35" in his
poem "Behold, our bodies are laid out in a long, long line." (Ben-
Nun and Garry 2003 [referencing Haim Gouri 1949])

From Sodom we went on to Kurnub, today Mamshit. We bypassed
the camel patrol and walked to Nevatim, to the village of Olei Cochin,
which had already been established as a kibbutz as part of the eleven
settlements officially established on the night after Yom Kippur, 1946.
We went through Tel Ruhama, where the town of Yeruham was later
established. The road went on and on, and when we met a Bedouin
and asked him how long it takes from here to there, he said—the
time it takes to smoke two cigarettes. And indeed, by the time we

had smoked two cigarettes, we had arrived at Revivim in the south of Israel, and we returned north to Kfar Giladi on a truck.

These marches served a variety of purposes. The most important of them—connection to the land. Knowing the land of Israel was the ideological basis for fulfilling the vision of a Jewish state in our homeland. Physically getting to know the land during these marches built an emotional connection between man and earth, and later on it motivated us through many of our missions and served us, providing us with the ability to cope with the layout and the topography, knowing scouting as a military skill, and keeping physically fit. True, the Palmach march was a tradition, but there was a high risk that we could get caught, and, considering our young age, it was very daring.

On one of the marches, I took the platoon from Mount Gilboa, south of the Sea of Galilee, all the way to Jerusalem, through an area where there were only Arabs. First to Nuris, an Arab village in the Gilboa region, and from there through Mount Bezek to Ebal above Nablus, and then to Sartaba—and on foot to Ba'al Hazor, the highest place in the Shomron (Samaria). From there we went down to Jericho, and we made our way up to Jerusalem through Wadi Qelt. Six days. At night we knew how to walk right next to the Arab villages without them noticing us. The geography of the land had been "imprinted" on our feet. When we reached Mount Bezek and we looked at the area, we felt like it belonged to us. It didn't matter if we went through an Arab village or saw an Arab worker. We needed to own the land so that we could establish a state. Period.

The Platoon Commanders' Training Course— A University of Sorts

In the beginning of 1943, when I was nineteen years old, I continued my formal training and was sent to the Haganah's platoon commanders' training course, the most elite course at the time. The course was like a military university for me and it was the height of my training courses, starting as a private and then as a part of the bomb squad, a squad commander, and a heavy weapons expert. Basic military education at a platoon level was what served me until after the War of Independence. Within a year, just as the war started, I switched from managing a platoon to a company, to a battalion, and then to a division. The transition was quick, without any further formal training. It was all possible because of everything that we had learned in the platoon commanders' course and the practical experience we had from the moment we enlisted. I didn't go to battalion officers' training course in the IDF until 1952, at which point the experience of a military course in an organized and established army was a whole different experience.

The course took place on a northern kibbutz in the Galilee, Kibbutz Dalia, and its commander was Moshe Carmel (who served as a general during the War of Independence and later as Minister of Transportation). The instructors were Moshe Lehrer (who was the head of the Manpower Directorate), Mondak Bar-Tikva, Israel Beer (who was later exposed as a Soviet spy), and Immanuel Nishry—all later on filled high positions in the IDF and in the public service of the State of Israel. Yehiam Weitz, whom I held in such high esteem, was an instructor's assistant and was killed on the "Night of the Bridges." During the course, I expanded my acquaintance with people from the Hish and the Haganah and left the bubble of the Sixth Company in Kfar Giladi. In 1943, we left Kfar Giladi as part of the companies' visit to the kibbutzim. We, the oldest platoon in the Jerusalemite Sixth Company, were based at Kibbutz Tel Yosef.

The feeling of unrest that we first felt while we were in Kfar Giladi persisted, and I remember a large meeting with a difficult ideological discussion led by Yitzhak Sadeh. We demanded answers for questions such as—why aren't we doing anything, only training and working? In addition, soldiers in the field demanded more aggressive action towards the British, even though it was still necessary to act with restraint. Some of the people decided they wanted to start their studies, because who knew when we might actually fight. A national decision established the service track in the Palmach, according to which, after two or three years in the Palmach, you were permitted to go study and remain as a "reserve soldier." Many took advantage of this option. I was not among them. The war, which broke out a few months later, interrupted the studies, and many of the fallen soldiers did not have the opportunity to put their talents to use. An entire generation of scientists was lost. Among the fallen in the well-known Convoy of the 35 were students I had known who were destined for greatness in various scientific fields.

When the winter came, the platoon in Tel Yosef relocated to the attic of the cowshed. We cleared out the straw and cleaned it out. The commanders—Yitzhak Rabin, Yohay Ben-Nun, and I—shared a room, and I remember meaningless conversations between young guys about girls and gossip. Yitzhak appeared to always want to hear everything, but he himself never shared anything. A completely discreet man, who took no part in any gossiping.

At the end of 1943 and the beginning of 1944, when he was at Kibbutz Sha'ar HaAmakin, Matti Peled was dismissed from the Palmach because of his fondness for "The Fighting Nation." He went to study at the London School of Economics and never returned to the Palmach. I was given command of his platoon. It wasn't easy. I joined a very tight group that had trained together, and they did not know me. Nevertheless, my foreignness did not interfere with my ability to put the platoon through intensive training, and, since they were lacking a clear and binding doctrine, they provided me with the opportunity to plan and design my own training courses. In Kibbutz Alonim all of the oak groves and the lands in the area of Kfar Yehoshua were at our disposal. The hostility from the Arab villages was like constant unpleasant background music that accompanied our military training. Bren describes one of these events:

Upon our arrival at Tel Amal, we started with short marches to get to know the area, and these marches were a central and important part of our training. On one of these marches we walked from Tel Amal to Tirat Zvi. There were ten of us, led by our platoon commander—Amos Horev. We had short sticks for self-defense—a weapon we were properly trained with . . . when we were just south of the city Bayt She'an, three Arabs walked in our direction—a youth of about eighteen years, and two young men about thirty-years-old. When we walked past them the youth started swearing at us, stopped about ten meters from us, and demanded, insolently, that we put our sticks down on the ground. He waved a slingshot over his head . . . and we knew this was the weapon that had determined the outcome of the battle between David and Goliath. We retreated about thirty meters, when the youth "succeeded" in getting free of the other men's hold. Somebody gave a warning and immediately we heard a sharp whistling sound—a rock flew over our heads. Still crouching down, our heads in our hands, we heard the command: "Take action!" We ran towards the three, our sticks at the ready. We easily separated the youth from the young men, and we hit him only enough to get the slingshot out of his hands. We warned them, and at Amos's command, we turned around and left. When we were about thirty meters farther away from them we heard them shriek and saw the three of them waving kaffiyot above their heads. We knew their "language." It was clear that the three had started a "Faz'a," which didn't surprise us. What surprised us was that the quiet fields—an Arab worker here and there—were brought to life. We suddenly saw Arab workers running towards us from all directions, and we hadn't thought there would be so many of them.

"Onward! Run after me!" Amos commanded, and started running towards Tirat Zvi . . . (Adan 1984)

The head of the kitchen at Tel Yosef was less than encouraging, and there was a shortage of cutlery, and we ate in tin and enamel plates. At Sha'ar HaAmakim, a kibbutz settled by Romanians, we ate good Romanian food in ceramic plates at large square tables. Quite an experience. We lived in a tent camp. In this platoon, among other people, were Yehonatan Dolinsky, Shaul Biber, Micha Perry, and Bren. A wonderful platoon.

Along with the rigorous training, we also took part in quite a few mischievous activities that were age-appropriate, relieved our stress, and gave us a reprieve from the heavy weight that our young, slim shoulders were carrying. One day, while I was with Yohay Ben-Nun preparing a platoon drill that would begin at Sha'ar HaAmakim and end in Nazareth, we arrived at a monastery wall. We jumped inside and saw a pool filled with water and naked nuns. We immediately ran away. When we got down from there, the sewage was running in open channels, and I slid down one for about thirty meters. We all laughed. Another little prank had to do with fish. Nahal Hasi, today Nahal Amal, starts flowing in the Gilboa and flowed through the kibbutz and in our tent camp. My room was above the pump that pumped water into the fish pool. The water was a set temperature, about 80 degrees Fahrenheit, which is the temperature in which fish can live and grow. As we were getting ready to leave the base for a vacation, I set off a small explosive in the fish pool and we all collected fish to take home. I would also hunt birds in the fish pool, and we called them black water-chickens.

I remember another little prank when a platoon that had settled in Ein Harod wanted to have a bonfire. I was asked to steal some geese that were being raised in Tel Amal and send them to the platoon. I went to the fish pool, shot a pelican, skinned it—I threw the meat in a can—and I sent it to them. They told me—Amos, the meat is tough, but it's edible.

Only 20-Years-Old—Already a Company Commander without a Preparatory Course

In June of 1946, I was in Jerusalem because I was sick with malaria again. I helped my dad in his workshop, and then it was "The Night of the Bridges." Nehemiah Shein, commander of the Sixth Platoon, was killed in this operation. Some of the soldiers I had been training also died. Yehiam Weitz, who had gone back to studying chemistry, was studying for his exams. He came for a day or two to participate in the operation at Nahal Kziv and was killed. When Nehemiah was killed, I was called to take command of his platoon—the Sixth Platoon, whose base was in Ein Harod, near Mount Gilboa in the north. I was only twenty years old when I was appointed to command one of the twelve platoons that made up the entire Palmach force at the time. After "The Night of the Bridges," there was a lull in the fighting for a while. The only thing I could do was increase the level of training. At that time, there weren't enough weapons, and it was not possible to have even a single platoon drill. The Palmach needed us to train all fighters in the platoon to be Mini Squad Commanders, and those were the instructions we got from Palmach headquarters. That's how the entire platoon commanders became Mini Squad Commanders. At the beginning, it seemed like the level of training was unnecessarily high, but later on we discovered just how necessary it was. The only practical training area that was hidden from the British was in Sodom at the Dead Sea. We were barefoot because our shoes were being fixed. We got our weapons from the hidden storage space in Kibbutz Beit HaArava and we provided our own food by hunting boars on the Transjordanian side of the border.

Five platoons as well as a new settlement in Jubb Yussef, near Rosh Pina north of the Sea of Galilee, were under my responsibility and command, and I personally created and led training programs and marches for all of them. I remember platoon training sessions in which I sent the platoons to get intelligence reports regarding different targets. We spread them out throughout the entire land of Israel. One team was sent to prepare a report on a kibbutz in Emek Hefer on the coastal plain in the central part of the country. The secretary of the kibbutz told me that a team arrived and asked for information. The kibbutz simulated enemy targets, and they should not have operated the way that they did. I court-martialed them. In the grapefruit groves of Ein Harod and Tel Yosef, at the foot of Mount Gilboa, there were concrete positions left over from the 1936 Arab Revolt, complete with steel doors and locks. I imprisoned the three members of the platoon in there for four days. But I also came to speak to them every day, so that they could understand why I had punished them.

As a company commander, I was also responsible for everything having to do with weapons and the weapon stashes where they were hidden. The weapons were extremely valuable, and we took great effort to procure and protect them. There were not enough weapons for everyone. That is how we began the War of Independence.

Only three of us knew where the opening to the weapon stash was: the guy in charge of munitions, who had been trained at using weapons; the quartermaster; and myself. My dad, who was an expert on weapon stashes, had advised me about the stash in the valley. After the British broke into the weapon stashes on Kibbutz Yagur, near Haifa, and searched in other kibbutzim, we had to hurry and extract the weapons from the kibbutzim. I transferred the stash to a farming area between Tel Yosef and Mount Gilboa. I decided on a location and together with the members of the kibbutz we dug a very deep hole. At the welding workshop, we built a metal container, a large cube, which we then lowered into the hole. We placed a meter-long access chute with a serious latch to ensure that rainwater would not get in. The container was covered by about half a meter of dirt. To access the chute, we would clean out the dirt. From the moment the stash was covered in dirt, even the people who had helped us didn't know where it was anymore. That's how it was kept secret. Using two pegs in the ground and two pieces of rope, I knew exactly where the stash was. It had rifles, machineguns, a mortar, and gelignite explosives. The gelignite emitted toxic fumes. You could suffocate, and there were no masks at the time. Despite that, we still went down into the stash. I would go down, do what needed to be done, cover it again, and then a tractor with a plow would come by, and after it had been re-plowed, once again people did not know where the stash was—other than the tractor driver and myself, of course.

When I would go to my parents' house to visit for a few days, I would bury my papers in one of the planters, as a sign for good fortune so that they wouldn't be found. I trained my boxer dog, Vicky, to be a serious attack dog. Once, as part of the British's standard surprise searches in the homes of those suspected of underground activity, we heard a knock on the door of our house in Tel Arza in northern Jerusalem. An officer walked in with two Scottish soldiers in kilts. Vicky attacked the officer. He fell to the ground and she put her jaws around his throat, without hurting him. I grabbed her leg signaling for her to let go. The officer stood up, pale as a sheet, dusted himself off, and left.

A First Company Military Operation—Liberating "Illegal" Jewish Immigrants from Atlit

Until the War of Independence started, the British still ruled, and we hadn't had any opportunity to experience operating an entire company. The absence of auxiliary weapons and communication devices also didn't allow for drills or training as an entire company. True, I was commander of a company, but I operated at the level of a platoon, that is until we carried out the big operation to free the immigrants from Atlit (a British detention camp on the coastal plain south of Haifa), an operation in which a company was activated. We did not know how to operate battalions. Only in 1944 did they begin to establish battalions in the Palmach, which at first were more of an administrative framework. The Haganah brought more than a hundred thousand immigrants, while the British did everything in their power to prevent Jews from entering Israel beyond the limited quota allocated. An open armed struggle was waged against the capture of the refugee ships and their deportation to Cyprus, which also included blowing up ships that were intended to transport immigrants from Haifa to Cyprus. The Palmach, being land-based, was not involved in immigration by sea, but did engage in transporting immigrants who were brought on foot from Syria and Lebanon. Some of them were arrested and imprisoned

by the British in Atlit with the intention of returning them to their
countries, where they would face the death penalty.

The operation took place on October 9, 1945. Yitzhak Rabin
planned the operation. Nahum Sarig was put in charge of carrying it
out; the first battalion commander of the Palmach. We had to gather
forces and weapons, to plan and execute all we needed to do behind
the backs of the British. We thought about how to block the British
military and police access roads from Haifa to Atlit from the south
and from the Carmel through Beit Oren. The first step was a discreet
assembly of all the forces in Kibbutz Beit Oren, which was done in
complete darkness the night before the actual operation.

My role was to be a scout to lead the force to the open area in
front of the detention camp, and then to carry out a violent, armed
blockade in case the army or the police arrived from Haifa. I had about
a dozen people. In the end, no British forces came to my blockade. A
small force came from Isfiya (also known as Usfiya) and was blocked.
The force that actually broke into the camp was commanded by
Yitzhak Rabin and Nehemiah Shein. How do you break in without
any casualties? First, we had already stationed Hebrew teachers there,
people who were trained in the Israeli-developed martial art known
as Krav Maga, and second, among the Jewish guards in the British
police force was one Jew who gave us access to weapons. To prevent
the use of these weapons against the forces breaking in, we removed
the firing pins beforehand, and so our forces were able to overtake
the guards without any casualties. We extracted 208 refugees. We told
them to hurry up. They loaded their belongings and children on their
shoulders, and we walked in a long line. We went straight up Mount
Carmel, towards Beit Oren, with me bringing up the rear with Yitzhak
Rabin. It was hard, we had to carry a few of them, and Yitzhak carried
a child on his back the whole way up.

As we approached Beit Oren, it became clear that the British army
was surrounding, or was about to surround, the kibbutz. We buried the
weapons in the forest. And then, next to Beit Oren, we saw a surprising

and inspirational sight: thousands of people from Haifa, who, on their own initiative, were coming to the area—and the force rushed to divide the immigrants up among them so that they would blend in. It made it easier for us to pass, and the British had no way to find the immigrants or arrest them. Yitzhak Rabin and I walked to Haifa, got on a bus, and returned to the valley, ready for the next operation.

That was the Haganah's largest armed operation up to that point, and it included a battalion or battalion and a half. A very successful operation. We were very excited. We had conducted a successful military operation, and it helped bring the tremendous motivation of the entire Yishuv (the organized Jewish community during the pre-state period of the British Mandate) to the surface.

While on Sick Leave—A Few Free Days Were Enough to Fall in Love

And I, in my own personal life, came down with malaria again and had to return to Jerusalem for tests and recuperation. This forced break affected my entire future life, and I thank the lucky stars that sent me malaria. From time to time, I would walk in the city until one day, in Zion Square, my gaze fell upon a tall girl, very pretty, her hair in a Russian-style braid. A few days passed, I went to the university to hear a lecture, and I saw her once again in the lecture hall, that girl whose name I did not know. I courted her and fell head over heels in love with her. From that moment, my life went on in two opposing and demanding circles: a combat commander in the Palmach who felt the weight of his people's existence on his shoulders and a young man in love who wanted to start a family.

After concluding my position as company commander of the Sixth Company in the Jezreel Valley in 1946, I was commander of the Eighth Company as part of the Palmach's Second Battalion until October 1947. Yitzhak Rabin was the battalion commander, and Zvi Zamir was the battalion instructor. I received command of the company from Menachem Rusak, a member of Kibbutz Na'an. We had a meeting in Kiryat Anavim to transfer command of the company, and it lasted a few days. I was starting to get the hang of things. It was an excellent company with five units scattered in different places: Kiryat Anavim, Ma'ale HaHamisha, Ramat Rachel, Beit HaArava, and in a settlement in Revadim in Gush Etzion, which was associated with the leftwing Hashomer Hatzair socialist Zionist youth movement. Despite the geographical separation, it was a platoon with an extraordinary atmosphere and a lot of motivation was forming. The best of our youth were part of it. I remember Aharon Shemi-Jimmy, Yitzhak Zebuluni from Kfar Hasidim, Dan Katz, Rafi Zilberman, Shaul Panueli, and Arkadi Harkavi, who was in charge of the homing pigeons and was killed in an attack on the radar station. A hundred and fifty soldiers were in this platoon and about one hundred more joined as part of "the Reserve," which included people who had already served for two or three years and had left for university, most of them to the Hebrew University. "The Reserve" was important because they helped maintain the framework and communications, and they trained with us when possible. The commander was Uzi Narkiss, a student at Mount Scopus. Following him, I appointed Israel Hadar Bigelman, nicknamed "Beigale." My headquarters were initially in Ramat Rachel, a rather dull kibbutz near Jerusalem with a depressing standard of living. The dining hall's tin roof would blow in the wind during our meals. I lived in a "lift," a type of large wooden crate with cracks, and it was cold and wet. Later, I transferred my "headquarters" to a shack that we put up near the cowshed in Kiryat Anavim in the Judean Hills west of Jerusalem.

In one of the research books about this period I found a description of the platoon that was under my command from the perspective of a bystander. And this is what he wrote:

After the Black Shabbat [on June 29, 1946, when British authorities began a widespread search for Jews suspected of engaging in anti-British activities], *Menachem Rusk left his position as commander of the eighth platoon, and Amos Horev (Sochaczewer) was appointed in his place. Amos Horev turned out to be charismatic, with organizational talent and wonderful technical skills. Physically, he was small and skinny, but he turned out to be a gifted commander, and so he was nicknamed "Little-Big Amos."*

He was the first platoon commander who didn't adhere to "commander etiquette" and would make sure to meet with his soldiers, listen to them, and treat them as equals.

Because of the distances between the platoons, we needed a vehicle, but the British were in control of the land. Vehicles were stopped and searched more than once. The weapons were stored in the most creative places. Amos used his technical and artistic skills to create weapon stashes and to play the right part with the British. Since 1946, the eighth platoon has implemented a professional approach in every field of combat. A certain pattern and order were created in field training and sports, marches, gathering of intelligence and creating files on the villages, munitions and technical plans. That is how Amos trained the eighth platoon for the challenges that they would face in the War of Independence.

Training Routine, Heated Arguments, and Sources of Income

We settled into a routine of training. The conditions were relatively good. We could walk to the Judean Desert, near Feshkha, where the British did not regularly patrol, maybe because it was too remote for them. I thought we needed to work the company to the bone with intensive training, including marches and platoon-size firing drills. It did not matter how many bullets we had, we always maintained a routine of drills and training.

Zvika Zamir and I met in 1945 and are close friends to this day. The special friendship we built did not prevent us from having heated arguments about the training program I wanted to run. I remember that during one of our arguments over an instruction program, I kicked Zvika out of the tent in Kiryat Anavim. We would hide the guns for the firing range in the doors of my pickup truck. I had a pickup truck and Zvika had a red Triumph motorcycle. One time we rode his motorcycle to Feshkha, and going down the wet road to Jericho, the motorcycle slipped, and we both skidded several dozen meters on the road. Fortunately, neither of us was hurt.

In Kfar Uria, in a relatively hilly area near Beit Shemesh, we had very convenient training grounds, far from any main road. To the south of us was Rafat, to the east Hartuv, and to the north Bayt Susin and Bayt Jiz. The quarrels with the Arabs from Bayt Susin and Bayt Jiz—usually over the invasion of grazing lands—were an introduction to some serious training. Training in those areas allowed us to get to know the land, which was extremely helpful to me during the battles near Latrun and in finding an alternative route to Jerusalem—the Burma Road—which I will tell more about later on. I developed a training method that I called "paratroopers drill," designed to teach the individual soldier to be familiar with the land and reach a certain rendezvous on their own. Every soldier's individual capability was an important component of our training at that time, and training in large formations was a rare event. In this specific training routine, I took a map and using transparent paper drew a walking route from point A to point B. At night, I drove a team of five or six people in the company truck. I covered the back so they would not see where we were going. Near Mount Hebron I dropped them off one at a time with a sandwich and a canteen—no weapons. It wasn't really dangerous. It was morning, each soldier had a map and the route. They had to place a cross on the transparent paper on top of the map using the surrounding view as a reference point and to try to identify where they thought they were on the map. After placing the paper on the map, they had to walk according to the route marked on it. The rendezvous was at Herodium.

Training also included the basics of gathering intelligence. We created a platoon of scouts that cooperated with the Shai—the intelligence and counter-espionage unit for the Haganah—which was the basis for the state's future intelligence services. The scout platoons made files for the different villages that included topographic and demographic databases, access routes, and water sources. With Leica cameras that we received from Shai, we took pictures of the village and its surroundings. The Haganah gave us five Palestinian pounds for each of those files, which we used to purchase any equipment we were missing.

Another way to make money for the company was loading and unloading potash that had been extracted from the Dead Sea. The platoon that was at Beit HaArava would load the potash onto trucks, while the platoon at Ramat Rachel would unload the potash and load it onto train cars. It was really hard work, but it earned us a lot of cash that was also used to get the equipment we were so desperately missing.

PIAT—Developing Anti-Tank Weapons before a Tank Was Ever Seen in Israel

As a company commander, I also dealt with technological issues whose importance was clear to me even when I lived in my father's house. I did a few simple things like developing mines, silencers, detonation pins for explosives, and more. The fact that we didn't have any weapons against tanks troubled me, because I assumed they would be needed when we were at war with a proper army that had tanks. One day I was skimming through a British magazine, "*Illustrated London News*," and in it were pictures of the war in Europe, including pictures of a British soldier, decorated with a Victoria Cross, firing a PIAT weapon intended for the infantry operating against tanks—on a German Panzer tank. In the inner pages of the magazine, was a detailed sketch of the weapon's structure, including the shell, a 2.5-pound shaped charge with an effective range of about 115 yards when aimed directly at the target.

The inspiration for the creation of anti-tank weaponry—the PIAT

I decided to try and develop a weapon like that for us. I had connections in the Arab village of Abu Gosh with Arabs who stole ammunition from the British military camp in Wadi Sarar. I paid them the fifty-seven Palestinian pounds that my dad had given me exactly for this purpose. They brought me a PIAT. Abraham Berman, from the Berman bakery, and I went to my dad and his workshops at the university, and we started developing things. A PIAT has two components: the warhead with the hollow charge and the missile launcher. We were the first in Israel to know what a "shaped charge" was—a hollow charge that is the warhead. Following the British documents I acquired, I learned about the use of hollow charges in the German army. We started developing a large hollow charge that could break through concrete buildings, which we used later in the battle at Dayr Ayyub. We experimented at Kibbutz Beit HaArava. After a while, I found out that a Jew named Jenka Ratner, one of the founders of Rafael (the Israel weapons industry), who did research for the British navy during World War II and developed weapons for the Haganah, was asking to see the PIAT. I gave it to Ratner—and I took myself out of the further development of the weapon. Ratner continued to develop it with Israel Military Industries. When the War of Independence broke out, the PIAT was manufactured at the workshops of the Israel

Military Industries in Tel Aviv, and it became our anti-tank weapon. No one in the army knew about my involvement. Later, when I had already become part of the IDF, I continued working with Ratner and together we developed a different anti-tank weapon, one similar to the Bazooka.

During those days, chasing weaponry was like chasing a life-saving drug. That was what we needed at that time. We received information from a Jewish guard in the Jewish police force working under British command during the British Mandate, whose name I have never been able to track down, who was on guard duty at the camp at Tel Litwinski, which is today Tel HaShomer. The message said there was a storage space with guns, machineguns, and anti-tank weapons—PIATs. A company from the Palmach's Fourth Battalion broke into the place, and during the battle, the Jewish guard was severely injured. At Beilinson hospital, where he was operated on, he asked Itzik (Isaac) Viman, "Tell me, Itzik, did they or did they not take the PIATs?" "They took them," Viman answered him, and the injured man responded, "They took them, so now it will be easier for me to die"—and he died. Before he died, he asked that someone make sure that his parents, who were still in Romania, would be brought to Israel and taken care of, along with his sister who was already in Israel.

Transferring Hidden Weapons Under the Watchful Eyes of the British

I used a large oxygen tank to transfer weapons from one unit to another. The weapons were at the bottom of the tank, and oxygen was on top. If you opened the valve, oxygen would come out. Or in a tank with cooking gas. I had a welding kit in my car for opening and closing the tanks. Once I lost a cooking gas tank that was filled with 9mm ammunition. I placed it in a pile of gas tanks in Kiryat Anavim, and it was taken to be refilled in Haifa. Another time, in a "pillbox"—guard posts that the British had set up—at the entrance to Jerusalem, my truck was searched and they didn't find anything. I had it filled with crates of vegetables. I wanted to continue on, but then they said, "Leave the truck, you'll get it back tomorrow from the Russian Compound." That was where the British secret police, the CID (Criminal Investigation Department), was stationed. I walked to my parents' house and could not sleep. I was thinking about how to behave the next day. Did they find out? Did they not find out? Should I go? Should I not go? I decided to go. They did not find out. I made a scene about the spoiled vegetables, and I drove off to get the hidden weapons to Beit HaArava.

Another event took place when I was riding the number 9 bus to Mount Scopus, where the Hebrew University was located. On my body, under my shirt and sweater, I had hidden electric detonators. The Jewish driver, instead of continuing on the bus route, drove to the Mandatory Police in Mea She'arim. He got off the bus, returned with a British police officer, and pointed at me. I immediately took the detonators and handed them to the person sitting behind me. I said to him, "Give these to my dad. Tell him I've been taken to Qishle in the Old City." (Qishle was a detention center near the Tower of David originally set up by the Turks.) The driver claimed that I had stolen his sweater. I told the police my mom had knitted it. The driver had a sweater made of the same wool! The idiot took me to the police. If they had found the detonators, I would have killed him.

Cat and Mouse—British Police Officers and Me in Jerusalem

One day, the Irgun Zvai Leuimi, a dissident Jewish paramilitary organization associated with the Revisionist Zionist Movement, blew up a Mandatory government building, and I went with a friend, Yaakov Hefetz, to watch. We stood across the way, at the bottom of a stairwell, and we laughed as we watched the explosion fail. Two British police officers in civilian attire caught me. Yankele made a run for it. They put me in the stairwell and beat me up. Yankele was sure they had taken me into custody in Latrun (where the British had a fort).

The second time, a while later, I was finishing up my business in the Old City. I arrived at Mamila, just outside the Old City walls, and walked towards the Jaffa Gate to get on a bus to Bethlehem, get off at Mar Elias and walk to Ramat Rachel to make it there before the curfew. Two Scottish soldiers in kilts were standing across from me. One of them pointed at me and said, "This is the guy." People had already been kidnapped and killed in similar situations. I was taken into the traffic police building and stood next to an Arab traffic officer who was directing traffic at the intersection of Ha'Neviim and King George, in front of the traffic police. I said to him *"shuf!"* ("look" in Arabic). I wanted a witness. The soldiers saw that I was not alone and did not hurt me, but called a police car and took me to the CID (Criminal Investigation Division) headquarters, a building that today hosts the Leumi Bank, near what was once the central post office. My ID and documents were all fake, of course. They interrogated me for four hours, until midnight, but I gave nothing away. At the end the interrogator said to me, "Listen, you're a kid, don't roam around the streets, go home." I told him, "What do you mean by roam around? There's a curfew and I will be killed outside. I need to get to my kibbutz, Ramat Rachel, and I will not leave this place now." They called an armored vehicle and took me all the way to Ramat Rachel. The guard opened the gate and I went to sleep in my shipping crate.

Teenage Mischievousness

We were still mischievousness, and we still wanted to be happy, even during intense training and heavy thoughts about the near future and the fate of the Yishuv. When winter came, the guys from the Palmach went to the kibbutz guest house in Ramat Rachel, which was never really in use during that time of year anyway. Each one of them loaded their bed and other possessions onto a tractor and made their way up the mountain. But it was only natural that we should celebrate the move with a traditional bonfire. The party was scheduled for Saturday afternoon, and for a party we of course needed respectable refreshments. In honor of the celebration, the platoon members who were staying at the guest house brought a cake that was intended for a kibbutz trip to Kibbutz Ashdot Yaakov in the north. And there were chickens that had come that day from America and were meant to be sold. Those chickens were supposed to make the kibbutz a lot of money, but they met an early demise. Kiryat Anavim was in a frenzy. That was not the first time that Palmach members were caught stealing from the kibbutz. On Saturday night, the kibbutz members held a meeting in the dining hall to discuss the outrageous scandal. They were considering throwing the Palmach out of the kibbutz.

A few years ago, at a memorial service in Kiryat Anavim, a man approached me and said, "Amos, you don't remember me? No? I stole chickens, and you kicked me out of the Palmach." It was in Kiryat Anavim, when I was commander of the Eighth Company, seventy years before! I suddenly remembered and said, "You stole very special chickens, and you ate them. Do you know what a terrible relationship we had with the kibbutz because of that?" Indeed, I had kicked him out of the Palmach—but then I brought him back.

Here and There I Had Some Personal Time— I Forgot to Buy the Wedding Ring

During that time, I was almost completely engrossed in the work of being a commander and preparing the people for the existential test to come. But at the same time, I was also taking the first steps in establishing my life with Shoshana Sapir, the student from Jerusalem whom I had met and fallen in love with. The kibbutz had designated a "lift" for Shoshana and me. The "lift," the very first room we shared, was exposed to the cold and the wind, and we needed about ten

Getting married in 1946—Sapir and Sochaczewer families

blankets just to survive the winter. One day, when we were visiting her close friend who lived in the Bukharan quarter, we sat on the stairs leading up to her house, and the words just came out of my mouth— "Shanka'le, let's get married." We told our parents a week before the wedding. On November 7, 1946, I arrived at my wedding straight from operations training—but I had forgotten to buy the wedding ring. Our parents arrived, but we still didn't have the required ten people for a quorum. I went down to the street and gathered another five people. We ate lunch with our parents, and that was how we started our life as a married couple.

CHAPTER 6

Gradually We Realized That a Real War Had Started

In October 1947, I requested leave to study mechanical engineering at the Technion. Back then, we still didn't yet know that the UN would permit us to have a state and that the British would leave. We didn't think there would be a war in the near future. My request was approved, and I had hoped I could devote more of myself to my wife, Shoshana, who was at the beginning of her pregnancy, and to building family life as she had always imagined it. My position was filled by Eliyahu Sela-Raanana. Shoshana was pregnant on the Moshav and I was at the Technion. In Haifa, I rented a room in an apartment belonging to the mother of my good friend Yohay Ben-Nun. Every Friday, I would return to Neta'im, to Shoshana, and on Sunday I would go back to my studies. Six weeks of studying passed, and then it was November 29. The UN reached its decision to establish a Jewish state in the Land of Israel. The next day, Arab gunmen ambushed two Jewish buses near Petah Tikva; seven passengers were killed. Arab rioters burned the commercial center in Jerusalem. The Palestinian Arab Higher Committee called a general strike. And I was called back to the Palmach. I deposited my suitcase and sketch board in the luggage storage at the Central Bus Station in Tel Aviv.

I told myself I would be back in two weeks. I was naïve enough to believe I would return to the Technion; I did not see the war coming. I thought it was tension again, maybe on a larger scale, but that was all. Slowly and gradually my friends from the Palmach and I realized that a real war was starting. My personal life was shaken as well, and by the end of the War of Independence in 1949, my entire world had been engulfed by the war. I didn't avoid any risks, challenges, or hardships.

And so there we were, Shoshana and me, two young people who had just gotten married and brought a child into the world, living nearly parallel lives and going through long periods of time when we were completely apart.

For five and a half months, from November 29, 1947, the day the UN decided on the end of the British Mandate and the division of the Land of Israel between the Jewish and Arab settlements, until May 1948, the day of the declaration of the establishment of a Jewish state in the Land of Israel and the departure of the British forces, the Palmach was the only recruited, organized, and highly trained force that was ready for action. On average, our people had about two years of training, and a few of us had five years of training. Our force was ready to withstand the surge that nearly determined the fate of the Jewish people and the state in the making. In November 1947, the Palmach consisted of about thirty-five hundred members, including reserve forces. It was organized into four battalions, and we quickly set up two more battalions—the Fifth Battalion under the command of Shaul Yoffe and the Sixth Battalion under the command of Zvi Zamir. Both battalions were dependent on soldiers from the Eighth Company of the Second Battalion, the battalion I had been commanding and training until just a month earlier. The Palmach was also dependent on people in reserve duty— people with guns, willingness to fight, the proper military mindset and thought processes, and operational capacities. At first, we had about one gun for every five soldiers and the ammunition had to be used very sparingly. In April of 1948, after four months of non-stop fighting, weapons arrived from Czechoslovakia in preparation for Operation Nahshon (to lift the Arab siege of Jerusalem, home to one hundred thousand Jews or about one-sixth of the country's

Jewish population)—guns, machineguns, and ammunition—and gradually things improved. The number of soldiers increased as well, and during the operations that followed Operation Nahshon, the Palmach battalions reorganized themselves into three well-trained brigades—Harel, Yiftach, and HaNegev.

The source of the high quality of our forces was, as mentioned, our thought process and the training based on it. We taught our forces to think about the most important principles of combat and to analyze different situations based on these principles. In fact, regarding combat, by that point we had reached the third and highest stage of our development from a youth movement to a proper military force. We fought mostly at night because then the enemy can't see you and you are less vulnerable. The few weapons that we had, mostly grenades and machineguns, got the job done. Night-time fighting was an inevitability. We had no advantage during the day, but we did have an advantage at night.

On May 14, 1948, after five and a half months of intracommunal fighting with Palestinian Arab forces seeking to prevent a Jewish state from coming into being, the second phase of the War of Independence began with the formal end of the British Mandate, the declaration of the State of Israel, and the invasion of the military forces of the neighboring Arab countries. During this phase, the IDF was established, and additional forces were brought together. We all worked together in full cooperation against the invaders until we won. Even when the Palmach headquarters were dissolved on November 7, 1948, its three battalions continued to exist in the same format and continued to fight as part of the IDF.

I fought in many battles, and I wish to retell them from my perspective as a fighter and as a commander. From this point on, I will be like a camera with a narrow lens that allows us to get as close as possible to the actions, dilemmas, errors, successes, smells, sounds, unspoken emotions, sweat, overwhelming fatigue, and everything that motivated me and my friends to fight to the end.

Six Weeks at the Technion and Back
to Fighting in Jerusalem

When I came back to Jerusalem from the Technion, I reported to the
Haganah Jerusalem district commander, Yisrael Amir, who gave me the
responsibility for commanding the fifth region. The region included
Jerusalem's Seam Zone, approximately from the old train station
near the German Colony, though the Montefiore neighborhood,
the Mamila cemetery, King George Street, north to Mea She'arim,
including the Jewish Quarter in the Old City—everything along the
border that abutted the areas where the Arabs lived. I was appointed
to this position following the failure of the previous commander to
handle the violent outbreaks by Arabs against Jews in Jerusalem and
the torching of the commercial center. This happened only days after
the UN's decision to end the British Mandate. I filled this position for
six weeks. I needed an apartment hidden from the British to house the
headquarters. Schmetterling, a lawyer who knew me because I went
to school with his daughter, allowed us to use his home in Mamila
for this purpose. The conditions were not easy, and we encountered
some serious difficulties at the beginning. It was still unclear how this
would all turn out.

I didn't lose touch with my friends from the Palmach, and
while still filling my position as commander of the fifth region, I
also participated in the battles guarding the convoys to Jerusalem on
December 9 and 26, the first in Sha'ar Ha'gai (literally, Gate of the
Valley), about fourteen miles west of Jerusalem where the road from
Tel Aviv begins a steep ascent, and the second at the Castel, on the
road about eight miles west of the city.

In the middle of January 1948, I took Yitzhak Rahav-Rabinowitz,
whom I had met in Jerusalem and who was part of the unassigned
Palmach marine unit, and we entered the Old City on a bus that
could navigate through the narrow streets. The Jewish quarter was
still populated. There were Haganah forces as well as some forces of

the IZL (the Irgun Zvai Leumi, also known as "Etzel"). I saw that it was a challenging situation—there were no steel helmets, not enough weapons, not even any sandbags. People were constantly injured by sniper shots. I left Yitzhak in the Jewish Quarter and went to take care of logistics and bring some of the missing equipment.

Later on, I thought to myself how those six weeks of studies had led to my beginning the War of Independence as the commander of the fifth region as part of the Haganah—and not as part of the Palmach or as commander of the Sixth Battalion, which had been formed on the basis of the Eighth Company that I had commanded and trained for so many months. If I hadn't gone to study—where and over which battalion would Zvi Zamir have been commanding, and what would our next moves have been? But in war in general, and in history in general, there's no place for asking, "What would have happened if . . . ?"

After the disaster of the Convoy of the 35 in January 1948, when a platoon led by Danny Mass, deputy commander of the Sixth Battalion, was discovered and massacred while trying to bring assistance from Jerusalem to the cut-off villages of Gush Etzion, I felt that I was most needed and could be of most help in the Palmach, in Zvi Zamir's unit, the Sixth Battalion, that had lost so many soldiers in nearly impossible missions attempting to guard the supply convoys to Jerusalem. His position was even worse after the eighteen soldiers from the Convoy of the 35 were killed.

At first, the Haganah refused to let me transfer, but I would not give up, and I turned to Zvi Zamir. "Enough, I want to come back to the Palmach, to your battalion. Danny has fallen in battle, and I will be your second-in-command." I was appointed as Zvi's second-in-command and was there until Yigal Allon had me transferred to the southern battlefront. The battalion's job of protecting convoys to Jerusalem as well as other jobs such as building armored vehicles and improving combat methods led to the establishment of what was then called the Sixth Battalion.

The War over the Road to the Besieged City of Jerusalem

The war over the road to Jerusalem intensified gradually, eventually becoming a series of almost daily battles. We experienced the first attack on an Israeli vehicle on the day after November 29, 1947, near Bayt Nabala. In his book, Zvi Zamir describes the beginning of the war of the roads to Jerusalem the day after the UN's decision, while I was on my way back to join the soldiers after a vacation at the Technion.

> . . . on December 2nd, 1947, there was a pogrom at the commercial center on Mamila street in Jerusalem . . . the next day I was called to the Palmach headquarters on Rothschild Avenue in Tel Aviv. At the time I was second in command of the organization's second battalion. Yitzhak Rabin, who was the Palmach's operations officer at the time, came out of the conference room and said to me:
>
> "You know what's happening in the country. Zvi, the second battalion is going to stay in the Negev, you are going to Jerusalem tomorrow morning . . . organize the members of the Palmach. You need to assist the region commander in any way you can and with everything you have. You are to command the eighth company and the Jerusalem reserve forces . . ." The Jerusalem reserve forces included 120 men and women . . . no explanation was necessary. We all knew what was going on throughout the country, and especially the dire situation Jerusalem was in. We also knew that Jerusalem's ability to defend itself would determine not only the fate of the city, but also the fate of the future Jewish state.
>
> "Your mission," I told my new soldiers, "is to secure the transports of vehicles heading to Jerusalem and returning to the coastal plain. We know the Sha'ar Ha'gai route as drivers, but securing transports on that road is a challenge we have yet to face. We will do what we must. We will learn, improve, and do our best."

We met on Friday, and on Sunday we started accompanying convoys, more than once under live fire . . . Several weeks went by before the Yishuv realized how bad the situation was and understood that this was the time to focus on getting food, supplies, fences, and weapons to Jerusalem. Not pianos. We internalized that very quickly because we were being shot at. People were injured, people were killed. But it's difficult to say that Jerusalem was shaken out of its routine during the first few weeks of the terrorist attacks . . . how do you set up for securing convoys in two days? Quickly . . . to this day I am in awe of the bravery of the soldiers accompanying the convoys. On trips with them I experienced the difficult conditions, the courage, the resourcefulness. The guys would look for trucks that had a bulletproof cargo unit, and if none was found, they would build posts from what was there—onion sacks or any other equipment—that would at least camouflage us.

We lost many friends on those convoys, but there was never a time when people did not show up the next day to complete their duties. That was how we had been educated. Our parents knew about every person who was killed or injured, and despite that did not prevent their children from going on their mission. And so it continued, and they drove and drove and drove. In my eyes, that is heroism.

The Palmach headquarters did not have an understanding of the bigger picture and had no way of assisting us . . .

I have no complaints about anyone. What could they say other than "do what you can." Each of us had been told at least once to do what we can, and we did what we could . . . (Ziv Zamir, With Open Eyes *[Kinneret Zmora-Bitan Publishing House, 2011], 33–36)*

At first, the drive from Tel Aviv to Jerusalem was on the old road through Bayt Dagan and from Latrun to Jerusalem, but the Arabs were shooting in Abu Kabir and in Bayt Dagan, two villages near Jaffa.

The route was changed, and we drove through the Hatikva Quarter of Tel Aviv (which itself had been attacked by Arab militiamen in December), Mikve Israel, Holon, Rishon LeTsiyon, Rehovot, Ekron, Mazkeret Batya, and Hulda. From Hulda, we got back on the road to Jerusalem. At first, the guarded convoys were small, but gradually, because of the deterioration in the situation and our understanding of just how efficient the protection we were providing was, additional vehicles joined—and the convoys got longer and longer. With each convoy we tried to be smarter and cleverer. When we received British guns, it was a great celebration. These were weapons that could be used at night to capture mountain ranges and to secure convoys.

We started driving, all of us armed, but the British stopped the convoys, searched for weapons, and did not protect us. We were forced to find more sophisticated ways to hide the weapons, and female Palmach members started joining the convoys and hiding grenades under their clothes. On the road with no protection, people were getting hurt. At first, the vehicles had no form of armor to protect them.

We knew from the first day that this was not the best way to accompany the convoys on the dangerous road to Jerusalem. We knew that our pistols and even the Stens were not weapons worthy of use against our attackers who were sniping from hideouts at a range that the pistols and Sten submachineguns couldn't reach.

In the meantime, people that we knew were falling in battle every day—and we collected the bodies. Sometimes, we could not retrieve the bodies immediately and could go back and get them only after it got dark, and we would see that more than one body had been mutilated.

Saving the Villages at Any Cost—the Disaster of the Convoy of the Thirty-Five

When I left the Jewish Quarter, I learned about Danny Mass's first attempt to get to Gush Etzion with thirty-five fighters. He tried going through the terraces in Bayt Jala, did not succeed, and retraced his steps. I knew Danny, a Jerusalemite who had graduated from the Rehavia Gymnasia and was an excellent caricature artist. He was with us in the platoon when we were still in Ayelet HaShahar. I went to meet him and told him, "There is no need to climb terraces. Take a different route, from Hartuv to the Gush, get as close as you can and take a leisurely walk up the path." I told him that in the two weeks that I had commanded Gush Etzion, during the tense months of August–September 1947, I sent a platoon with its weapons, on foot, from Hartuv to the Gush and it made without encountering anyone. I remember being in Kfar Etzion when a messenger came from Ein Tzurim looking for the commander. Everyone pointed at me. I was sitting on the ground in shorts, and he said to me, "Don't mess with me, I'm looking for the commander." I looked very young and it didn't occur to him that I could be the commander. I had just said to Danny, "Leave the second it gets dark, so you have enough time before daylight. The walk from Hartuv to the Gush takes about four-five hours. If you leave at 8 p.m. you'll have at least eight hours of darkness." He agreed. I sent a scout from my company, Yitzhak Zvuluni from Kfar Hasidim, who had already done this route at night. I went back to my position in Jerusalem, and I heard of the disaster only the next day.

Zvi Zamir, who was the battalion commander, told me what happened before the platoon left and shared the reasoning for his decisions and estimations about what eventually happened:

Approximately ten thousand Arabs participated the attack on the Gush in January 1948. This attack was stopped by a daring counterattack of a Palmach platoon under the command of Aryeh Tepper, which had been sent to Kfar Etzion as part of their commitment to protect the Gush. After the attack there was a lot of pressure on the Jerusalem district and the Haganah to provide immediate assistance in the counterattack, expected the next day. Instead of evacuating the Gush, it was decided to augment the protection there with the best people and weapons possible.

Given the Palmach platoon's success in stopping the first attack, the Sixth Battalion was supposed to send a reinforcement platoon. Soldiers from the Second Platoon of the battalion were sent on this mission. The soldiers of that platoon knew the road from Hartuv to Kfar Etzion from drills they had done in the area, the last of which had taken place only weeks prior. These were the best of our soldiers, and transferring them to be reinforcements in the Gush had a negative impact on the Sixth Battalion's ability to protect the transports and supply deliveries to Jerusalem. Additional fighters were sent from Hish.

The force that was supposed to leave from Hartuv was running late because the weapons arrived late. The commanders of this battalion, led by Danny Mass, faced a difficult dilemma whether to postpone the mission until the next night, or leave late and risk exposing the troops in daylight. The Hartuv district commander tried, unsuccessfully, to communicate with Jerusalem and Kiryat Anavim to report that the force had left late. I don't know what Danny's reasoning was and why he decided to leave that night, but probably they were concerned about the fate of the Gush, which we expected would be attacked the next day, and were worried about what might happen if reinforcements didn't show up." (Zamir 2011, 39–40)

Danny Mass and his men were driven to Hartuv in a truck. By the time they got ready and cleaned their weapons, which had arrived critically late, it was the middle of the night, between January 15 and 16. Some suggested postponing, but he refused. The battle took place in daylight, an hour's walk away from the Gush. They were only thirty-five men. The Arabs? There were many hundreds of them. That day, I was in command of a convoy from Jerusalem to Tel Aviv. When we arrived in Rishon LeTziyon, there was no longer need for protection, so I left the convoy, took a bike, and rode to Shoshana in Neta'im. I didn't hear from Danny the next day. I said to Shoshana, "Shanka'le, something terrible has happened, there has been no word from Danny Mass." Later, on the news, everyone learned what had happened. The things that we publicized were awful—it was hard to identify the dead. They had mutilated the corpses.

My deep grief, which the stress of war did not leave much time to dwell on, was mixed with anger that came from my core, and only years later did I dare express it in words, "I know myself; I would not have left late." I would not have wanted to be in that kind of a situation in daylight. At night, I know how to figure things out, so not everyone would have been hurt. Later, I had a similar situation when trying to conquer Tzuba, by the Castel. I postponed an operation because there was a chance we would end up operating in daylight. I was criticized for it. I was told, "You didn't follow an order." Correct, I refused, but we conquered Tzuba on a different day, and no one got hurt.

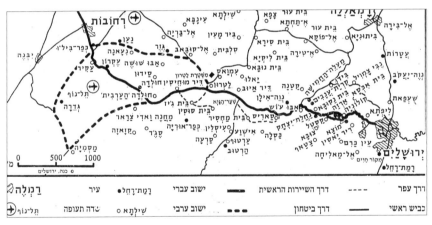

Map of the battle areas for securing the supply convoys to Jerusalem

A Series of Failures—"Can't You See It's a Lost Cause?"

January 22, 1948. Two convoys were attacked, in Saris at the turn to Neve Ilan and on the Castel. Two truck drivers were killed in one of the convoys. The corpses were taken out of the truck and placed in the armored vehicle in a sitting position. It was winter back then, and they froze. I drove the armored vehicle to Jerusalem. I was asked to transfer the corpses to the Wallach hospital morgue at the entrance to the city. The morgue was full, and they wouldn't accept any more corpses. I went from morgue to morgue, all over Jerusalem, but couldn't find a place to leave the bodies. I went back to the Wallach hospital and said, if you don't accept them, I will place them on the sidewalk. And that's exactly what I did.

On February 3, a convoy was attacked on the Castel. Ten guys were killed in a daytime attack. On February 20, I commanded a retaliation at Beit Nekofa (Bayt Nekoba).

The large number of fatalities combined with the challenging situation had a negative impact on our morale, and the atmosphere was dark and gloomy. One of our units was posted in Neve Ilan, a kibbutz established by people who had been part of the French Maquis (resistance members who used guerrilla warfare against the Nazis) and was headed by Rafi Zilberman who had been in Hashomer Hatzair and had served under me in Tel Amal. Rafi entered my room in Kiryat Anavim, pulled out a gun and shot a bullet into the ceiling. I asked him, "Tell me, Rafi, have you lost your mind?" and he said, "What difference does it make, Amos, my turn to die will come tomorrow or the next day anyway." I did not have such a fatalistic approach, but some did. The unit at Neve Ilan secured the turn on the road to Abu Gosh and from there to Jerusalem. They had a machinegun on a tripod. On March 1, 1948, Rafi went out during daytime, with a small force, to attack the people who had been shooting from the mountain range above the turn at close range, and he was injured. There was no way to extract him while under fire. They laid there until darkness, and Rafi finally died of blood loss. Why did he go attack them without permission? Maybe as a result of the atmosphere at the time.

The number of vehicles in each convoy grew, and with it so did the number of casualties. In the middle of March, I was preparing to take a convoy up to Gush Etzion. The convey was getting ready near the Schneller camp, and I decided I would take this convoy out at night. Unlike most of the other people at the time, I highly appreciated a nighttime operation. This was true because of the element of surprise, because you can't snipe at night, and because the Arabs were not used to fighting at night. The convoy was canceled. I went down to the Judean Foothills to lead a food convoy to Jerusalem.

On March 24, there was a six-hour-long battle to protect a convoy leaving Tel Aviv. Several vehicles made it to Kiryat Anavim, but the last vehicle returned to Hulda. A rescue force was sent from Kiryat Anavim to help the convoy. Yitzhak Rabin was part of it. It was a challenging time, with many losses.

During the last week of March 1948, we failed with three different convoys. On March 27, the Yehiam convoy, which left from Nahariya to Yehiam in the Western Galilee, suffered the loss of forty-six people. On that same day, the Nabi Daniel convoy, under the command of battalion commander Zvi Zamir, was attacked on the way back from the Gush Etzion to Jerusalem. After two days of fighting, the British army rescued anyone who hadn't been able to make it back to Gush Etzion and had barricaded themselves in an abandoned building. The British collected the weapons and gave them to the Arabs, along with armored vehicles and buses. Sixteen were killed and forty were injured in that battle. Regarding the third, on March 31, the Hulda convoy that I was commanding was supposed to lead supplies and reinforcements to Jerusalem. We were caught in a battle that lasted for hours, and then we returned to Hulda, having lost twenty-two soldiers in that battle. And so, in three days, eighty-five people were killed in three convoys; at that time the entirety of the Palmach's forces was no more than three thousand soldiers. The situation was dire.

On March 28, the Fourth Battalion was called up to Hulda to serve as backup for the forces fighting for Jerusalem and the road leading to it. That same day, I led a supply convoy that organized itself in Hulda. Twenty-six trucks, four buses, and seven armored vehicles—that was the total of the Hulda convoy of March 31. Other than the supply convoy, I was also supposed to join Uzi Narkiss's company. I decided, without asking for permission, to take the company early, while it was still nighttime. And so I led Uzi and his company in armored vehicles, at night, without any interruptions, and not a single shot was fired. We got all the way to Sha'ar Ha'gai, where the company set up in the northern mountain ranges to respond to the massive firing that we knew would be coming from the southern mountain ranges. Once again, I was witness to the advantages of moving at night. Some thirty to forty minutes later, I was already back at Hulda with the armored vehicles, preparing to leave with another supply convoy. The road was empty and quiet. It was about 9 p.m., and it was dark. That was when we got the order from the high command: "Wait for backup and take it with you."

I responded, "We must leave immediately, under the cover of darkness, or we will lose the element of surprise." It was difficult to accept my idea that we should only mobilize the convoys at night. At the time, that was considered thinking outside the box, but it was the result of our situation and lack of supporting weapons with which we could protect the convoys. It was also difficult for the enemy to snipe at us in the dark. And still, until now, not a single convoy had left in the dark. But they paid me no notice: "After the loss we suffered in Nabi Daniel, you must wait for backup and take it to Jerusalem." "We will lose people." I tried in vain to change the order. "That is an order," I was told—and the conversation was over. So, I waited for the arrival of two companies.

It was pouring on the dirt road from Hulda and all the way down to the paved road, and we sunk in "quick-mud," all the while dealing with the challenges of the terrain and a truck that would not start. A tractor had to come and move the truck so that the convoy could proceed. And while all this was happening, an irregular armed Iraqi force was gathering and setting up near Wadi Sarar, backed up with civilians from Arab Hulda, Ramla, and Lod. We had no intelligence about how many armed fighters there were. Shots were fired and the battle began, in daylight. The battle lasted many hours. In one of the weapons stashes, we had a three-inch mortar, which we had taken apart in case we were searched by the British. With the help of a soldier, we got the mortar out, wiped it down, put it together, and I starting firing from the ground, completely exposed, at the forces that were closing in on us. At first towards Wadi Sarar, then towards Arab Hulda. And then the bipod broke, and I had to stop firing.

We would not have made it to Jerusalem, and so we decided to go back to Hulda.

At that time, almost every armored vehicle had a self-destruct charge meant for committing suicide so as not to be captured. The cruel abuse of our people if they were captured alive was well-known, and we did everything we could to avoid it. The commander of the last armored vehicle in the convoy was Yoram Tarbes, a soldier from the Sixth Battalion, a legend who was already writing physics books. "A large number of injured soldiers, Arabs on top of me, I'm blowing the charge," he told the operator. Afterwards he gathered the injured and blew himself up together with them. The convoy went back to Hulda; twenty-two soldiers had been killed, most of them in the armored vehicle that self-destructed. Soldiers from both backup companies were also injured.

At the time, I didn't see the similarities between the complications and the severe losses in the convoy that Zvi Zamir had commanded, the Nabi Daniel convoy, and the Hulda convoy. At first, Zvi was told to delay the return until they finished loading an economic asset—a reluctant bull—and additional equipment, and I was required to wait until backup arrived. That delay enabled the Arabs to put up blockades and gather forces that critically injured the soldiers of the convoy. Both of us, Zvi and I, followed the order to wait. In both convoys, when at risk of being captured by the Arabs, the armored vehicle commander blew the vehicles up with his men in it.

Yes, it was a dilemma, and we felt a strong pull to refuse orders and do things as we saw fit. We bit our tongues and followed orders. It was not the first time during those months of the war that I and the other commander faced this type of dilemma.

We retreated to Hulda. A British officer appeared in a small patrol car, and asked, "Who is the commander?"

"I am."

"Want to see the blown-up armored vehicle?"

"Yes."

I took a pickup truck. It was daylight. I rode with a driver. The officer got into the patrol car on his own, no one would shoot at him. His unit was parked further down, on the asphalt road. A conversation in English was starting up next to the armored vehicle while our corpses were scattered around and Arabs were watching us. He told me: "Can't you see it's a lost cause?" I responded, in the English I learned in school, "The situation is bad, but it's not lost." He responded, "You'll call us back again one day." At night we gathered up the fallen soldiers, and the next day we buried them in the Hulda cemetery.

Joseph (Yosef'le) Tabenkin and I drove to Tel Aviv and the Palmach headquarters in the Red House. Our clothes were still stained with blood. We reported to the general staff about the terrible incident. I don't remember officially being asked to come, but it was important for us to report and remind them that I had recommended that we leave at night rather than in daylight—a recommendation that was not accepted.

In 1987, to mark thirty days after the death of Yosef'le Tabenkin, Zvi Zamir recalled:

> Twenty-four years after the battles ended, a happy and rejoicing Josef Tabenkin, who had been commander of the Harel brigade, came to my house and asked a series of questions that hinted at the big question: why did you follow through with the mission under those circumstances? And in a slightly less polite way, "Why didn't you fight back? Why didn't you refuse?" I responded to him with the brief words that later on I wrote in my notes for the speech I would give at his memorial service: "I don't have an answer and I didn't have an answer other than responsibility, obedience, and naiveté." (Zamir 2011, 38)

It was one of the most challenging missions in my entire life. We knew that guarding the convoys was as good as a potential suicide, but not a single one of us missed a single day, and no one deserted. We all knew that without the supplies that we were bringing to besieged Jerusalem, the fate of the city would be sealed.

A Change in the Way We Guarded the Convoys—Operation Nahshon

The disasters of the three convoys—Yehiam, Nabi Daniel, and Hulda—brought an end to that method of transporting the supplies and guarding the convoys. Out of that bitter week, Operation Nachshon, a critical turning point in the War of Independence, and one formulated while the British were still in Israel, was born. Until the Nahshon Operation, we had been conducting a passive war, focusing mainly on defense, and our main goal had been guarding the convoys. Here and there, despite our small numbers and lack of weapons, we succeeded in capturing mountain ranges, which helped secure the convoys. Sometimes we even succeeded in conquering an enemy post or two, but then we had to vacate it as soon as the convoy passed because we did not have enough people to take up places in the post. Nahshon involved a completely new approach. It was the Haganah's largest operation so far. Its objective was to conquer land and keep hold of it, not merely to defend certain convoys. We were still very short of weapons, and we had to empty all the weapons out of some of the settlements (Yishuvim) in order to fulfill the mission.

Preparations for the operation had started, and more soldiers were taking part in the operation than ever before. The Givati Brigade, a large brigade with five battalions that had fought in Ashdod under the command of Shimon Avidan, joined the operation, and Avidan was appointed commander. The Palmach's Fourth Battalion also joined, under the command of Yosef'le Tabenkin. Since I was part of that battalion, he made me his second-in-command for the duration of the operation. Battalions from the Alexandroni Brigade also joined us, along with a battalion from the training branch that included people from the special staff and participants in different courses.

On April 1, in preparation for the operation, a large number of weapons arrived from Czechoslovakia by air and by sea. This was very significant. Suddenly, we felt as though the operation was taking shape and that maybe, just maybe, a company could be a company, a battalion could be a battalion, and we would have supporting weapons. For the first time we had German Mauser guns, manufactured by Skoda, and light machineguns—MG34—which we called "Magladim."

Operation Nahshon commenced on the night between April 5 and 6 and ended on the sixteenth. It was a daytime operation, from Hulda to Jerusalem. Many battles to try and conquer the areas surrounding the road to Jerusalem had preceded this operation. On the night between April 2 and 3, we conquered the Castel. The Arabs prepared a counterattack and took it back. At that time, I was in Jerusalem with the convoy, which I couldn't take back to the Judean Foothills because the Castel was under their control again. Another attack from our end took place. I went to the operation's officer of the Jerusalem district, Zion Eldad, Zion the Redhead, and I heard that the commander of the Motza area wanted to retreat. I said, "Have you lost your minds? We don't have the Castel yet, and if he leaves Motza, Jerusalem will be completely cut off." They asked me what to do. I asked them not to retreat until nightfall. "I will get to Motza," I said. To keep Motza under our control they gave me soldiers from the Noam unit, named after Noam Grossman, who died during an operation in Ramallah. Meir Zorea, nicknamed "Zarro," was available and joined us. We drove to Motza and captured the sanatorium, so that at least that place wouldn't fall under their control. We had an armored vehicle which we had stolen from the British, and it had an Ordnance QF (Quick Fire) two-pound gun. On the way we hit a landmine, but nobody was hurt.

We had already conquered the Castel a few times. We conquered it, a convoy went by, we left, and the locals returned. During Operation

Nahshon, we conquered the Castel and a Jerusalem unit held it and stayed there. When the unit was in trouble, Palmach forces would send reinforcements. And then we killed the leader of the Jerusalem area Arab militias, Abd al-Qadir al-Husseini. As a result, there was a massive counterattack. It turned out they wanted his body. We lost many people in that battle, which gave birth to the saying, "The privates are retreating, and the commanders are covering the retreat."

In the morning, Yosef'le Tabenkin gave me the news that we had conquered the Castel, and he put me in command. I left Motza at 5 a.m. and took command over the Castel. I was there for a day. There was another attempted attack from the north, but it did not succeed. Al-Qawuqji was firing at us using Krupp 7.5 cm Model field guns. It was the first time we had witnessed an artillery attack. It was a new psychological state that we needed to explain to keep people calm. I explained it, and that was that.

We didn't receive orders to bomb the houses in the villages, but I bombed the Castel in bitterness and rage, feeling that what had happened there should never happen again. The Castel was the first village we bombed, and we left only the building at the top of the village. I remember saying, "This place will be an eternal disgrace [to the Arabs]." After that, we bombed all the villages from which the inhabitants had fled, so that the people who had fled would not return and so that we would not have to fight time and again to get convoys into Jerusalem.

After preparing the ground surrounding the road to Jerusalem, on April 5–6, the Nahshon convoy, which I commanded, ascended the road to Jerusalem, the first convoy after the fall of the previous three—Yehiam, Nabi Daniel, and Hulda. We knew the Arabs had bombed water carriers. We added a truck full of railroad ties to the convoy for the purposes of building bridges. The convoy stopped at a turn, part of it still exposed to shots fired from the Qalunya village. I got off the vehicle with two other men, and we filled the ditch with the railroad ties while we were under fire. And then a British military convoy arrived, heading away from Jerusalem. It drove over the railroad ties, and after the last armored vehicle had passed, the officer got two teams with Bren machineguns and covered us until I got the entire convoy through. The Arabs fired, blew out a few of our tires, and we suffered no further casualties. The convoy made it to Jerusalem safely.

The Nahshon convoy went down to the Judean foothills with a different commander. I collected the corpses at the Castel together with Beni Marshak, the Palmach's "Politrok." We were barely able to recognize them because they had mutilated those corpses, too. Some of the men had committed suicide. We gave them a temporary burial at Ma'ale HaHamisha, because digging graves into rock is a difficult task. We then transferred the bodies to the site where the Harel Brigade cemetery is now located, in Kiryat Anavim. Almost every night, on our way to battle, we would pass by kibbutz members digging graves in the rocks.

Between April 10 and 11, after we had conquered the Castel, I took part in the conquest of Qalunya, an Arab village that had been a threat to the conveys, near what is now Motza. I operated a Davidka (mortar) to try and assist the convoys. We found British and Yugoslavian explosives in the village. We fought against British soldiers who had defected and there were also British defectors who were fighting with us. Two tank crewmen brought two Cromwell tanks with no ammunition. The village was conquered and bombed.

Widening the Corridor Leading to Jerusalem

Tzova

After conquering the Castel, between April 18 and 19, I commanded a company sent to conquer Suba. Suba was a village atop a hump of land with extremely tall terraces. The plan was to approach after dark up to a distance of 275–325 yards from the village and then bomb it with Davidka shells holding forty–fifty kilograms of explosives.

You fire, destroy houses, people run away, and that allows you to go in. It turned out that the access route had been blocked by stone blockades, and taking them apart took a long time. I saw that daylight was approaching, and we were concerned about being shot by snipers. I gave the command to abort the mission, despite the anger that we felt about that. A few weeks later, when we had the appropriate assistance weaponry, including 120 mm mortars and 65 mm canons, we conquered Suba. Not a single soldier was lost.

Biddu and Bayt Surik

We conquered the village of Bayt Surik April 20–21. Some of the villagers fought back and some ran away, and when we were done, we bombed the village and left. I found rolls of film in an Iraqi soldier's pocket, and later, when we developed them, we saw pictures of dead Jewish soldiers who had been murdered in the Gilboa. We fired the Davidka at Biddu, which was nearby, and all the Arabs ran to Nebi Samuel. Suddenly, a black Cadillac appeared; my childhood friend, Yohay Ben Nun, had "stolen" the car from the Haifa port and had come to join us in battle. Yohay was a company commander in my platoon in Tel Yosef. Later, he joined the Palmach's navy seal unit, which was part of the Palmach's Fourth Battalion, of which he eventually took command. Since they had nothing to do in the Haifa port, he decided to join the Harel Brigade. That is who that man was, a very brave man, and sometimes I even thought to myself that he may just have been too brave.

I was with Yohay at Biddu. We went into an ancient, white, stone house, went down to the basement, and I said to him, "look, human-sized oil jugs, wooden plows, maybe from the time of the second Temple." We went out, bombed that building along with part of the village, and then left altogether. We had no intention of holding on to these lands because we didn't have the additional forces to do so. Every operation of this sort gave us what we wanted—a wider corridor and a steppingstone to another operation. It was as though we were firefighters. We scrambled from one operation site to the next, not even enjoying the fruits of our victory because we did not have enough soldiers to do so.

In a book memorializing Yohay, I found a description of what we had both experienced at Bayt Surik and Biddu over those two nights and three battles:

> We went to attack Bayt Surik, where there were Iraqi forces. We jumped from terrace to terrace as we headed towards the village. I remember Amos Horev beside me. We entered the village and as I moved my hand to get my pistol, I realized I was empty handed. While jumping on the terraces my pistol must have slipped out of its holster. Luckily, an Iraqi soldier's body was lying before us and next to it was a short Italian gun with a belt of bullets. I took the gun and the bullets and entered the village. The battle was over relatively quickly. The sun was already coming up and dawn was breaking, and I said to Amos, "I'm going to look for my pistol." Amos responded, "I'll come with you. I'll help you look."
>
> We went back and started retracing our steps, heading down. The terraces were endless, and it felt like looking for a needle in a haystack. The ground had been plowed and it didn't seem like we were going to find it. In the meantime, the morning choir had started to "sing," and snipers were shooting at us from all the surrounding mountain ranges. We took cover behind the terraces, we sat down, and I lit a cigarette. As we're sitting there Amos said, "what is that black thing sticking out of the mud?" I told him it was a Flint rock. He said, "Right, it's a Flint rock." We finished smoking the cigarette, and when we got up to leave Amos said, "Still, I'd like to see what this Flint rock is." He went over to the rock, and out of it came a mud-covered pistol. That was the mood in those days. A pistol is something you would never abandon. We happily fired all 14 rounds, and joined our forces which were heading to the village of Biddu.

When we got nearer to the village, the Davidka was set up and fired, creating a big explosion. Then we saw the sad scene of hundreds of villagers leaving the village . . .

We entered the village and didn't meet any enemy forces. An old Arab man was sitting at the edge of a well near the entrance to the village, blinking blind eyes and trying to understand what was happening in his surroundings. I remember the feeling I had then and the concern that some trigger-happy soldier would use this "opportunity" to fire at the line of refugees and kill them. But then we got the order not to open fire—and everybody put their safety catches back on. We're not proud of this, nor is the Palmach, it's not what we do, but these things did happen during the war.

Fighting in Jerusalem and its Neighborhoods

The Harel Brigade, whose main job was to guarantee the land routes to Jerusalem, was called on to fight inside Jerusalem on a number of occasions. On April 25–26, we conquered Sheikh Jarrah. The British arrived with tanks and wanted to forcefully remove us. Yitzhak Rabin was able to reach an agreement according to which we would pull out. It was important to the British, because once the mandate was over that was their planned exit route from the area.

Katamon and San Simon

Twice, we went out to conquer the San Simon Monastery. Our first attempt, on April 26–27, was a failure. On the second attempt, we came from the west, and after a very difficult battle, we conquered it. Among the soldiers were Raful (Rafael Eitan) and Dado (David Elazar), who would both later become IDF chiefs of staff. Yosef'le Tabenkin told me to take a platoon and the Davidka and head towards the monastery from the direction of where the Museum of Islamic Art is today, on Palmach street. I used the Davidka to bomb the building. At 4:00 a.m.

or 5:00 a.m., we detected an ambush together with Uzi Narkiss, and we weren't injured. I crossed the stone wall with two other soldiers, I entered the monastery and took control over it. I was surprised to see dead people in the posts surrounding the monastery and along the fence. I found out that they didn't have helmets, and that they were all hit in the head while on their posts. There was a pile of bodies in the monastery, some of them women, some of them nuns. The battle was over.

And then, the capture of Katamon, the entire slope all the way to the German Colony, and then into town, mostly to leverage our success. If we had had more forces, we could have conquered the entire city of Jerusalem and kept our success going all the way down to the Dead Sea.

With the Last of our Strength—The Road to Jerusalem is Blocked Again, and We Fight Again

Even after Operation Nahshon, we were still having a hard time getting convoys up to Jerusalem. The convoys had grown bigger, sometimes up to 250 trucks. We failed again and again. We were sitting in the Castel, but the entire mountain range, from Saris to Sha'ar Ha'gai, was under control of the Arab forces. We hadn't held onto Bayt Mahsir or the mountain range. Despite Operation Nahshon, Jerusalem was under siege again, and we used the last of our strength to fight and conquer Bayt Mahsir, which was necessary to prevent Jerusalem from being cut off again.

Bayt Mahsir, which today is Beit Meir, was a large, barricaded village from which it was easy to control the road from Sha'ar Ha'gai to Saris. The battle there was different, with a different objective. Conquering Bayt Mahsir was of special importance because without it we would not have been able to reopen the road to Jerusalem or even to create the right conditions for opening the road. The length of the battle was also different. It went on for a few days, between May 5 and May 7, and we didn't just charge up and conquer the place. The

Harel Brigade had to fight in face-to-face combat. First, we took care of the posts that had been set up around the village, and only then did we get to the village itself to capture it. This mission also required great physical exertion. We were using the last of our strength and the last of our supplies, including our limited gasoline and ammunition. I joined Yiska Shadmi after conquering the post north of Bayt Mahsir. They were in the height of a counterattack. We threw grenades at the people charging at us, fired every weapon we had, and held them back.

The battle for Latrun and the opening of Burma Road would not have been possible if we did not control the entire area of the corridor to Jerusalem to Bab al-Wad and the ridges facing south from the Latrun road. Despite the Seventh Brigade's conquering Bayt Susin and Bayt Jiz, without Bayt Mahsir Jerusalem would have remained cut off. It can definitely be said that the victory at Bayt Mahsir allowed for the opening of the Burma Road.

CHAPTER 7

A Nation Fighting against
Regular Armies

The mandate was over, the British had left, and on May 14, 1948, the establishment of the State of Israel was declared. As soon as the British left and the declaration was made, Arab states' military forces invaded and joined the Arab forces within Israel, the same ones we had already been fighting against for the past five and a half months. A completely new phase had begun in the war for the survival of the newly-established Jewish state.

We didn't celebrate the declaration of the establishment of the state, and I don't remember any excitement. There was no time to celebrate because we were engaged in battle, and from our perspective the troubles occupying us hadn't stopped. Gradually, and while fighting, we became part of the IDF as it was being transformed into a regular army. We continued to fight as part of three Palmach brigades, with increasing cooperation with the new units.

I was the Sixth Battalion's second-in-command; our battalion had been fighting since the beginning of the war. By the middle of May, the battalion was so exhausted and worn out that it barely still existed and needed to be reorganized. So many people from that battalion had been killed. Those who had survived were split up between the other two battalions—the Fourth and the Fifth. As a "freelance" commander, I helped the other battalions on special operations.

An Attempt to Conquer the Old City of Jerusalem—"I'm Not Asking for Advice"

We, the Palmach, were not supposed to take part in battles within the city, but David Shaltiel, the commander of Jerusalem from the Etzioni Brigade, asked that we assist with military deception. His plan was to conquer the old city through the Jaffa Gate, whereas we advised attacking from the Rockefeller Museum. He responded that he was not asking for advice. I went along with Ra'anana and Uzi Narkiss to prepare the distraction. Ra'anana and I were very tired. We went through the Jewish Agency building and rested in the conference hall. We put down our Thompson submachineguns and spread our bodies out on the table, hands, legs, and all. Two important people walked in, Golda Meir and Zalman Aran, later a long-serving Cabinet minister. We didn't even stand up in their honor. And then Golda stood over us and asked, "Is there hope?" We knew the situation was not great, and in the background the Egyptians were advancing and were almost at the entrance to Jerusalem.[1] But regardless of all that, we said, "Of course there's hope, there's no problem whatsoever." What could we tell her? Golda's eyes lit up from the reassurance our response provided. Then I understood. People who were not involved in the fighting itself saw the situation from a very different perspective.

Our brigade created a distraction on the night between May 18 and 19, conquered Mount Zion, opened the Zion gate, and reached the Jewish quarter. But only part of the old city had been conquered. Shaltiel had failed, because of the Jordanians' strong barricade at the Jaffa gate.

The Battle for Latrun and the Price of Arrogance

The British had built a fort in Latrun to control the road between Jerusalem and Tel Aviv. They withdrew from it on May 14, 1948, with the end of the British Mandate. On May 16, it was occupied by the British-officered Arab Legion, the army of what was then known as the Emirate of Transjordan. Our conquering the Latrun fort was vital since the only road that connected Jerusalem to the Judean foothills went right past it. The entire area was heavily defended by the Legion—not just the fort and the Latrun Monastery—filled with military posts, cannons, British armored vehicles, and about three thousand soldiers. There were no tanks in this battle, and we only had an armored vehicle that carried homemade machineguns.

Ben-Gurion ordered Shlomo Shamir, commander of the Seventh Brigade, to conquer Latrun at any and all cost. As far as Ben-Gurion was concerned, Latrun was crucial for the fight over Jerusalem. The brigade attacked Latrun on the night between May 24 and 25—and failed. I was at brigade headquarters and I witnessed the disaster. It was a hot day and the horrible buzzing of the flies bothered us terribly.

This painful failure was preceded by a meeting that perhaps could have predicted the future. A short while before the battle, we received a message asking us to come to the Okava razorblade factory near Rishon LeZion to pick up 150 additional people, all Holocaust survivors who had been in the British internment camps in Cyprus, and to bring them to the Harel Brigade. I left Jerusalem on May 19 in a single armored vehicle. Heading to the Judean foothills along with me were Nathan Shaham, Benny Marshak, and Ben Dunkelman, a Canadian officer who had been fighting in World War II and had joined the Harel Brigade as a volunteer. When we went past Hulda, we were asked where are you from? We yelled that we were from Jerusalem, but they didn't believe us. The road we took bypassed Latrun, which was already in the hands of the Arab Legion, and the snipers shot at us only after we came out of Sha'ar Ha'gai, near the monastery. Later, this road served as part of Burma Road.

When I came to get the soldiers, whom we needed as badly as oxygen, they were in the courtyard of the command headquarters, where the chief headquarters are located today. I heard about the Seventh Brigade's operational plan to break open the road to

Jerusalem. They were planning on attacking Latrun. I met with Vivian (also known as Chaim) Herzog, the operations and intelligence commander of the Seventh Brigade. I told him that I was going to get reinforcements. He said something along the lines of, "Why are you debating and looking for roundabout ways? Just wait, in a day or two we will break open the road leading to you. You will be able to drive to Jerusalem on a bus." It was explained to me that this was going to be a real battle, with cannons and everything.

When they started bringing the injured and the dead back from the battle for Latrun, I understood that I would not be taking a bus to Jerusalem after all. For me, this was a painful encounter with a military culture that didn't value the way we had been fighting in the Palmach, that placed its hopes on battles fought in the British style.

Jerusalem No Longer Under Siege — The Story of Burma Road

As we were retreating from Latrun, the Seventh Brigade, with the help of the Harel Brigade, conquered two villages south of Latrun, Bayt Jiz and Bayt Susin. Conquering these two villages enabled us shortly after to locate the alternative road to Jerusalem.

When I was at the Sharona headquarters' courtyard, running late to meet reinforcements, I was met by Yisrael Galili, the Haganah chief of staff, who told me that there was an American officer in the Seventh Brigade, Colonel David Marcus (a West Point graduate who had volunteered to help us under the name of Michael Stone), who evidently did not know his way around the terrain. Galili asked that I take him along with me to get to know the area. I received a note from Yigael Yadin, then head of operations, which I was asked to pass on to the commander of the Seventh Brigade, Shlomo Shamir: "Amos S., from the Moatza [the Palmach headquarters], will take care of transferring the backup forces and will also be in charge of all attempts to make contact with Jerusalem. Please allow him to move around freely."

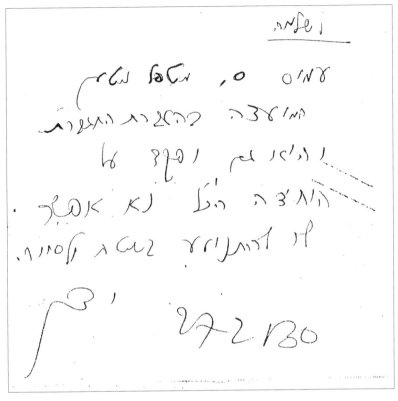

Yadin's letter to the commander of the Seventh Brigade

To Shlomo,
Amos S. is taking care in my name for the
Moatza (The Palmach Headquarters)
in transferring reinforcement
and he will also command
that unit. Please enable
him to move in the area and to patrol.
Yadin

On the way from Tel Aviv to Rishon LeTzion to receive the
reinforcement soldiers, we drove in the jeep of a Palmach officer
named Gavri'el Rapaport, known as Gavrush, from Kibbutz Beit Alpha,

who had stolen the jeep from the Etzel. In the jeep were Colonel
Stone, Shlomo Shamir, the commander of the Seventh Brigade, and
me. I said to Stone, "Come up the hill with me, we'll see Latrun." I
asked for the unit at Bayt Susin to cover us, and we went up. Below
we saw corpses of our own soldiers, killed while retreating. I said to
Stone, "Knowing the area, we can break a way through to Jerusalem.
We can bulldoze our way to Jerusalem." We came down from the
viewpoint and drove to Hulda. Together we continued to the "Okaba"
factory, and we took the reinforcement of 150 soldiers in buses to
Bayt Sosin. We gave each soldier a three-inch shell—150 people, 150
shells—when in all of Jerusalem there were only thirteen shells for
three mortars.

The soldiers carried the shells on foot on the dirt road behind
the mountain range, at the entrance to Sha'ar Ha'gai. Shlomo
Shiloach from Givat Brenner (a kibbutz one mile south of Rehovot),
nicknamed Shlauchi, a company commander in Harel, led them to
Sha'ar Ha'gai in the dark, and from there to Kiryat Anavim. Eight
kilometers, two hours of walking. After that section, when you come
out at the comprehensive school for Bayt Jiz and Bayt Susin, you
arrive at the hard part, 1.5-2 miles, allegedly impassible by vehicle.
In the entire area there were only huge rocks and boulders—not even
a single tree.

On the night between May 29 and May 30, after completing
our mission and bringing an unprecedented amount of people and
weapons, Gavrush and I left from Bayt Susin and drove on, thinking
that maybe we would find some way to get through the hardest part.

It was night, we arrived at the terraces, and we fell asleep. In the
early hours of the morning, while it was still dark, we heard noise
coming from the east. Luckily, we didn't open fire at the figures that
appeared before us: Ra'anana with a jeep pushed by eight people. The
moment the two jeeps were together, we had a road in Wadi Abu-
Abed. We had not planned this in advance. We hugged and kissed
each other.

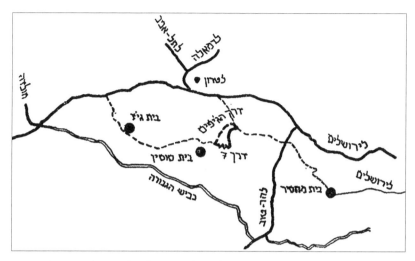

This was the road—that was how the Burma Road was discovered

We immediately drove to report to Yadin. I was brought in to see Ben-Gurion, who approved without delay the sending of reinforcement jeeps, including his own. We got two 65 mm cannons, a machinegun, ammunition, and medical equipment from logistics, all to be brought to Jerusalem. We loaded about six tons of equipment. Colonel Stone wrote a note to the head of logistics, Ephraim Ben-Artzi, and in it he wrote, "Please give Amos two guns and a mortar for Jerusalem."

At night, we drove back to Hulda in jeeps, thirteen in number, with six tons of equipment, and we started the ascent. One jeep fell into the valley. We were busy trying to get it out and didn't have enough hours of darkness left to continue the drive: we had gone through an area that was not under our control. We went back to the Hulda grove and were so tired that even the bombing of Hulda by Iraqi planes did not wake us up.

That night, we tried again. Gavrush, a virtuoso driver, Ra'anana, and I in the front, people with tools clearing out rocks. A force from Harel was waiting on the other side of the mountain range. After a few hours, thirteen heavily loaded jeeps made it to the other side. Immense excitement. We drove to Jerusalem. At Kfar Bilu, I loaded a crate of cucumbers—Jerusalem was under siege. Dawn started to break as we arrived near Shneller Camp, and I saw an acquaintance from a Jerusalem unit wearing a New Zealand hat. I stopped beside him and said, "Nice hat, give it to me." He immediately said, "Give me a cucumber and I will give you the hat." I took a cucumber out of the back crate and got the hat. The poor guy hadn't seen a cucumber in three months.

The importance of what we had achieved was not the quantity that we brought, but rather the fact that we were able to bring cargo to Jerusalem. Thirteen jeeps, each with half a ton of cargo, drove from the Judean Hills and entered the besieged city of Jerusalem, where no one could come in or out, and now here were people—coming and going. We had established a political fact of the utmost importance: Jerusalem was no longer under siege—and all this was just a few days before the first lull in the fighting.

If I had to rank my contributions in this war, this would be among the most important ones: locating the jeep roads through Ha'Ayalot

Colonel Stone's letter

that a certain reporter called the Burma Road. Ra'anana from the Fourth Battalion, myself, Gavrush, and a few others had accomplished this exceptional feat. Gavrush and I went from west to east; Ra'anana, Avraham Chen, and others went from east to west. And now you could transfer supplies and even lay down a water line to the city.

Our resourcefulness and the ability to locate this road were the result of combined knowledge and experience from all our years in the Palmach. Years prior to that we had trained and patrolled, learning to get to know the area well. It was the training area of the Eighth Company, my territory. Kfar Uria, and after it Hartuv, Hulda, Neve Ilan, Kiryat Anavim and Ma'ale HaHamisha became a Jewish chain. On the parallel mountain range were Saris, Bayt Mahsir, Dir Amar,

Engineering operation to lay a water line to besieged Jerusalem and paving the "Burma Road."

Kisle, below that Eshtaol, Tsor'a, which were all Arab villages at the time. The inhabitants had left. We had bombed it all.

For two weeks, we used the path we created to take supplies up in jeeps, six tons at a time. The water system from Rosh HaAyin had been cut off by Qawuqji and the Jordanians long before we completed the road for the trucks. After we opened Burma Road, we placed a water line that reached to the water pumps at Sha'ar Ha'gai and provided Jerusalem with water. It was a huge engineering operation.

During a lull in the fighting, the Seventh Brigade started using bulldozers to pave the path that we called "Derech Sheva"; no one got near that path. The road reached its end at a cliff. Trucks came from Tel Aviv to the cliff, carriers loaded the equipment on their backs and took it down to the bottom of the cliff, and from there everything was brought to Jerusalem in trucks. They recruited the carriers in Tel Aviv.

True, we weren't the ones who got the bulldozers to pave the way, and we weren't the ones who brought the big trucks, but you can't deny the Palmach their original achievement—locating the Burma Road—which drastically changed the situation in Jerusalem. It was a rare, once-in-a-lifetime achievement.

Jerusalem and the Harel Brigade

The time of the convoys to Jerusalem had come to an end. I viewed it as a huge political achievement. Even though we were neck deep in fighting, we kept our thoughts and opinions about the bigger picture open. In the midst of the harsh, painful everyday fighting, the fighting forces were drained of their ability to understand the political implications of the situation. The fact that we had been able to break the siege and reconnect Jerusalem to the outside world was vastly important for the establishment of the State of Israel. It was around this time, during the first lull in the fighting, that Matti Megged had interviewed and documented the feelings of both the soldiers and the commanders of the Sixth Battalion:

At first we only vaguely felt how committed we were to Jerusalem, but over time this vague feeling turned into something more tangible that united us . . . this commitment to getting food to Jerusalem took hold not only among the soldiers who accompanied the convoys, but among all of the soldiers of the battalion. This feeling of commitment, obviously, took on a very simple, material, everyday form, but behind it was the greatest goal: saving the city for the Jewish people and the up-and-coming state. (Matti Megged, The Sixth Battalion Tells its Story (*A pocket book for the Hebrew soldier, Israel Defense Forces Department of Culture 1949*).

Even between battles we never stopped working to improve our coordination and performance. On April 16, 1948, at the age of twenty-six, Yitzhak Rabin formed the Palmach Harel Brigade in the Jerusalem mountains, which he commanded until the end of May. He was then replaced by Yosef'le Tabenkin. The brigade held command over the rest of the battalions that were fighting in Jerusalem and the surrounding areas; the Fourth Battalion was under the command of Yosef'le Tabenkin, the Fifth under the command of Menachem Rusak, and the Sixth under the command of Zvi Zamir. At first it consisted of about thirteen hundred people. We lost 431 soldiers, a third of the force.

This Harel Brigade was not a particularly harmonious bunch. There was tension between the battalion commanders, and there were major differences between the battalions. Each one had come from a different place and a different framework in the Palmach. And yet, none of these factors took away from its main achievement: that if it weren't for the Harel Brigade Jerusalem would not have remained under our control. The Harel Brigade was essential to our cause, perhaps also as a result of the fatalistic approach it developed. There is a lot of power in fatalism and acceptance. This was the brigade that lost so many soldiers but never stopped fighting. The Harel Brigade tried not only to maintain the connection between Jerusalem and the lowlands and to assist the Jerusalem forces in the war inside the city, but also expanded the corridor to the north, and then to the south.

When I look at *Sefer HaPalmach* (the Palmach Book) and the calendar of events recorded in it, I think to myself, "Oh my God, did we actually do all of this, every day and every night?" Indeed, it was a long, continuous war. We each did one long shift, with no break, because there was nobody to take our place.

On the southern front, we began a new chapter in both the fighting and the overall situation, completely different from anything I had encountered in the war near Jerusalem as part of the Harel Brigade. That being said, the Harel chapter of my life had made its way deep into my heart and built me up to become who I was in the rest of my professional life. It helped define my values, the ones by which I live, think, and act to this very day. I was fortunate to have been part of a group of people, a military organization, without which the State of Israel would not have existed. I'm not saying that others didn't have a part in that, but when you put everything in proportion, it is clear that we were the main factor, which is why I am comfortable with the claim to our central role in the War of Independence. I say this and take full responsibility for it: without the Harel Brigade, we would not have had Jerusalem, and if we had not had Jerusalem—we would not have the State of Israel.

Two More Failures—Latrun Remains Jordanian

Before the second attack on Latrun, we experienced another failure. In response to an order, a company was transferred from the Sixth Battalion to the Seventh Brigade. I met the company commander, Jacob Yaki Veg from Kibbutz Rehavia; earlier, he had been a platoon commander in the Eighth Company under my command. He said to me, "Amos, I have a bad feeling." Indeed. They broke into the Latrun police building but were unable to bomb the entrance. The forces that were supposed to follow them in did not arrive, and they were compelled to retreat. Yaki Veg was killed, though Eytan Yarkoni got out alive in his armored vehicle.

As part of the second attempt to conquer Latrun, on May 30–31, we, the Sixth Battalion, were supposed to ascend from the east along the Legion's line of cannons. We got about halfway up, and the attempt failed. Mistakes were made. The Yiftach Brigade participated in the attack, and Amos Lapin Ben-Arie, who was a platoon commander in the Eighth Company, conquered a Jordanian post. Moshe Kelman, the battalion commander, was supposed to follow us up and break through the line of cannons. He made a mistake and went up to a different post which he thought was ours—and the mission failed. With my own eyes, I saw the Jordanians killing our injured soldiers.

I didn't want to drive back after this failure. Pensively, I walked to Abu Gosh. When I arrived, I saw one of our Jerusalem veterans, Katinka, pale as chalk. I asked, "What happened to you?" and he replied, "Somebody just left to tell your parents that you were killed." Amos Ben Arie had fallen, and they mistakenly thought it had been me. I was able to get to my parents in time to prevent them from having a heart attack.

During the two attempts to conquer Latrun, Operations Yoram Alef and Bet, 123 people were killed, many were injured, and others were taken prisoner. Latrun remained Jordanian until the Six-Day War.

Latrun May Have Remained Jordanian but We Conquered Its Surroundings

The Sixth Battalion was headquartered in Saris, by the upper pumps. Zvi Zamir was battalion commander, and I was his second-in-command. Yitzhak Yakov, nicknamed Yatza, was my assistant. The units were spread out in the field. Under the command of Losik Chen, company commander, we completed the conquest of Suba without any losses. We bombed Suba with 120 mm mortars with time fuses in order to penetrate the buildings, along with 65 mm cannons. The village was

half-empty when we entered it. The Arab fighters had fled. I looked
back with satisfaction at the criticism that had been directed at me a few
months back when I refused to conquer Suba without the appropriate
means, in daylight, which would have meant risking soldiers' lives.

It was decided to expand the corridor leading to Bayt Nuba (June
17–18). Instead of banging our heads against the wall and attacking
Latrun as the Seventh Brigade did, the Palmach command tried an
indirect approach—closing Latrun off from the north and cutting it
off from the road to Ramallah, a maneuver we repeated later at Kiryat
Gat against an Egyptian brigade. I commanded two companies in
the east section, one from the Sixth Battalion and one from the Fifth
Battalion. Siko, later to be Professor Pinchas Zusman and director
general of the Ministry of Defense, was a company commander on
the western section. We went up the hard way. Mules carrying the
ammunition slid down the hill. The connection between myself and
the company commander was lost, and in order not to repeat the
mistake made when Moshe Kelman misidentified the post, I lit a fire,
to signal to him—"I am here." We easily conquered the mountain
range when it was dark. I organized the units. Counterattacks by the
Arab Legion started in the morning. They took some serious hits, and
we succeeded in conquering the posts of Bayt Nuba.

Yeruham Cohen, an officer in an elite intelligence force that
gathered information from behind enemy lines who at the time was
Yigal Allon's adjutant, recalls:

> *Zvika Zamir, commander of Harel's sixth battalion, who was
> part of the operations in the Jerusalem corridor, tasked the force
> with a mission, under the command of Amos Horev. They were
> to minimize the Arab Legion's hold south-east of the Latrun area
> and cut it off from its other side near Ramallah. It was one of the
> most daring and challenging missions of the War of Independence.
> The fighters made their way on foot, carrying most of the unit's
> equipment on their backs, assisted by two transport mules (both of*

which tumbled down the hill and died). The force made its way from Ma'ale HaHamisha to Neve Ilan, conquered the village Bayt Tul, and from there continued until it was near the village of Bayt Nuba, which lies in the back of Latrun, where it barricaded itself on one of the hills along the way. The enemy, who understood the dangers of being surrounded, struck with a strong counterattack but was held back, despite its advantage and its superiority in terms of both people and equipment. Our people struck the enemy very strongly, and the enemy lost almost an entire company.

At the end of the operation, Amos Horev and Zerubbabel Arbel reported to Yigal and suggested taking advantage of the conquest of Dir Rafat and looking for a suitable route to Jerusalem, that would serve, even if only temporarily, as an alternative for the blocked road to Latrun. It could also serve as an alternative to Burma Road, which was inconvenient and difficult to traverse. Yigal gave his approval, and a day later both returned with a map, and a new route marked out on it. The next day Yigal went out to inspect the new route, and it was approved. A temporary road was prepared, which later became the foundation for the paving of the "Route of Heroism." (Yeruham Cohen, In the light of day and in the dark, *Amikam Publishing House 1969, pages 162–164*)

"The Sixth Battalion Will Yet Arise"

The Sixth Battalion, under the command of Zvi Zamir, had started its war during the battles over Jerusalem on November 29, 1947. It had suffered so many losses that it was completely worn down within the first five and a half months of fighting over the road to Jerusalem. During the first lull in fighting, which started on June 10, 1948, we went down the Judean foothills to Camp 80 in Pardes Hanna, determined to reestablish the battalion. Not in the classic way, but by starting anew. Our commitment and dedication to this battalion was evident in the book, *The Sixth Battalion Will Yet Arise.*

I was very involved in the process. We received backup, people who came from abroad, Hungarians who didn't speak Hebrew or Yiddish. We trained them intensively. As part of the organizing that the IDF was doing, some of the battalion's fighters were transferred to other units, mostly to the Seventh Brigade, under the command of Haim Laskov, a fomer British soldier and later the IDF's fifth chief of staff. On the night the lull ended, the rehabilitated battalion was preparing to ascend to Jerusalem with new weapons: 120 mm mortars, 65 mm cannons, Canon de 65 M model 1906. As we were getting into a line as a convoy, a group of Palmach soldiers suddenly showed up. They had been detailed to Laskov and demanded to join us. Officially, they defected. In my opinion, this was an expression of the deep connections between the Palmach fighters on the one hand, and on the other hand it was an expression of the alienation and distrust between the Palmach and the former British soldiers. For Haim Laskov, for whom leadership and role modeling were natural and innate, this was a harsh blow. It may be that this incident negatively impacted our relationship with him for a while.

An Encounter Between Cultures—the Palmach and the Former British Soldiers

The transition from being an almost entirely independent unit to joint missions with a brigade of former British soldiers who had served in the Jewish brigade during WWII was not a simple one. The difference between the Palmach commander and the commander who had come from the British army would manifest itself in constant tension during the War of Independence, when the IDF was founded, and we all had to join one national framework.

This contrast was also noticeable in the differences between the commanders' training courses run by the Palmach and those run by ex-British soldiers, from squad commander and up. For the Palmach, even in the squad commander course, which was the most elementary course, we studied the principles of war and emphasized the individual soldier's broad set of abilities so that they could think for themselves. This is what our fighting situation demanded, since a small group of soldiers, and sometimes even individual soldiers, could find themselves nearly alone in the field on more than one occasion. In contrast, in the training received by the former British soldiers, the emphasis was on repetition of specific fighting models.

The encounter between Zvi Zamir and the Seventh Brigade commander provides a clear example of the difference between the Palmach soldiers and the former British soldiers. Zvi Zamir recalls:

> The commander of the 7th brigade, Shlomo Shamir, nicknamed
> Fistuk [pistachio], who was an Israeli high-ranking commander in
> the British army and well-liked by Ben-Gurion, requested that I meet
> with him. I knew the 7th brigade was planning an attack on Latrun.
> We were in Tel HaShomer, and he said to me, "Run organizational
> drills with your battalion soldiers." And I said to him, "Wait a minute,
> what do you mean organizational drills? There is a war [out there],
> and how exactly do you plan on fighting this war with the armored
> vehicles you took from us? Now, since these armored vehicles only
> travel on a paved road, and not a dirt road, I think the people should
> be training in the movement expected of them as part of the offensive
> plan, not organizational drills." This is how he responded. "They
> didn't teach you how to think." I replied, "Fistuk, all they taught me
> in the Palmach was how to think." (Boaz Lev Tov, "Interview with
> Zvi Zamir" [Yitzhak Rabin Center, June 8, 1998])

I had a similar encounter with Haim Herzog, the intelligence and operational officer of the Seventh Brigade, as we were preparing for the first battle to conquer Latrun. He was assured of their success and treated my need to find a bypass route to Jerusalem with disregard and disrespect. He also openly expressed disdain for the primitive fighting, as he saw it, of the Palmach—without the customary firearms used in modern standard armies.

When there was an encounter with former British soldiers, they gave us the feeling of—"Who do you think you are? We, the soldiers of the Jewish brigade of the British army, have a clear military canon, and, justifiably, see the British major as an expert. On the other hand, you Palmach people are not military experts." Indeed, we were not classic military professionals. We were not bound by fixed, strict patterns, nor by an organized canon. From the beginning of our journey in the Palmach we were shaped, and we shaped other commanders, to be thinkers—not just brave. There were things that we understood almost instinctively, and we adapted our techniques to the unique reality we experienced. Lacking communication devices, when there was no way to receive commands from high-ranking officers, we needed commanders who could analyze the situation on their own and make decisions on the spot.

As our forces grew in numbers and we worked outside the framework of a squad or a platoon, it became more challenging. I have no doubt that commanders who properly internalized the British military doctrine would have had a hard time, if not a total lack of success, acting properly based solely on the information and equipment we had back then. For example, there were times during the siege on Jerusalem when we only had twenty bullets per gun and thirteen bombs for two mortars. In March 1948, guns and machineguns arrived. The first proper gun I saw as an officer was Czech. It appeared at Hulda for the Nahshon Operation: Mausers, light machineguns—MG34—called "Magladim," and a Besa machinegun from Czechoslovakia. For the first time, every soldier had a weapon.

The Storm of Reorganizing as One Army of the State of Israel—"The Altalena"

The lull in fighting and the time the Sixth Battalion had to recuperate was not yet over, and on June 20, 1948, the battalion already received an order to head out to the coastal dunes of Kfar Vitkin to prevent the

Irgun (IZL) ship "Altalena" from unloading people and equipment at the beach. They already had succeeded in unloading some but following an exchange of fire they returned to the sea. Zvi Zamir and I returned to Camp 80. The next day I drove to the Palmach headquarters in Tel Aviv. The "Altalena" had docked just across from there. In his book "Service Notebook," published in English "The Rabin Memoirs," Rabin wrote about the events of this difficult day, when Jews shot at Jews. He arrived at the Palmach headquarters at the Rich Hotel, where the French embassy stands today. Yigal Allon appointed him the Tel Aviv commander as well as the commander of a Palmach force that was gathered at the Palmach headquarters and was preparing to prevent an IZL attempt to take over the building:

Back ups of IZL fighters were pouring onto the beach from the ship at sea and from Tel Aviv. Just minutes after 10 am they opened fire at the headquarters. We fired back at the shooters, IZL fire teams who were spread out along the beach in large numbers . . . the IZL fired a PIAT towards the Palmach headquarters. . . . That seriously exacerbated the situation. . . . I reached the conclusion that there was no other choice other than to push the IZL fighters away from the building. Amos Horev and I go up to the roof of the building and throw grenades towards the fire teams that were spread out on the beach. The fire ceased. (Yitzhak Rabin and Dov Goldstein, "Service Notebook" The Rabin Memoirs [Ma'ariv Library 1979]) (IZL)(National Military Organization)

From Harel to the Southern Front–Betrayal?

I didn't leave the Palmach, but I did leave Harel, and there were those who considered that an act of betrayal. It was not easy for me. True, the dire situation in the south justified my decision, but I do not deny the fact that I also had personal reasons that were not directly related to the situation.

At the end of the first lull in fighting, when the Sixth Battalion, in which I was second-in-command to Zvi Zamir, was restored and back in action, the head of the brigade, Yosef'le Tabenkin, wanted me to establish an "armored" battalion, the Tenth Battalion. While I was learning from the head of the Seventh Brigade, Ben Dunkelman, what an armored battalion is, Yigal Allon approached me and asked that I join him at the southern headquarters. Yigal had established the southern headquarters and commanded it. It was responsible for military operations from Bethlehem to the south. It was almost a completely Palmach unit. Its second-in-command and head of operations was Yitzhak Rabin, and I was appointed Yitzhak's second-in-command. I left the establishment of the Tenth Battalion to my second-in-command, Shiloach. It was a great honor to work with Yigal, and I did not for a moment regret my decision.

At the time, Harel was very "cliquey." I didn't like those dynamics. They made me feel uneasy. The relationship between Yitzhak Rabin and Yosef'le Tabenkin was strained. Rabin was his commander when he established the brigade, and when he left for the southern front as Yigal Allon's second-in-command, Yosef'le Tabenkin was appointed commander of the brigade. Yosef'le was part of a tight-knit group, mostly from Ein Harod. But he wanted me, I was one of his many seconds-in-command. Despite that, I preferred to leave. There were people with personal squabbles in the southern front as well, but it was a little "cleaner" there. I had the feeling that I was breathing cleaner, fresher air.

CHAPTER 8

The End of an Era—
The Palmach Had Shaped My Path
for the Rest of My Life

The Haganah was a large organization comprising tens of thousands of people, partly recruited, partially trained. Sort of like an army of reserve-duty soldiers who only show up for service once in a while. The Palmach, on the other hand, wanted to be a fully recruited force. Its goal was to establish a military force capable of handling unexpected military challenges. The founders of the Palmach didn't know when exactly war would break out. It was clear there would be a war, though it was clear that it wouldn't happen so long as the British were here. But what would happen after they left?

When the state was established, we were the people's army, the best of the IDF. At the beginning, we were a few hundred fighters, and we all knew one another. By the War of Independence, the Palmach had grown to 3,120 people. Of them, 2,200 were recruited fighters and 920 were trained reserve-duty soldiers, nicknamed "the Reserve." It was an unusual military organization because the soldiers also worked at the same time in their civilian lives, and so they lived in cycles of working and training. The work was actually conducive to our abilities as fighters. We lived as part of the kibbutz movement, and we were not disconnected from society. We trained intensely, preparing for armed battle. At its core, the Palmach was a massive youth movement that had learned how to fight.

We started out as a group of teenagers who left home and cut ties with almost everything outside the Palmach. We were a group that trained, walked the land, and built a secret military right under the noses of the British. We were not gangs, we were a real army, made up of squads, platoons, companies, and, later on, battalions. During the war for Jerusalem, we created a brigade, and then two more, that fought under the command of Yigal Allon the entire time until we conquered Um Rush (later known as Eilat). We were able to progress from the "Jo'ara Academy" to training platoon commanders and, ultimately, to operating in brigades.

It's difficult to explain this experience of the Palmach and the underground forces. Every underground force had its own romantic halo. We, my generation, skipped our youth. We were like fish in water only in the kibbutz. We walked around with pins hidden under our lapels that said H.R., which stood for "Hebrew Recruitment." Our friends who went to the British Army's Jewish brigade walked around in uniform. They looked at us in a funny way. Explain to them why they can wear uniform and we cannot, because we are in the underground force. Because you want to explain it to them, but you can't. We didn't show our pins to anyone. The British officers didn't know they were hidden under our lapels.

We operated completely covertly. At times, the Palmach would provide me with fake IDs with names like Davidson or Amos Sapir. I don't know who forged those documents.

We weren't particularly clever. We just understood the simple rules that existed back then. The enemy understood these rules, too: This is a war; there will be a winner and a loser. But what was our ultimate objective? We wanted it to be our first and last War of Independence, and we wanted peace afterwards.

It may be that the Palmach's unique way of operating was the reason that such a small organization gave the IDF five chiefs of staff (Yitzhak Rabin, Haim Bar Lev, David Elazar, Rafael Eitan, and Mordechai Gur—also, Moshe Dayan started his career in the Palmach) and over twenty major-generals (among them Yigal Allon, Zvi Zamir, Avraham Adan, Yeshayahu Gavish, Yohay Ben-Nun, Matti Peled, Yitzhak Sade, Yitzhak Hofi, Danny Matt, Elad

Peled, Eli Zeira, Dan Laner, Uzi Narkiss, Shlomo Gazit, Gad Navon, Rehavam Ze'evi, Asaf Simhoni, Herzl Shafir, Shmuel Gonen, Mordechai Hod, Yohanan Ratner, myself, Motke Ben Porat, Aharon Davidi, Samuel Mola Cohen, and Shimon Avidan), along with high ranking individuals in the Mossad and the General Security Services (including Mike Harari and Rafi Eitan, and Avraham Shalom, head of the GSS [Shabak]), and many others. So as we can see, the Palmach did indeed have a huge impact on the structure of the IDF and the future general staff.

In addition to its contribution to the security of the state, which was a natural next step for the Palmachniks, you can also see the contributions made by the many writers, artists, and academics who were also fighters in the Palmach and helped build settlements. Some seventy settlements were established by graduates of the Palmach, and about forty of them became kibbutzim.

Looking back at my personal experiences and how they became embedded within me, I recognize a few explanations that can answer the question "What was the Palmach?" more completely than the factual descriptions of how it was formed and in which battles it played a major role.

Commitment at All Costs, the Failures, the Losses—and Harel Moves Forward

We experienced failures in the brigade, and there were missions we didn't complete, such as the convoys to Nabi Daniel and Hulda, the battle in Nabi Samuel, and others. Wrong decisions were made, some the result of commanders' mistakes, some due to the lack of proper equipment. The failures intensified the arguments between us regarding the best course of action. These heated arguments came from a place of real responsibility and were not intended to point blame or to get on somebody's good side. That was not part of our military culture or character. To this day, I am confident that my approach, according to which we should operate at night and not during the day, was best. If the conditions aren't right, it's better to wait for a better time. Ignoring that is what happened to the convoy led by Danny Mass, which left late; it's what happened to the Hulda convoy that left during the day when the ground was muddy, and it's what would have happened that time when I was asked to ambush buses on the way to Ramallah in response to an Arab operation. I said I was willing to do it at night, because anyone who would attempt to do it during the day would not come back alive. And, indeed, the person who conducted that mission was Noam Grossman, and he did not come back alive. After the operation, the Arabs in Ramallah held a victory march with the heads of our fighters on the tips of their spears.

There were failures and successes; that is the nature of war. At the end, the question is, did the number of successes exceed the number failures? Did we achieve our objective? And, in the bigger picture, did we correctly assess the situation and do things right? We were busy with decision-making and preparations during a time of great uncertainty, and I don't know a single system that can be completely immune to any sort of failure.

Did we break down after failures? Did we break down after Nabi Samuel? No. The Harel Brigade was strong and vital, perhaps partly as a result of the development of its fatalistic approach. There is, apparently, strength in fatalism. You make peace with the situation you are in and say, "Yesterday was him, today is me." To see Harel marching through Jerusalem after Nabi Samuel, carrying their weapons and singing the Palmach song to raise morale in Jerusalem. And who went to conquer Katamon? The same people who had just fought for Nabi Samuel. Conquering Bayt Mahsir was also one of those battles in which only our absolute commitment, even when there was no strength left, could have brought us victory. Without that commitment, it would not have been possible to reopen the road to Jerusalem or to use the Burma Road route.

Without rank and order exercises—Discipline and Hierarchy

Today, when talking to people about the Palmach, what comes to mind is an image of a disorganized, undisciplined, and unruly group. But that was not the case. There was discipline and order in the Palmach. That being said, the style was quite different from the one the ex-British soldiers had been accustomed to. We had drills even when we were only working on the kibbutzim, proper military drills down to the last details. True, we weren't in khaki uniforms, but they were drills nonetheless, with the girls in dresses and the boys in white shirts. There weren't too many external codes of etiquette, no uniforms, no salutes, but entering the platoon commander's tent was not an everyday thing, and it was always accompanied by a sense of excitement. There are those who would say they "were shaking" before entering the tent. We may have been wearing torn clothes, but our discipline was iron strong. True, we didn't know how to salute. When we were incorporated into the IDF, they did use the formality of saluting. Once, I entered the headquarters in Qastina, the battalion policeman saluted me, and I walked over and shook his hand; only later did I learn that the IDF was using this new language.

What between Refusing an Order, Avoiding Action, and Default

At that time, our network of connections with the Haganah headquarters was pretty loose. We received assistance mostly in the form of intelligence, if there was any, and a little bit of help from logistics in getting canteens, tents, and blankets. The rest, more or less, we took care of on our own. From this it can be understood that the Haganah had very little influence or effect on operations we did in the field. On the strategic level, we were told what area we would be operating in, but each company decided for itself how and when to operate. Later, this was also true when we were organized in battalions, and the same was true when we had finally established the brigade. We were young and inexperienced in dealing with some of the problems we had to deal with. We lacked equipment. We pulled solutions out of thin air, alone and with no guidance from people more experienced than ourselves. Our thinking was very strategic, we knew what the main objectives were, and we, the commanders, were a part of the discussions about them.

The importance and significance of decisions made by a squad commander or an individual soldier in real time were unlike anything that would happen in a regular army. Every framework, from the company on up, was initially intended to be more administrative, not to handle operational decision-making. We operated in the field as though we were firefighters, going from place to place within our designated area. I don't know what the Yishuv leadership and the Haganah headquarters were thinking at the beginning of the war, in the five and a half months prior to the invasion by the neighboring Arab country armies. This issue merits a separate study and description; I am focusing on what the individual soldier and commander in the field could see and know.

Within the Palmach fighting forces, we had ranks and maintained a chain of command regarding orders and the responsibilities for planning and executing missions and operations. Until the moment of execution, there would be heated arguments between us, and after that, when it was time to execute the plan itself, we did it to the best of our abilities and with every last ounce of strength we had.

There a few incidents in which I was faced with a difficult dilemma as to whether or not to execute a mission as I had been commanded. During the first attempt to conquer Suba, I avoided following an order, when an analysis of the situation in real time, in daylight, made me abort the mission. I knew that in doing so I was preventing the deaths of our soldiers by snipers, since we had no weapons to use as backup. There was criticism, people said we should have broken through. I said we had already lost ten men trying to go up the Castel on January 26 in daylight with no assistance. You could lose a lot of men fighting a battle in daylight in Arab territory because of snipers. A few months later, after the first lull in fighting, we conquered Suba with the proper weapons and no casualties.

During the mission to lead a crucial convoy of supplies and backup fighters to Jerusalem—the Hulda Convoy—I followed the command to wait for the required backup fighters, even though I knew it was misguided and dangerous. I tried to convince the others that we would lose the element of surprise if we didn't leave after nightfall, but my opinion was not accepted because the need for backup fighters in Jerusalem was so critical. And so, hours went by and the sun came up. The Arabs from the surrounding areas gathered, a harsh battle ensued, we lost twenty-two fighters, and the convoy didn't make it to its destination.

During the Nabi Daniel convoy, an assigned rescue team in Ramat Rachel didn't help the injured heading back from Gush Etzion, because their commander thought they wouldn't make it to the people in need and would not be able to rescue them.

There was a clear distinction between disobeying a given order and acting without getting permission from a higher-ranking officer. And indeed, I did not ask for permission to lead Uzi Narkiss's company at night to capture mountain tops and protect the Hulda Convoy that was scheduled to come by.

Today, when I watch exposés on television, I notice that they are making an effort to focus on and emphasize failures, being "smart in hindsight." True, there were failures and errors were made, but our failures never included defection, or carelessness, or indifference. Much of our knowledge and many of our decisions were based on accumulated experience. Real-time decision-making cannot be taken out of the context in which we were living: in many cases we didn't have communication devices, there was no one to consult, and there was no one to receive the commands in real time—you were the sole commander in the field. Each of us, essentially, made many decisions that would not be possible today in an established, organized army with advanced communications between the fighters and commanders. Knowing this, it is quite understandable why the Palmach officer training courses emphasized the thinking, independent commander in the field. I am convinced that the training methods and culture that developed in the Palmach proved themselves in the statistics of the War of Independence, certainly in the beginning. I don't know if commanders who were trained in an established army, such as the British army, would have been able to handle the situations and conditions we faced.

We Had More Dead Friends Than Living Friends—but We Kept Going

What guided us all was a deep understanding that this war was a life-or-death situation. That knowledge affected many things, including our sadness. We, the fighters who remained alive, had more buried friends than living ones. Knowing that led us to continue fighting even though we lost people every day. I don't think it was the importance of Jerusalem that kept us going. There was nothing unique about the supply convoys to besieged Jerusalem, in Katamon and San Simon, other than the fact that you fought for your life and for the lives of tens of thousands of Jews in Jerusalem.

When thirty-five men died on their way to rescue Gush Etzion, there was no time to dwell on our grief. All I did was insist that I would replace Danny Mass as Zvi Zamir's second-in-command in the Sixth Battalion, which had lost eighteen excellent fighters in one day, and we continued to lead the convoys without stopping for even a second.

Half of the thirty-five fighters who had gone to Gush Etzion and died were students at the Hebrew University in their third and fourth year of studies. Some were our friends. Scientists. The most talented of them all, in my opinion, was Tovia Kushnir—from a young age, he had been a wonderful botanist, flowers have been named after him, and he could have won a Nobel Prize in botany. And the physicist Yoram Trebes, who fell in the Hulda Convoy.

There was a guy named Pinchas Mishkov Pinchik. We had a term in the Palmach—"a Mishkovist," referring to someone who is told what to do and then does it a hundred times better. Someone who volunteers too much. He studied chemistry, worked at HEMED, the Haganah's scientific research branch. He came to me and said, "I'm a medic, what am I doing at HEMED?" I sent him to Gush Etzion. He was killed, and when I went to see his family, I was met with hostility, and for years I would take a detour to avoid going by his parents' bookshop. We understood the parents and their anger. The commanders would make an effort to go to the families in Jerusalem and inform them of their son's death, and most of them wished to support us even in their time of deep mourning and grief. Yes, there are deaths on my conscience that could have been avoided. But we must be strong and move on.

We lost many of our friends during the convoys. From December 1947 to May 1948, we lost seventy-three of our friends and ninety-six were injured, but not one of us missed even one of the convoys to which we had been assigned. At that time, since there were no other arrangements, the Jerusalem fighters lived with their parents and left for missions from their parents' home, and the parents didn't try to stop them.

In the War of Independence, we lost 1,187 Palmach fighters, which was about a third of all of the fighters lost in the war.

There are times when I feel a lump forming in my throat. The personal incidents that touch my heart. I knew so many of the fallen.

Sometimes, in those days, during the hard moments, mostly when we headed down to the Judean foothills with the convoys and met the people sitting in cafes, you would ask yourself, and we would talk about it: "Damn it, the entire country is a frontline, but the entire nation is not an army, so what's going on?" But we didn't think this way very often, as we did not have time to ponder things that had no practical application. After the war, we didn't feel like the sadness and the grief made its way to the general public.

No Orders from above Were Given to Bomb and Destroy Villages

I was not instructed to do so, but I bombed the Castel in bitterness and rage and with a deep feeling that what had happened must never happen again. To allow the convoys to pass through to Jerusalem, we bombed all the empty villages, so that the population that had fled could not return, and so that we, who did not have enough fighters to hold the position, would not have to fight again and again.

We understood the meaning of distinguishing between collective injustice and human injustice to an individual. There is a very clear conflict. At the time, there was no argument about one simple thing: we wanted a Jewish state so that we could live, and that is our right, and we knew we had to make it happen. We believed that wholeheartedly. Part of that belief, and maybe even in direct correlation to that, was the Arab custom of not taking live prisoners and then horribly and cruelly abusing the bodies.

Commit Suicide Rather Than Be Taken Hostage

I did not hate the Arabs, but I knew that I could not be captured alive. I took that into consideration during the fighting. We killed Arabs when we fought them. But not as revenge. Never. It was a war in which the Arabs knew that if they surrendered, they would probably live, while a Jew knew that if they surrendered, they would be murdered and their body abused. From day one, it was clear that we must do everything in our power not to be captured alive. When we found our friends' bodies, disfigured so badly that they were nearly unrecognizable, we understood even more clearly just how horrible this war was.

I will never forget the corpses I collected with Benny Marshak after the battle at the Castel. We barely recognized them. Some had time to commit suicide. Every armored vehicle had a simple explosive device, known as a *shidit*, whose sole purpose was to prevent us from being captured alive.

That's what happened on the Hulda Convoy, when we lost the battle. Yoram Terbes, commander of the armed vehicle, activated the *shidit* so that he and his soldiers, most of whom were wounded, would not be captured alive by the Arabs who had swarmed the vehicle.

And that's what happened on the Nabi Daniel convoy with Zrubavel Horowitz, commander of the special armored vehicle known as the "Roadblock Breaker." After he helped rescue a few of the fighters, he blew his armored vehicle up with the crew inside, so they wouldn't be taken hostage by the Arabs surrounding them. Horowitz was from Tel Yosef, and later on he was awarded a Medal of Valor.

Where does one get the strength to do this—and not just once? We knew that this was a war of life or death. We also knew the rules of the game, that you cannot be taken alive.

CHAPTER 9

Operations Officer on the Southern Front—Like One Big Family

I joined the southern front at one of the lowest points in the war. When the Egyptian army forces advance and when it seems impossible to stop them when they reach the outskirts of Jerusalem. At a time when the Negev settlements are cut off and the Negev Brigade is besieged. At this time the IDF had already been established and was at the beginning of its organization, first headed by Major General Yaakov Dori, and after a few months due to his illness he was replaced by Major General Yigael Yadin. On Ben-Gurion's decision, the Palmach headquarters, the "Council" headed by General Yigal Alon, was dissolved on November 7, 1949. But in practice, the divisions of the Palmach—Harel, Yiftah, and the Negev—continued, and we continued to be the Palmach until we captured Eilat and ended the War of Independence.

I decided to accept Yigal Allon's offer to join the southern front because I wanted to make a difference. I was a staff officer, not a commander. I dealt with operations, and I was involved in all the planning. I took part in the crucial meetings that Yigal led, and I learned a tremendous amount. I had been in the field a lot, and I had seen how things happen. Anyone who reads the operational orders written by Yitzhak Rabin and approved by Yigal Allon will find it difficult to believe that Yitzhak did not attend a private military school and only went to the platoon commanders' course in Jo'ara in 1943. Being with them at headquarters during those months deepened my appreciation of them both.

The team, which included Yigal, Yitzhak, intelligence officer Zrubavel Arbel (who was nicknamed "Chifaf"), and me, was like one big family, with more than a few disagreements and arguments about operational topics.

I loved working with Chifaf, the best combat-intelligence officer I have ever met in my life. We met in the Harel Brigade, where he was also the intelligence officer. Chifaf was my kind of person, and it was mutual. Sometimes it seemed that we were always on the same wavelength. We also did things that were wrong.

An Egyptian expeditionary force of about ten thousand soldiers had crossed our southern border immediately after the declaration of the establishment of the state of Israel on May 14, 1948. The Egyptians moved in two lines from Gaza. One line moved along the coast towards Tel Aviv and the other went through Be'er Sheva to Hebron and Jerusalem. Few know or remember that they made it all the way to Kibbutz Ramat Rachel, next-door to Jerusalem. Tel Aviv was being bombed from the air, and there were tough battles on the ground in an attempt to stop them. Kibbutz Yad Mordechai was conquered by the Egyptians after five intensive days of fighting. The Egyptian advance on Tel Aviv was stopped near Isdud, modern-day Ashdod, only towards the end of May, but essentially, all of the Negev towns in the south were cut off. Thirteen of our villages in the northern Negev were under siege, among them the kibbutzim Dorot, Tze'elim, Sha'ar Ha'Negev, Nirim, Zikim, Revivim, and Nevatim. The Palmach's Negev Brigade, commanded by Nahum Sarig, was besieged across from Gaza. The Egyptians had cut it off from the rest of the state. It suffered harsh war conditions from the start. The siege started at the outposts in Hulayqat, southeast of Ashkelon.

The Egyptian army had a lot more equipment that we did, and their strength was in their defense, not offense. Along with the many operations, we also went on violent patrols, like small attacks, during which we learned about the Egyptians' offensive tactics and their capabilities. Later, this knowledge helped us plan and execute large-scale operations on the southern front. It was a product of Yigal Allon's "roundabout approach."

On the southern front, we completely ignored political constraints. We understood things in the most basic way possible, since we were fighting a war for the life and existence of our nation. But Ben-Gurion stopped some of Yigal's initiatives, some of which, as I understood them, could have affected the results of the war.

During this phase of the War of Independence, all the units at the southern front, and Harel among them, had transitioned from small-scale to larger-scale fighting, according to the standards of that time. If at the start of the war we transitioned from fighting in squads, to platoons, to battalions, and finally to brigades, now we could refer to the fighting units as divisions. In the south, this was even more evident. Slowly, more weapons were added, including artillery, air force, half-tracks, and a few tanks—seven or nine low-grade Hotchkiss tanks, and, later, three Sherman tanks—and we were no longer rationing weapons. Some of the units had been fighting since the beginning of the war, and the Palmach units were especially worn down. The transition from defense to offense revived our spirits and bolstered the fight in us. It drastically changed the situation.

For the Harel Brigade, fighting on the southern front was different than the fighting in the Jerusalem hills in several ways. The fighting in the Jerusalem area took place on hard mountain terrain. In the south, there were open expanses of land, nowhere to hide, and no way to get closer to the enemy. This type of terrain calls for a high level of mobility with armored vehicles and special forces. Another difference—the experience at headquarters, under the command of Yigal Allon. There was a unique atmosphere. It wasn't the slap-on-the-back type of friendliness, or a lack of boundaries, but we were free to express an opinion and to deal with things on an intellectual level, which led to the positive results on the southern front. When it came to decision-making and risk assessment, there was a military chain-of-command. Discussions and clarifications were conducted openly, and every opinion was heard. In my opinion, had this not been the case, some of the creative ideas that turned into actual missions might never have come to fruition. The atmosphere, the conditions on the southern front, and the operational needs all suited me well. Thinking outside the box is just part of who I am. I see things differently. I have always had a strong sense of adventure, and I have made sure to put it into action. But one also learns from failures. When I had the strength and the opportunity to act, I did. And when I didn't, I kept my thoughts to myself.

Yigal Allon commanded over most of the operations in the Galilee, in the center of the country, and in the Negev, and he expanded the boundaries of the State of Israel well beyond the initial division agreed upon in the United Nation's Partition Plan in November 1947. At a later stage of the war on the southern front, during operations Yoav, Horev, and Ovda, Allon commanded six brigades. The brigades were employed in a strategy of an indirect approach, i.e. avoiding a frontal

On the southern front (left to right): *Yigal Allon, Amos Horev, and Yitzhak Rabin*

attack except for those cases where achieving our objective could not be achieved in a roundabout way. The headquarters initiated and managed many operations, and I've chosen to tell about a few turning points in the war that can demonstrate the way we thought, the teamwork at the headquarters, and the special, specific gravity and unique way of Yigal Allon.

Operation Yoav—Beginning with a Failure and Then the Turning Point

Operation Yoav, October 15–22, 1948, was intended to break the siege over the western Negev settlements and push the Egyptian forces back. Many forces took part in this operation: the navy, the air force, and three brigades, two of them from the Palmach; later, these forces were joined by armored battalions, the Ninth Brigade, and the largest artillery force that the IDF had ever operated. A real army, operating in a very wide area, with Yigal Allon commanding over all these forces. I choose to mention only a few of the aspects of this complex battle, particularly those that portray the larger picture.

The operation started off as a failure. The attempt to conquer Iraq al-Manshiyya on October 16 failed. I remember this bitter failure. Dozens of losses. Our tanks, small French Hotchkiss tanks, were damaged and unusable. We didn't yet have an organized doctrine for armored units in battle. The tank crewmen, who were new Olim (immigrants) from the Soviet army, knew how to operate a tank, but that wasn't enough.

In this difficult situation, after losing the element of surprise, Yigal excelled in making decisions to attack from places the Egyptians did not expect. He was certain that we should not try to attack Iraq al-Manshiyya and conquer the Hulayqat outposts without tanks. Yigael Yadin disagreed. In the end, Yadin told Allon, "You are the commander in the field, it is your decision." The battle in Hulayqat was a hard one, revealing the Egyptians' ability to fight static warfare and their weaknesses in mobile combat. The first attack, on October 17, failed, and two days later, on the nineteenth, at night, Givati overpowered the Egyptians in face-to-face combat. We were using spears; the Egyptians were using Vickers machineguns. It was Operation Yoav's first great success, the turning point. That is how the road to the besieged Yishuvim was opened. We continued our fighting momentum, despite a short ceasefire, which we broke.

During Operation Yoav, we cut off the road from Ashkelon to Beit Guvrin at two different points, and next to modern-day Kiryat Gat we captured a large Egyptian brigade that was stuck in the Fallujah Pocket. The Alexandroni Brigade, under the command of Itiel Amichai, surrounded it with no intention of attacking. We thought that with no supplies, they would eventually surrender. Two months passed, and they didn't surrender. And then, as part of Operation Horev, the brigade attacked the pocket on December 28—and failed epically. A whole company was annihilated, over ninety soldiers were killed. Rabbi Shlomo Goren was the one who tried to identify the corpses. We continued south. The siege of the Fallujah Pocket continued for four and a half months, and Ben-Gurion and Allon commended the Egyptians' ability to stay there. The Egyptian brigade cleared out only as part of the Armistice Agreements in February of 1949.

In addition to the harsh battles, I also remember stories that to this day still make me smile. For example, the story about Ben-Zion Rabinowitz, "Batz," the engineering officer of the southern front. The Egyptians were bombing an Arab village near Fallujah. The people came back from the village and told me: "Batz is gone." I said, "Then go find him." They couldn't find him. "Before we give up," I said, "let's check again." And then we heard him. Turns out that, during the bombing he leapt to find cover and fell into an ancient well. Usually, in order to find out if there is water in a well, one throws a rock down, creating a stone cone in the center. Batz stood on the tip of the cone, his head above water. We rescued him. It was a good thing I insisted on looking for him.

Conquering Be'er Sheva—Decision and Conclusions

The Negev Brigade was exhausted, but Allon chose them specifically to complete the next mission, the conquest of Be'er Sheva. Among other reasons, this was an effort to help raise morale. But our momentum was stopped after the conquest of Be'er Sheva, on October 21, 1948, because inhabitants of the area looted the food storage units in Be'er Sheva in response to the harsh conditions in which they had been living for so long. These events prevented us from taking advantage of the situation and heading north towards ad-Dhahiriya and Hebron. An attack on the city would have been a total surprise for the Egyptians and the Jordanians. We headed to Hebron only the next day, but the Jordanians already knew and were prepared. We reached the bottom of the mountains and were stopped.

Operation Horev to Eliminate the Egyptian Forces—The Courage to Act and Take Risks. Success but Ben-Gurion Orders Us to Stop

Operation Horev, the largest of all, took place between December 22, 1948, and January 7, 1949. On most of the fronts throughout Israel, the fighting had stopped, which enabled the IDF to gather a large force from the Alexandroni, Golani, Harel, Negev, and the Eighth Brigades. Planning was done at the southern front headquarters, and the operation was commanded by Yigal Allon, Yitzhak Rabin, the operations officer, and me as his second-in-command. The plan was based on our rich experience. We acted as one, well-oiled machine. We already knew how to operate in large forces, and we knew how to estimate our strength and the Egyptians' strength just as we knew to estimate their weaknesses.

Indeed, the key to planning this operation and its success was knowing the Egyptian weaknesses. When our forces put a wedge between their different units, they would respond by moving their forces towards the wedge. And we would arrive at Wadi Abiad in a roundabout and unexpected way. The large numbers of the forces, the targets, and the objective of pushing the Egyptian forces out of Israel and into the Sinai Peninsula were all brought before headquarters for approval. In discussions about the plan, we raised concerns about sending forces into the rough terrain and dunes of Wadi Abiad. There were those who thought it was a one-way route, because dunes are shaped like a sawblade, and to go up against the direction of a sawblade on the way back would be very challenging. Leading up to the operation, I was supposed to head a raid on the airport in Arish to damage the Spitfire planes that were fighting against our Messerschmitts. In the end, this did not happen. And I had already thought up a route through Wadi Abiad.

We did our "homework" and checked how passable the wadi was, searching for a route that would bypass the Egyptians and enter Sinai in the area between Nitzana and Rafah. The key to success was getting to know the land and the maps of the Nabataean cities: Mamshit, Ruhayba (Rehovot), and Ovdat. My plan was to move down the old path through Wadi Abiad, between Nitzana and Ovdat. During our patrols, while driving with Meir'ke Pa'il, we drove over a land mine near Kibbutz Halutza. The jeep was destroyed, and we were thrown into a sand dune. The driver was injured, but the rest of us were unharmed. At the meeting to approve the plan for Operation Horev, we remained firm in our opinion that while this route had some risks, the plan was reasonable and necessary. Our plan was finally approved, including passage through Wadi Abiad, but at headquarters they didn't trust our scouts' reports. I anticipated the upcoming commotion and worried that the operation would be delayed or even canceled.

A senior engineering officer showed up in Be'er Sheva and wanted me to show him the route we would take through Wadi Abiad. I understood that if he saw the path, there would be no operation. He would refuse to take the risk. I told him I couldn't take him to the path without approval from Yigal, and Yigal was in Qastina. We drove to Qastina and Yigal wasn't there. We went back to Be'er Sheva, it was already getting dark, and that was that. The operation was a go.

The opening move was to put a "wedge" in the middle of the Gaza Strip so that the Egyptians would move their forces from Nitzana to Gaza. The Golani Brigade accomplished this. Then something awful happened. It started to pour. We were trying to transfer ammunition and food on camels. In the ensuing battle, many were killed. But the wedge served its purpose: The Egyptians moved their forces.

In the next stage, we used the Wadi Abiad passage, moved through the Nabataean city of Ruhayba (Rehovot), and arrived directly at Nitzana. The Eighth Brigade, under the command of Yitzhak Sadeh, moved down Wadi Abiad, struck the Egyptians who fled, and conquered Nitzana. The picture of the Egyptians' shoes on the sand dunes was incredible. We breached the route from Hulayqat south and surrounded the Gaza Strip. We cut off the line from Rafah to Revivim near Auja al-Hafir. We entered east Sinai and arrived at the airport in Arish. It had not been easy, but we did it. A big operation, a huge victory, with success that could immediately be put to good use, and all while still in motion.

We had suffered many loses, but we had struck the Egyptian army and chased it into Sinai. We came prepared to follow through with the plan: to reach the Rafah intersection all the way to the sea, to surround the Egyptian army that was left in the Gaza Strip, and thus complete the conquest of the city of Gaza. At that time, there were about two hundred thousand Arabs in the Gaza Strip. We could have handled their needs and maybe even have found them an appropriate solution. Maybe if we had, we wouldn't be facing the much larger problem today, since now there are almost two million people living there.

At the time, as completion of this phase was within reach, a political decision was taken to retreat. In response to a British and American ultimatum, Ben-Gurion ordered a retreat from Sinai all the way back to the international border. Yigal tried to convince him to conquer Rafah, but Ben-Gurion refused. There is no argument about

At the southern front during a sand storm (left to right):
Yitzhak Rabin, Yitzhak Sadeh, Amos Horev

the fact that the army is a tool and that it must follow the commands of the political echelon, but I can't help expressing the feelings I had at the time. We were in a winning position, earned through a hard war in the desert with quite a few losses. This was not just another victory, it could have been the last battle with the Egyptians, and we were in a position of power. Yigal ordered me to drive to Nahum and give the order to retreat. So, I drove through a sandstorm to tell Nahum Sarig, commander of the Negev Brigade, which was deployed at the entrance to Arish, that by order of the political echelon he must relinquish what he had achieved. I gave him the order and went back to Be'er Sheva.

On January 7, 1949, the air force shot down five British planes in an air battle over the western Negev and northern Sinai. One of the pilots ejected and was taken prisoner. We ran towards him to try and save him. Yitzhak Sadeh was also there; he gave me a small piece of silk from the parachute. Shoshana, my wife, made a shirt out of it for our little son, Yehiam. The operation in El Arish was canceled, and a ceasefire was put into effect that day.

Over sixty years later, I was on a tour of Ruhayba (Rehovot) an ancient Nabatean city in the Negev on the perfume road. My friend, archeologist Yoram Tzafrir, had done some excavating, and we returned there in his memory. While I was standing there, I was flooded with the memories of that place, where we had taken one of the boldest and most daring steps in Operation Horev.

Conquering Mount Hebron—Possible, but "We Need to Take Advantage of the Next Opportunity"

As our journey as a nation began, we were living in a world that had not yet settled down after World War II, that terrible war that took about fifty million lives and turned another fifty million people into refugees. We understood that as the world settled down and became stable again it would become harder for us to conduct irregular activities or to capture additional territories. We had an unusual opportunity, which—and forgive me for my choice of words—I would describe as "God-given." I felt a great sense of success with every additional yard we conquered. I said, "Let's get this Hebron issue over with." That was my approach.

At the time, there were about one hundred thousand residents in Hebron. The Egyptian army had left, and the Jordanians were there. I arranged a trip just before Operation Uvda—Yigal, Yeruham Cohen, and me—to the Harel Brigade, which was deployed by Solomon's Pools, southwest of Bethlehem near the road to Hebron. The point of this trip was for Yigal to see how close Mount Hebron was. I convinced Yigal that the next operation had to be the conquest of Hebron. I didn't speak of Samaria (the Shomron), that was a different front, I had nothing to do with it. He went to Tel Aviv and suggested it, but

Ben-Gurion objected. Politically, he preferred conquering lands from the Negev to Eilat, and I would say that he had good reasons for this. The British hadn't come to terms with the fact that the Negev would be ours and wanted to give some of it to the Egyptians. We thought we would still have time to take care of Hebron later, but we didn't know that Uvda would be our last operation. In my opinion, not conquering Hebron was a missed opportunity.

Yeruham Cohen, Yigal's adjutant, writes about this:

The next day Yigal Allon left the southern front headquarters, Amos Horev and myself with him, and together with the commander of the Harel Brigade, Yosef Tabenkin, we made our way to the front lines of the brigade. We drove in the pouring rain in an open jeep, but when we reached the front post the skies cleared and the Hebron mountain range and the wilderness, the stolen lands of Gush Etzion, were revealed to us. It was visibly clear that the enemy forces that had defended the intersection were weak from holding off the Harel Brigade. At this point it became apparent that not conquering Hebron was an entirely political choice, there was no military issue. It was afternoon. Yigal decided to go to Tel Aviv, to the higher echelons, to try and change this decision. Around midnight he came back to headquarters, his face sullen. He didn't say whom he had spoken to but said only: We will have to take advantage of the next opportunity." (Yeruham Cohen, In the light of the day and in the dark, Page 187, Amikam Publishing 1969)

Not long after that painful end to our plans, on March 8, 1949, Operation "Yitzuv" became a go. Its objective was to conquer the area of Ein Gedi near the southwestern shore of the Dead Sea. Yigal Allon asked me, "Is this according to the Partition Plan?" I didn't go check, maybe it was, maybe it wasn't, but I said, "Sure, it's according to the partition plan, we can take Ein Gedi." And so it was.

At the End of the War—War and Negotiations Lead to a Ceasefire

Yeruham Cohen, Yigal Allon's close adjutant, describes the situation as the war was coming to an end:

> *Major-General Allon received an appointment as a member of the Israeli delegation to the negotiations of a ceasefire with the Egyptians. It was going to take place on the Island of Rhodes, under the mediation of the United Nations. Since he was against any kind of negotiations with the Egyptians before they released the Gaza strip, . . . Allon asked the Chief of Staff to release him from this delegation. But since nobody else on the delegation knew the forces and the terrain down south well enough, Chief of Staff, Yaakov Dori, said he would release him only if either Yitzhak Rabin, head of operations, or Zerubbabel Arbel, the intelligence officer, would go in his stead. Since Allon wanted to gather all the necessary information about the southern Negev and Eilat in preparation for Operation Uvda, which was already brewing in his mind, he decided to send Rabin. . . . Rabin wasn't happy about the appointment . . . and suggested his second in command, Amos Horev, to go instead of him. [. . .] I had had enough of diplomacy and politics.*

Preparing an Operation Far, Far Away

Yigal Allon did not accept Rabin's request, and left with no other choice Rabin flew to Rhodes to negotiate with the Egyptians. I remained as Yigal's second-in-command, and as the active operations officer I worked on Operation Uvda all the way to the Red Sea. An operation far, far away. I assumed that the distance demanded transporting supplies and forces in large carrier planes. We also needed to locate a landing point. I went to Yadin along with Dan Tolkowsky, the air force operations officer. I spread a map out and presented the plan, and it was approved.

We had two objectives. First, to locate a landing strip and a water source. The second, to find a route on which a motorized unit could head south.

We sent a patrol. We received two men from the air force for this purpose, Bodenkin, a road engineer, and Applebaum, a Dakota pilot from the United States. They left from what is now Sde Boker, drove to the end of Ras a-Ramon—the Ramon crater—and from there to the Egyptian border, but found no landing strip. Chifaf and I flew in on a Piper plane and joined them. A Piper could land just about anywhere. We started to descend in jeeps along the border. We found a landing strip at the foot of Kuntila, in a place called "Valley of the Moon," at the foot of a mountain known today as Hezekiah. Haim Gouri described the scouts' experience as they witnessed the beauty of the place: "The view exceeds the senses' abilities [to grasp it]." We found a plain that allowed for every soldier to make camp; later it was called Sde Avraham. From there we moved on to Ras Radadi, a border point between Mandatory Palestine and Egypt. We reached the bottom by jeep and then climbed up on foot, and when we reached the peak, we saw the blue waters of the Gulf of Eilat, Um Rashrash, and two corvettes—British war ships.

We continued south, looking for water. We found a spring called Ein Al-Qatar, known today as Ein Netafim, about six miles north of the gulf. Our map wasn't detailed enough, but we knew the Egyptians had a border post called Ras Al-Nekab about six miles north of Um Rashrash, and across from a post located about seven and one-half miles west of the Jordanian border, which the Jordanians had taken over after the British left. Our assumption was that the Jordanians still had somebody at that post. As to the Egyptians—we were already negotiating a ceasefire with them.

There's a path on the border and (at various points) within Egypt that leads south from Nitzana and goes up the granite mountains towards Um Rashrash. During Operation Uvda, Bren's company was supposed to go down to Um Rashrash on this path, and we thought that they might get caught in battle with the Jordanians at Jabal Masri. And then I did something that should not have been done. I said to Chifaf: "Let's check if the post at Ras Al-Nekab is manned." Yigal Allon had told us that the operation would be covert and so the scout patrol going out beforehand must not be spotted. We went up from Ein Netafim with five soldiers and found that post abandoned. A battle would have broken out had the Jordanians held the post. The Egyptians, who did not know about the patrol's objective until that point, must have seen us on our way back. They didn't fire at us but must have passed the information on to the Jordanians. We were at the closest spot to Eilat before operation Uvda. At the end of our patrol, we returned to the southern front, to Qastina, and told Yigal, "You need to court-martial us." "Why?" he wondered. "Because we were spotted, we did something we should not have done." Yigal looked at us and said, "You know what, let's wait two weeks." By then the operation was already over.

CHAPTER 10
The Battles Ended and I Moved to the Negotiations Table

The war had ended, but we still didn't know what the future would hold. There was a ceasefire, but shots were fired in the Gaza Strip every once in a while from both sides. People were being killed.

The State of Israel gradually transitioned from fighting for its existence to the different sphere of negotiations, and we were speaking with the enemies' political echelons. The negotiations about a ceasefire took place in Rhodes. Yeruham Cohen, Arnan Azaryahu, and I were on the ceasefire committee, which dealt with the practical details of implementing the treaty with the Egyptians, and we met in the few houses that had not been destroyed in Nitzana, on the border with Egypt.

I felt no emotional difficulty building friendly relationships with the Egyptians. Colonel Valentine, from the American military, headed the meetings. The Egyptians did not respect the laws of war; they tortured prisoners. One day, Colonel Valentine showed me a picture of Egyptian casualties that had been published in *Time* magazine to prove that the harm that we did was no less than the harm committed by the Egyptians. The next day I brought him a picture of the casualties of a convoy whose soldiers had clearly been tortured horrifically and whose bodies had been desecrated. He never brought the topic up again.

I had my first opportunity to meet and talk to the other side face-to-face. I formed a special connection with one of the Egyptian delegates, Colonel Mahmoud Riad. I invited him for a meal at my house in Neta'im. He asked to tour Israel—and I took him for a tour in the Emek (Jezreel Valley). It was on May 1, and he saw red flags up in all the kibbutzim. We became friends. Later, he became the Egyptian minister of foreign affairs and the secretary general of the Arab League. When I was on a trip in Egypt, after the peace treaty in 1979, I tried to contact him, but it didn't work out.

Mahmoud and I worked closely together. According to the treaty, Beit Hanoun, on the northwest edge of the Gaza Strip, was a no man's land, and no one was allowed to enter. Arabs tried to enter, causing an incident: one of our patrol units killed ten people. I drove there with Mahmoud Riad in his jeep. An Egyptian police officer was whipping a farmer. I looked at Mahmoud and said to him: "You are hitting your brother!" and he responded, "We are Africans, they are Asians . . ."

The borderline for the ceasefire ran through Wadi Shalalei, north of Beit Hanoun. People from either Kibbutz Erez or Nir-Am came to me and said, "There is something very important in the Beit Hanoun

Members of the Egyptian-Israeli Ceasefire Committee: fourth from the left, Colonel Valentine, the chair of the committee; second from the right, Amos Horev

The Ceasefire Committee on a food break with the members of the Egyptian delegation. First on the right, Colonel Mahmoud Riad, head of the Egyptian delegation and a future Egyptian minister of foreign affairs.

area: the aquifer. Push for a change in the line of the border." I said to Mahmoud, "Let's divide the no man's land in two, and Beit Hanoun will be Egyptian." I took the map and marked the division on it. Thanks to my initiative, the border at the northern part of the strip is straight. The idea was approved, and this change supplied our people with water.

The besieged Egyptian brigade in Fallujah was released according to the ceasefire agreement. In the area where the Egyptian brigade had retreated, a few Arab villagers who ran away from their villages had found shelter. We lost about ninety fighters in the battle; an entire company of the Alexandroni Brigade was wiped out. I said to Mahmoud, "We have a terrible desire for vengeance." He asked, "What do you suggest?" I said, "We will remove all the refugees that are left after the brigade moves out." He arranged a meeting in Tarqumiyah with British officers from the Arab Legion, and I coordinated the removal of all the Arabs from the Fallujah Pocket to the Jordanian side.

Through this I learned the meaning and significance of the written word in a signed agreement. I knew how to speak to the Egyptians. There was no lawyer next to me, but I consulted with Chifaf, the intelligence officer of the southern front. I said then, "We just arranged a ceasefire, we will act 'by the book,' and now we make peace." So I believed, but I was very quickly proven wrong.

By that time, I felt it was okay for me to go out and fulfill my dream of studying. I was a soldier when necessary, but I wasn't born to be a soldier my entire life. Later, of course, I learned my lesson: even when there is a ceasefire, you must always prepare for the next war.

I went on to study engineering, and I continued to serve in the IDF for many more years, carrying with me my experience and the lessons learned from the War of Independence, both as a soldier and as commander transporting convoys to Jerusalem—and then as an operations officer on the southern front.

CHAPTER 11

The Palmach and the Harel Brigade— Legacy, Forgetting, Erasure, and Remembrance

Explaining What Should Never Be Taken for Granted

The younger generation takes many things for granted. It sees us as if we were soldiers in the IDF today with bulletproof vests and steel helmets and communications devices. They cannot imagine a different army—barefoot and weaponless, no communications devices, and no steel helmets. Historians and television investigative reporters ask, "Where was the Convoy of the 35's communications device?" Try to explain to them that there was no communications device, when today every car has a phone and we are all close and well-connected thanks to these amazing devices.

About thirty years ago, I was asked to explain what had happened at Bayt Mahsir to educational officers, counselors in youth movements, and soldiers. As I stood there, I began to experience feelings that had dissipated over the forty-eight years that had gone by, and I could reexperience the magnitude of what had happened. Among other things, I told them, "Things should not be taken for granted. It was a given for us, the Palmach, that this was how we needed to fight, but it was not a given that these would be the results. It might be a given to you that these were the results, but it absolutely could have ended differently."

Today, when I watch investigation programs on television, it hurts me to watch the lightness and the arrogance with which mistakes are judged. We experienced failures and difficulties, too. My heart breaks a little at the ignorance, superficiality, and out-of-context analysis of those times, what they included and what was missing.

Stopping the Erasure of Public Memory and Consciousness—the Battle for Historical Truth

Ever since the end of the war, my friends and I have experienced a mixture of doubt, disrespect, being ignored, and even fear on the part of others. We were not considered professional military personnel. By the way, I am not offended by that. No one said that professional military personnel were preferable to a person who thinks or to someone who does his military duty because the situation demands it.

We can point to a few positive things, even though we were not trained in professional military frameworks. I have a feeling that if we had been those types of people, we never would have dared to do everything that we did. We acted correctly, considering the resources we had and the enemy we were fighting against. Later, some people claimed that we were an organization that tried to separate itself and that we behaved in an elitist manner.

I am in favor of elite organizations. I know that the term elitism is difficult to hear, but excellence is a principle without which we cannot survive and progress. We definitely had the pride of a unique fighting group that maintained a high degree of excellence. We weren't looking for the average, we were looking for the record-breaking.

In addition, people suspected, with no justification, that we were a political movement. Indeed, at the beginning, the Palmach was hosted by kibbutzim from all the different political movements. The Yishuv leadership lacked the means to fund the Palmach, so how could we operate? What could we live off? In 1942, the Hakibbutz Hameuchad, the kibbutz movement aligned with the Ahdut HaAvoda party, to which many senior Palmach leaders belonged, accepted Yitzhak Tabenkin's suggestion that a platoon of Palmach members be placed on each kibbutz for work and training. Other political parties joined the initiative later on. That's how the Palmach was able to fulfill its purpose. We operated on a monthly cycle. For two weeks we worked on the kibbutz without pay, then we trained for two weeks. The kibbutz agreed to this first and foremost for ideological reasons. It supplied us with a place to sleep and enabled us to conceal our training from the British. They also provided us with food and clothes, which the Palmach could not afford. The kibbutzim had a vital role, and without them the Palmach would not have survived. There were people with different ideologies in the Palmach. I have no doubt that Ben-Gurion's approach to us affected the general approach. Ben-Gurion saw the Palmach as an organization that was politically affiliated with the leftwing opposition; this was not what he had envisioned for the army, and he did not believe that we were fulfilling the security needs of the state-in-the-making. In addition, Ben-Gurion had a tendency to minimize and sometimes even completely disregard our role in that crucial first part of the war and our massive contribution to the second part of the war, even after the IDF had been established and three brigades from the Palmach had been integrated into it. In a long interview in 1987, I said, "I am saying this while taking full responsibility, that if the Harel [Brigade] had not existed, we would not have Jerusalem. If we didn't have Jerusalem, there would be no State of Israel. It's not that if we didn't have Harel, we would have had someone else, there was no one else!"

The Palmach slowly made its way into the new military framework of the IDF, all the way to the highest ranks. Who other than the Palmach had been at the headquarters in the southern front? Who, other than the Palmach units, had commanded those many forces? What was in their hearts? We operated in the Palmach style when fighting in the south. It is possible that Ben-Gurion recognized the southern headquarters as a natural continuation of the Palmach, whose headquarters he wanted to dissolve. Yigal Allon represented us all. You said Yigal—you said Palmach, and Ben-Gurion decided to fire him from his position as commander of the southern front.

He understood, more than anybody, Yigal's unique position, not only as a man and a commander, but as a representative of an entire movement. I cannot bring myself to accept the way in which he was fired. He heard about his own dismissal from his hosts while he was visiting the French army in Algeria. From Israel, Ruth Allon, Yigal's wife, and Shoshana, my wife, sent him a telegram.

As the years went by, we came to understand that we must put effort into perpetuating the memory of the events that took place and preventing a shift in the national remembrance. That shift, possibly, is a result of the fact that most of us did not become political leaders. The War of Independence was tantamount to a revolution, and usually revolutionary leaders of coups become political leaders, and then there is continuity between the achievements of the revolution and the way they are presented in the battle for the general public's consciousness. We weren't there, and along with the political changes, the process of rewriting history to fit the agenda of political leaders proceeds.

The question, among others, regards the textbooks that the Ministry of Education chooses to print and what it chooses to emphasize. You can declare dozens of times that we dealt with the bringing of masses of illegal immigrants to Israel and that we brought this or that many Olim to Israel, but then some textbook comes out and divides everything into percentages based on the political leaders in charge at the time. It is suddenly revealed that that there is no connection between the book and reality, and that the textbook creates an alternative historical "truth." It is clear to me that we, who were not willing to get involved politically, carry the responsibility for this. Personally, I was involved in the most important thing for the State of Israel at the time, and that was security, the IDF. Friends of mine, like Issachar Shadmi (Yiska), Zvi Zmir (Zvika), David Elazar (Dado), and Moshe Gidron (Musik)—we all served in the IDF and in the security forces for decades, but, as I mentioned, we did not take it upon ourselves to be involved in the political leadership. There were a few of us who did, like Moshe Dayan, Yigal Allon, Moshe Carmel, and later Yitzhak Rabin, but they did that independently and only after they had completed their service in the IDF.

Memorial Projects—to Remember and Inculcate What Happened Here to Future Generations

A group of friends, myself included, felt that we must do something to commemorate and inculcate what had been, to introduce the next generations to the crucial role the Palmach had played during the different stages of the War of Independence, to let them get to know how their legacy had been shaped, and to teach them about the first years of the IDF. Each of us did what we could, and for me it was an opportunity to do as much fundraising as I could. The project expanded, and construction began on Beit HaPalmach (Palmach House) in Tel Aviv, initiated by the Dor HaPalmach Foundation.

The exhibition at Beit HaPalmach is based on a dramatic-theatrical experience, and its aim is to allow visitors to share in the events of the Palmach and in its role in the War of Independence and the establishment of the State of Israel. Visitors experience a theatrical journey that includes documentary materials, following a group of youngsters who are joining the newly founded Palmach. This journey reveals the chain of events, the historical background, and the Palmach's character and activities, which remain an integral part of Israel's landscape.

Beit HaPalmach is also a memorial place for the fallen Palmach soldiers, and it contains a vast treasure of photos and films, a space for rotating exhibitions, and a place for ceremonies and events related to the heritage of the Palmach. It has become a place that is alive with visitors, young and old, soldiers on various training programs, Israeli citizens, and tourists.

The Harel Brigade is commemorated through a number of monuments. One of them is in the military cemetery in Kiryat Anavim

(1951), in which most of the fallen brigade soldiers are buried, and another is in the Givat HaRadar complex (1975). The book about the Harel Brigade was written later.

Later, commanders in the Harel Brigade—Uri Ben Ari, Zvi Zamir, "Yiska" Shadmi, Ra'anana, Motke Ben Porat, Aviva Kaplan, Nathan Shaham, myself, and a few others—initiated the building of a uniquely designed memorial monument to the brigade, sponsored by the Dor HaPalmach Foundation. We oversaw every detail in the establishment of the monument for the fallen soldiers of the Harel Brigade, until it was erected in Jerusalem in an area adjacent to the Supreme Court. The monument was designed by the well-known sculptor, Dani Karavan, who had also been in the Palmach and had previously designed the monument for the Negev Brigade, together with landscape architect Zvi Dekel and typographer Yanek Iontef. The stone wall, which had been designed to look like the wall of Jerusalem, eternalizes the names of the brigade's 431 fallen soldiers, and the path above the stone wall leads those who take it through the stories of the battles in which the brigade soldiers fought. The two brigade commanders, Yitzhak Rabin, the founder and first commander of the brigade, followed by Yosef'le Tabenkin, its second commander, are also memorialized, even though they were not among the fallen soldiers of the War of Independence. Haim Gouri wrote a poem for the monument and it is engraved in the stone. Upon his request, his name is not mentioned. That was him, the man who was so good at expressing what we needed to express.

To establish a relationship with the younger generations, we initiated a tradition of holding the Yom HaZikaron (Day of Remembrance) ceremony at the monument we had built in Jerusalem. As alumni of the Hebrew Gymnasia in Rehavia, we arranged with the school that the juniors and seniors would organize and prepare the ceremony at the memorial every year. The students arrive in white shirts, walk around the monument that tells the story of the brigade, and a Palmach member from our generation talks about that time. Then we lower the flags to half-mast, and the ceremony concludes with the singing of HaTikva and the Palmach anthem.

Every Yom HaZikaron, a national ceremony also takes place at the military cemetery at Kiryat Anavim, where about half of the 431 fallen soldiers are buried. A tradition has grown up there, and at the conclusion of the national ceremony, which is identical in all military cemeteries, the massive crowd stands up, and after singing HaTikva continues to sing the Palmach song—from beginning to end. We, who are still alive and whose numbers are waning, always gather under the same tree—some standing, some in wheelchairs, some with walkers—we look, and without saying a word, we feel encouraged by the interactions with the fallen soldiers' descendants, and with the many young people who come and want to touch history.

Even at Ninety Years of Age the Struggle for National Memory Continues—"We Have Sha'ar Ha'gai!"

After the assassination of Rabin, the state built Rabin Park, which spreads over about fifteen thousand dunams, from Kibbutz Harel all the way to the Castel. In 2006, Minister of Environmental Protection Refael Eitan, who had been in the Palmach, appointed a committee led by Uzi Narkiss. I was part of that committee, and our job was to maintain the park, giving special attention to Sha'ar Ha'gai. We worked there for a few years. About eighteen million shekels were put into this project; some of that sum came from state funds and some of it came from the Jewish National Fund. Among other things, the ruins of buildings in Sha'ar Ha'gai, which date to the days of the Ottoman Empire, were restored. You can see them from the road. In addition, the cave that we had wanted to turn into a battle-heritage center on the way to Jerusalem was prepared for that purpose.

Uzi Narkiss passed away, and Motke Ben Porat's and my appointments to this committee stand to this day, but the government changed and so did the priorities regarding the shaping of national memory. At the end of 2011, we were notified of the government's decision, 3779, from November 30, 2011, that abrogated all decisions made by previous governments and determined that a memorial for Rehavam Ze'evi ("Gandhi") would be established in Sha'ar Ha'gai, inside Rabin Park. We responded with a letter to the secretary of government, signed by five major generals in the reserves, all veterans of the Palmach (Yeshayahu Gavish, Zvi Zamir, Elad Peled, Shlomo Gazit, and me), two brigadier generals (Motke Ben Porat and Yiska Shadmi), and a colonel in the reserves (Uri Baidetz, chairman of the Nature and Parks Authority). In our letter, we emphasized one simple thing: Gandhi did not fight here, this is not his legacy, and we object to the initiative. Obviously, the answer we received, in March 2012, which reaffirmed that decision, did not satisfy us. Four years later, we were surprised to find out that suddenly a budget had been found to pave an access road to the place, after years of delay, and we decided to act. We appeared in newspapers and on the television. Based on the responses we received, we knew that the public was with us.

The battle for that area in Sha'ar Ha'gai was meant to protect the legacy of all those who fought in the battles that took place on that road, not just as part of the Harel Brigade. We asked to meet with the president and the prime minister. The president saw us very soon after and was supportive. This is what he told us: "Formally, I can't intervene in the government's decision, but I will speak to the prime minister." Six weeks later, the prime minister, Binyamin Netanyahu, agreed to see us. We—Yeshayahu Gavish, Zvi Zamir, Haim Gouri, myself, and Assaf Sela, son of Ra'anana—met with him. The prime minister invited those who were in charge of the Gandhi memorial. We said our piece, he listened, asked questions. At the end of the meeting, he told his people to take care of the situation. They met with a member of the Beit Ha'Shita, Moshe Peled, who had dealt with the Gandhi memorial, and with Ze'evi's son, Yiftach Palmach Ze'evi. But the son would not give in.

The public was with us, the president was with us, and in my opinion, so was Bibi (Netanyahu's nickname), but it never came to fruition. At our advanced age, we couldn't keep it going, and so I suggested to my friends to appeal to the Supreme Court to abrogate the government's decision. I thought the appeal would add publicity and strength to the protest, which would also have some effect on the political level. My friends were unsure. I met with Yoav Horowitz, Bibi's bureau chief, who told me that the issue was progressing, but he couldn't tell me when it would be resolved. We started a protest vigil every Friday morning at Sha'ar Ha'gai, organized by the next generation at the Dor HaPalmach Foundation. Dozens of people showed up. The number of people grew, and at the final events there were hundreds of people. Drivers passing by honked in support. After years in which it seemed that we would not be able to guarantee the Palmach's rightful place, and specifically the brigade's rightful place, in the history of the state, we were very encouraged by the public response. To be honest, we were amazed that we did not find ourselves, a bunch of ninety-year-olds, alone in the protest. The media was also on our side, but the decision was not changed.

I was ninety-three, and I couldn't wait. I went back to my friends and convinced them to appeal to the Supreme Court. I thought that if we won, perhaps Netanyahu would thank us for providing him with a ladder to get down from his high horse. If the Supreme Court rejected our appeal—well, then we would know that morally, and in terms of the people who supported us, we had done everything in our power to change the decision.

Before we appealed to the Supreme Court, prominent attorney Gilead Sher wrote a letter to the prime minister that explained our appeal, and this time, with no time to waste, I received a call from Yoav Horowitz who said they had reached a settlement.

On April 25, 2017, a meeting was held in the prime minister's office, with Netanyahu and his people, ourselves, and the Ze'evi family. At the end of the meeting, a joint statement was issued to the press. It was agreed, according to the Ze'evi family's preference, that the Sha'ar Ha'gai area—Bab Al-Wad—would be named after the pioneers and the soldiers who accompanied the convoys, and that the legacy of Rehavam Ze'evi would be memorialized in one of the settlements.

And now, it was time to build our own legacy and fill it with content. That is what I am working on with Motke Ben Porta and Assaf Sela, Ra'anana's son.

CHAPTER 12

The War Is Over, What's Next?

The war was over, Operation Uvda was behind us, and during our free time we could think about what was coming next. What about me? What about my family? In the background, my feelings were in turmoil, following the dissolution of the Palmach and my anger about the injustice that our commander, Yigal Allon, had suffered. Today, looking back, I can see how the decision to go study, specifically at MIT in the United States, came to be. Then, in those days, I didn't see how different events had affected the course of my life from that point on, or how they had affected the decision to go into the technological field and not to continue as a commander.

The issue of going to study had come up during the war while I was at the southern front. Yigal Allon knew I wanted to go study, he looked for a way to get me a scholarship, and he found one.

Another event that probably also contributed to the decision to go to study occurred while the Israeli government was visiting the fort in Eilat on March 1949. I briefed them about the situation, and when I was done Ben-Gurion asked me, "Amos, what are your plans?" He knew me, he had kicked me out of his office during the War of Independence when I made a comment he didn't appreciate. I answered that I was in the process of leaving the army, I'm going to study. He didn't say another word on that topic. Moshe Dayan thought I was leaving the army because of the way that Ben-Gurion had treated Yigal Allon, and one day he invited Shoshana, who at the time was studying at the faculty of agriculture in Rehovot, to ask her why I was leaving the army. She told him, "You are wrong, it's not the problem with Yigal. Amos wants to study." And so the path to academia opened up for me.

After Operation Uvda, we had an activity on the southern front
in conjunction with professors from the Weizmann Institute of
Science, among them Professor Israel Libertovsky, whom I knew
when I was younger from the scouts' group. The conversations were
about minerals, copper in Timna, scientific research, and more. I also
knew Professor Ernst Bergmann from the Weizmann Institute, and
during one of our conversations I told him I wanted to go study. He
arranged a scholarship for me at the University of California at Davis
in Northern California's central valley. Even though I had wanted
to study at MIT, I thought about going with Shoshana to Davis, so
that she could continue her agricultural studies, in which she was
excelling. In the end, we went to MIT because that's where I was sent
by the army after having signed an extended service contract.

Fate Chose the Most Advanced Technology Possible

I was asked where I wanted to study, and I chose not to return to the
Technion because at MIT there were three semesters per year instead
of two, which allowed for replenishing the shortage of engineers after
World War II. MIT was considered the best place in the world for the
study of technology. In January 1950, I traveled to the United States
and was the first officer who went to study as part of their service. I
chose to leave the military mainstream for the technological path.
It was clear to me that as a result I would not move forward in the
operational-commanding field in which I had grown and developed
in the time between my teenage years and the end of the War of
Independence. My choice destined me for certain types of positions.
It is plausible that if I had stayed in the army, in the operational field,
which I liked, that Dayan would have promoted me from operations
officer and his second-in-command in the southern front to head
of the southern front headquarters, which had become a separate
command in the IDF's new structure. From there I could have become
a major general, and perhaps even general commanding officer for the

Southern Command in 1955, until I would have retired from the army in 1960. As I've said, my studies opened up a whole different path before me, and this new road provided me with unique opportunities to take action and make a difference.

My First Time away from the Land of Israel

I was abroad for the first time. In total, it was a forty-hour flight through Rome, Paris, London, Shannon (in Ireland), Iceland, and Goose Bay (Canada), until we arrived in New York. I stopped for two days in Paris and met with my dad's older brother, David Sochaczewer, who now called himself Shocat. He had been an engineer in the Polish military and then was a leading engineer in the steam turbine field in the Schneider Company located in the French city, La Croix. He married a non-Jewish woman or a Jewish woman who had converted to Christianity. Their son, Jean-Michel Shocat, had been baptized. There was no contact with the son or with any of his children, and this branch of the family was lost to the Catholic Christian world.

I walked around Paris like a curious child. It was the first time I drank coffee from a large mug that felt like a bowl to me, and for the first time in my life I watched a strip show at the Crazy Horse club.

My encounter with New York also was filled with "first times." Lieutenant colonel was a high rank at the time, and I was welcomed at the airport by emissaries from the Ministry of Defense. They gave me four hundred dollars, which was a lot of money then. I wasn't used to dealing with money, and I didn't notice that a one-dollar bill and a ten-dollar bill looked the same (except for the amount written on them), and so I gave the guy who took my luggage up ten dollars instead of the customary one. When I was invited to eat out at a diner that was under the delegation's offices, I was astounded by the abundance of food. I ate a bowl of strawberries with whipped cream and quickly wrote to Shoshana about it.

On the train to Boston, on my way to MIT, I started to form relationships that would be a part of my future life. I was wearing a suit with the Palmach symbol on the lapel. Some guy was walking up and down the train. Suddenly, he asked me in Hebrew, "Can I sit next to you?" I responded that he could. It turned out he was Jewish, born in Romania, brought to the United States by his family at a very young age. He had been an officer on a battleship in the Pacific Ocean during World War II, and now he was a law student at Harvard. He recognized the symbol. I told him that I would be living in a hotel. He said, "Why a hotel? I live in the Harvard dorms, there is an attic, come live with me." That was Harold Haim Katz, and we have been friends ever since. Harold was a member of the Socialist Zionist Movement "Avuka" (Torch). His friends from Boston were among the founders of Kfar Blum. After the World War, he joined the Aliya Bet, which organized the illegal immigration of Jewish refugees, was caught by the British and detained in Cyprus, and then was imprisoned in Atlit before coming back to study in America.

We lived together in Cambridge for three months. After that, we both wanted to move and found an apartment for forty-five dollars a month, near MIT, in workers' housing, across from a soap factory. After a while, another law school alumnus, Richard Green, a member of the *Harvard Crimson* newspaper, joined us.

When I arrived in Boston, I bought a new Dodge car for $1,000, and paid in installments. The gearbox was automatic, but I didn't have money for a heating system in the car. I didn't know that I would have to deal with a temperature of minus 20 degrees Fahrenheit. When Yohay Ben-Nun came to study at MIT and we drove in the car, we would go from one café to the next to warm up a bit and then continue.

Before I left, Yeruham Cohen—a member of the Palmach who had been commander of the elite intelligence force that gathered information from behind enemy lines, had been Yigal Allon's adjutant, and who knew the ways of the big world—took me to a tailor in Tel Aviv to have a suit made. That's what I traveled with across the ocean. I didn't know how to tie the tie. The pants had a lining, and my foot went between the lining and the fabric. Trouble. I arrived at MIT with the suit, hat, and tie; I looked ridiculous, and I felt extremely uncomfortable. I wrote to Shoshana to send me my uniform. Everyone had been in the World War and they were all wearing khaki. She sent them, and I started walking around looking like everyone else, in khaki.

It was not difficult to get accepted to MIT, and my high-school graduation diploma, which I had gotten thanks to my mom's common sense, was enough for me to get in. I left with the diploma in my pocket, and that was it. I remember standing in front of the famous entrance gate to MIT. I walked in and was asked what I wanted. "To study here," I replied immediately, and I was sent to the man whose job it was to accept new students. After an hour-long conversation, he informed me, "You have been accepted."

The beginning was hard and took tremendous effort. For years, I fought when the British were in the Land of Israel, but I didn't know any more English than what was taught at the Gymnasia. Harold Katz helped me a lot with this and with other basic required skills. In the technical writing course about technology and science, I got back my first assignment, and it was filled with mistakes. My teacher said to me, "No redundancy," meaning, not to repeat things. I arrived here after a nine-year break from studying, and on the first day I was already cursing things out. In a letter to my parents I wrote, "Hello dear parents . . . sometimes, when I feel bitter, I ask myself, who the hell needs this? Can't I just live like a normal person anymore?" I told myself I was a fool for not having stayed in the army. But I never broke. Everything worked itself out in the second semester.

Most of the students were ex-soldiers who had served in World War II, which is why they had three semesters a year, instead of two. And that's why I was able to complete my degree in less than three years, and if you added additional hours, you could even finish your degree in less than two years. Thanks to this arrangement, I finished my degree in two and a half years. Starting on day one, I studied sixteen hours a day, trying to close the gap from when I had left my studies all those years ago. I didn't want a repeat of what had happened when I went to the Technion, when events in Israel cut my studies short. I felt a sense of urgency.

That Is Where We Started to Become a Family

Three years after I married Shoshana and only two years after our eldest son, Yehiam, was born, we started to become more of a family, without the difficult separations because of the battles that were taking place far away. Indeed, it was not easy to leave again, this time for studies, but we both loved studying, and so I went through the first eight months of university on my own, working hard and spending all my time and patience on my studies and on getting acclimated to living outside of the State of Israel without the strain of war. Shoshana joined me, and three months later, so did Yehiam, then three years old. Two more years went by and Nira was born, and now we were a mother, father, and two children. A family like many others.

We also had another circle that was very much alive and present in our lives. These were Israeli friends who joined us—Avraham Zakai, Yohay Ben-Nun, and five other officers from the navy. We were a small community of Israelis and Americans, each and every one a special person. I remember this as one of the best times in our lives. We developed a close friendship with Sonia and Shimon Peres, who was the head of the Ministry of Defense's purchasing delegation. They had a home in New York that seemed to be the continuation of their home in Kibbutz Alumot. In Sonia, I saw the best of the Land of Israel. Yohay Ben-Nun and I came to their house often. They had small children, and we felt right at home.

It was all good, until there was a crisis of trust with Shimon, which went on for years. We stopped visiting them at home. I renewed the relationship with him only after a long time, when our work lives were intertwined, mostly when I was very involved in the French issue, of which he was the architect.

Shoshana ran a household that was always open to guests. We lived on my salary and the lectures. When the UJA (United Jewish Appeal) invited me to speak, they paid me $100–$150 per lecture. I traveled to Maine in the evening and returned the next day directly to the university. During vacation, we went to New York for a week, and we went to a play every night, watching great actors performing on stage. We were experiencing a whole new world—to us, two young Israelis away from Israel for the first time, away from the tension and struggles of establishing a new state, this new world was immense.

Financially, we lived very frugally, and I remember that as a student I didn't receive a paycheck, only a reimbursement for receipts I submitted. When I asked to be reimbursed for our son Yehiam's kindergarten, my request was denied. I assumed that if the army was funding only my tuition and living expenses, I should study, and that was all.

I called the military attaché, Chaim Herzog, nicknamed Vivian. We were both lieutenant colonels in the War of Independence, and we knew each other. "They don't pay," he said. I asked, "Vivian, you send your kids to kindergarten, right? So why shouldn't I send my kid to kindergarten? How am I supposed to pay for it?" I angrily ended the conversation between us and chose to accept MIT's offer to be a paid research assistant, and that provided me with the money to pay for kindergarten. On May 8, 1952, Chaim Herzog sent a letter to the head of the personnel department:

> . . . I'd like to add that despite his academic success—Lieutenant Colonel Horev is also excelling at poor discipline and constant lack of satisfaction with the conditions given to IDF students here . . . and so I do not recommend that he remain in the United States following his graduation.

Not much time had passed before I received a letter from the head of the personnel department, Nahum Shadmi, my friend Yiska's father:

> *. . . I am also obligated to direct your attention to the fact that we demand behavior that is appropriate for an officer of your rank, and we hold you personally responsible for said behavior. . . . We hope that you can amend your behavior . . . upon your return to Israel, it is only fitting that we place you in a position that befits your rank based solely on your academic success, which we are all satisfied with.*

I have no doubt that this correspondence was hanging over the unfriendly welcome I received from Chief of Staff Maklef when I returned to the IDF with a degree from MIT.

Two and a half years passed, and I completed my studies, but not before people tried to convince me to stay for doctoral studies. A letter was even sent on the matter to Chief of Staff Yigael Yadin which said, "In view of the need for men of great ability and high character in the civilian and defence industries of the free nations, it seems to us desirable that a person having demonstrated the high degree of competence of Colonel Horev should be given training to the highest possible level . . ."

I fell in love with the United States in those days, even though it was during the time of Senator Joe McCarthy. I fell in love with Boston, a wonderful city, and with Cambridge, the city of universities. If I were to live in the United States, I would only live there, but I wanted to go back home. The good life in the United States didn't keep my mind away from thoughts about my home, the Land of Israel. I was concerned there would be another war because we didn't end the previous war properly. Ten years later, while I was Chief Ordnance Officer, I went back to MIT for another period of studies with the intention of completing my doctorate. At the request of Yitzhak

Rabin my studies were put on hold two years later, and I immediately returned to the army. I had completed the mandatory courses for the degree, but I hadn't had time to complete the required research, and so instead I did my doctorate in the university of life . . .

CHAPTER 13

Aiming High but
Stuck at the Bottom

Since I came accompanied by a letter of complaint—"our military attaché has notified us that despite his academic success, Lieutenant Colonel Horev is also excelling at poor discipline and constant lack of satisfaction with the conditions given to IDF students here . . ."— Chief of Staff Mordechai Maklef did not exactly receive me with open arms, and I was conscious of his sour expression. No wonder that the gates of re-entry into the IDF were not fully opened for me, and that even the knowledge that I had acquired in the best engineering institution in the world, combined with my experience from the years during the war that had just ended, were not enough to overshadow my "disciplinary issues."

As a Palmach man, upon my return I was immediately thrown into the struggle between the Palmach people and the people from the British army. This struggle was everywhere, in every branch of the IDF as it was in formation, and it was so strong that it had an impact on me for a few more years. It was a necessary struggle about all aspects of the military way of thinking, and as is natural, it was accompanied by fights for high and influential positions.

I was a lieutenant colonel in the War of Independence, at the time this was only one rank below a major general (Shimon Avidan, who commanded the brigade, was also a lieutenant colonel, as was Rabin). Before I left, they wanted me to be an instructor in a battalion commanders' course, and when I returned, Maklef sent me to attend a battalion commanders' course in Tzrifim. The instructor was Eli Zeira. Later, I was appointed head of the Order of Battle branch, working under the head of the planning division, Yuval Ne'eman. I had known him during the war as a second-in-command, Avidan's operations officer in Givati. The position had nothing to do with my degree in mechanical engineering or with my experience on the southern front. I sat in a shack and worked on the army's organizational structure in an attempt to build a balanced system of personnel, which included dealing with reserve forces, retirement, and recruitment for missing positions.

"So, Create It"—As Head of the Weapons Department

Fortunately, I met Dayan. One day, Dayan, who was already known to be the next chief of staff, saw me at the headquarters base in Ramat Gan. "I'm driving to Haifa, want to join me?" he asked. Of course, I immediately agreed. We drove and talked the whole way. When he was commander of the southern front, I had worked closely with him, and there were things about him that I liked. We were both true Zabarim (native Israelis), even if in our own different ways. I told about what was going on in my life. "And what do you want to do?" "To create a weapons department," I answered. "So, create it," he responded, as simply as that. That expansion of the branch into a department was a very important step.

It had been four years since the War of Independence. We hadn't even had time to lick our wounds. Planes and ships were few and their quality was low. I created what I considered to be a team of professionals, and they became the weaponry department of all branches other than the air force. Within the system, I embedded the advanced scientific infrastructure of "operative research." This system was developed in the academy as a mathematical way to do statistical experiments with the objective of predicting the quality of a weapon system's performance. One of the products of all of this was the procedure of developing weaponry.

Looking Ahead—Developing Missiles in the '50s Despite the Cold Shoulder

The first thing I did was approve the ship-to-ship missile program, "Gavriel," also known as "G-25" or "Luz," which was meant to protect cargo ships. Rafael (Rafael Advanced Defense Systems) was the first to initiate the development of missiles, and I asked to use this knowledge for the military. The protection of cargo ships required missiles because you couldn't arm them with cannons. I gave the mission to Rafael, which was then the national laboratory, and their developments were manufactured by Israeli Aerospace Industries and Israel Military Industries.

The navy didn't want the missile with a massive warhead that Rafael developed because it was difficult to operate the joystick, which could only move up or down and left or right. The "Luz" was developed to be a surface-to-surface missile ideally suited for the ground forces, but the head artillery officer didn't want it. I told him, if you don't act now, your forces will not have missiles. That's usually what happens when you don't think even the slightest bit ahead. As a result, during the Yom Kippur War, the ground forces didn't have missiles that would have enabled them to hit from a distance the bridges that the Egyptians built for their invasion. Another option was considered—that of using the "Luz" as an air-surface missile in the air force, to be used against the Dakota planes—but in the end no decision was made.

Sometime later, a great engineer named Uri Even-Tov, who had worked in the Israeli Aerospace Industries, developed an altimeter that replaced the problematic control of the joystick. The "Luz" once again became a ship missile named "Gavriel"—a successful instrument that made a fortune for the army and had a positive impact on the development of the navy.

As head of the munitions department, I took the first steps in developing relationships with other militaries, which became an important factor in the future development of the IDF. Later, mainly as Chief Ordnance Officer, it was one of my main efforts. In 1953, I traveled to the French military with the Deputy Chief Armaments Officer, Emanuel Pratt. It was the first of many such trips.

Traveling abroad made for some interesting personal stories as well, such as my planned trip to Vietnam. Dayan, the chief of staff, was very interested in the Battle of Dien Bien Phu between the besieged French and the Vietcong. Before the fall of Dien Bien Phu on May 8, 1954, he decided to send two officers to see how the French were fighting there and what weapons were they using; he wanted to know if there was anything of importance that we could learn from them. Nobody believed the French would be defeated. And who were those two officers? Gandhi, (Rehavam Ze'evi), head of operations, and myself. We had French suit-uniforms tailored for us and we were supposed to fly to Paris, from there to Indochina, and then land in Dien Bien Phu. A short while before we were scheduled to depart, the airports in the area were put out of commission, and as we had no place to land the trip was canceled. We were supposed to stay there for a month, and had we made it in time we probably would have been killed or taken prisoner when the area surrendered. I believe in miracles. I also believe in good and bad luck—this time, good luck was in our favor.

CHAPTER 14

A Messenger with a Note in His Hand—"You Are Hereby Appointed Chief Ordnance Officer"

A year had gone by, and Eli Zeira, Dayan's adjutant, showed up at my office with a note, signed by Dayan, notifying me about my appointment as head of the Ordnance Corps. That was the beginning of a tumultuous phase, during which I was imbued with the sense that the responsibility for technological advancement in the IDF was on my shoulders and that I could combine my fighting experience with the technological knowledge I had acquired.

At the beginning of 1954, when I was appointed to this position, I had to go against accepted opinion and promote obtaining and developing weapons. Everyone around me was under the impression that the War of Independence had been the last war and that we should not be expecting another war any time soon. Reality hit us when the Suez Crisis (the Sinai War) broke out, followed by the Six-Day War.

I was thirty years old, an "upgraded" Palmach soldier who had studied at the best engineering school in the world at the time (MIT), and I was "dropped" into a system filled with devoted, experienced people who had created the IDF Ordnance Corps from scratch in the years leading up to and during the War of Independence. I arrived as a lieutenant colonel to a position marked for a full colonel. I didn't know anybody, except for my driver, and no one there knew who I was and no one wanted me to be there—I was an outsider in my own corps. The muddy road to the garages in Tel HaShomer symbolized, more than anything else, what the corps' status was. I brought the head of the operations division and told him, "At least find me some kurkar [a type of gravel] so that we won't sink in the mud."

The corps' early days dated to World War II and the beginning of the War of Independence, when the first members of the corps gained their knowledge and understood their needs from the Haganah, which was an underground organization, and from the logistical system the British army used during the World War.

The Haganah's Ordnance Department was the core from which the Ordnance Corps was created. Emanuel Pratt planned its foundations between 1949–1954, as well the technical-military principles and their implementation and management. This period was characterized by financial deficits, frequent organizational changes, and perpetual struggles about what would be included in the Ordnance Corps. The main struggle—in addition to the power struggles over influence and control—was an argument regarding the most suitable logistical formation for the IDF. This was all happening while Emanuel Pratt and the entire state were in the process of coming together after the War of Independence. Pratt was in the center of all those "storms" and tried to lead them all in whatever direction he thought would be best for each corps, until in 1954 he chose to quit, carrying with him harsh feelings of anger, bitterness, and frustration. As time goes by, his unique contribution to the construction of the foundations of what would later become a corps rich in achievements and resources becomes clearer, but he couldn't see it at the time. Dayan accepted his resignation, and I was appointed in his stead.

Years before, when I was completely taken up by what was happening in the field, and my involvement in weapons and their supply was minimal, I felt firsthand how poorly the Ordnance Corps was doing—there was only one gun for every five soldiers, we went barefoot, and we fought with almost no supplies or equipment. I wasn't aware of the struggle at the beginning of the War of Independence, or that that struggle even turned violent at times, or that the Haganah's chief officer in terms of providing weapons actually was instructed to confiscate weapons from the Yishuvim for the Hish and the Palmach. This situation ended in April of 1948, when shipments of small arms arrived from Czechoslovakia. They had a considerable impact on us, the field soldiers.

In November of 1947, the acquisition of weaponry from abroad became the paramount mission of the Haganah headquarters, and it was no longer the responsibility of the ordnance department. There were no engineers in the core group of the future Ordnance Corps. None of the members of the department had served in the military and none knew the rules and procedures of an army. From their perspective, anything relating to ordnance was the responsibility of the quartermaster. It was a tight-knit group whose members were not happy to welcome "strangers," which is how they regarded the former members of the British army. This approach was prevalent in other areas of the Haganah as well and strengthened the sense of cohesiveness among that group of ex-British Ordnance Corps soldiers, who were first being brought into the Haganah. Written in one of the journals from Pratt's office we find the words, "We have finally started recruiting professionals from the previous war."

When I arrived, I found cliques, and the ex-British soldiers formed the strongest clique of all. In addition to differences in knowledge and experience, the corps was a meeting place for people who came from completely different cultures. The external etiquette, how people spoke to one another, was all completely different from what I had known in the Palmach. From my perspective, ex-Palmach soldiers, who were all Technion alumni and whom I recruited based on their relevant experience and mostly based on their ability to combine technological knowledge and field experience, did not form cliques that negatively impacted the attainment of our objectives.

Looking back, the competition between the ex-British soldiers and the ex-Palmach soldiers only improved the thinking and the work we did, which combined military and technological abilities. Each person brought their own technical expertise. Most of the ex-British soldiers specialized in weaponry that was just beginning to come into the IDF or had not even made it there yet. The more pretentious and better educated among them brought ideas of how to build a Jewish version of the British Ordnance Corps, the Royal Electrical Mechanical Engineers (REME). They also came with the understanding that ordnance was a vital part of an active army and that organizing it was no less complex and vital an issue than arranging the fighting forces, which was the military leaders' focal point. When it was initially formed, the training of the professionals, even among the officers, did not meet all the military's ordnance needs. Other than Emanuel Pratt, none of the experienced REME people had had any commanding or military staff training, and none of them had any experience with ordnance staff work in action.

In addition to the main group of ex-Haganah REME and ordnance department soldiers, we also had soldiers who had fought in the British and Soviet armored and combat engineering corps.

When I took over its command, the Ordnance Corps did not meet the standards for military combat, and expectations were limited to what I would consider logistics responsibilities and nothing more. To assess its functioning, we needed to conduct drills with their participation. We found crucial defects, such as "duplication and confusion in the division of responsibilities between the regional workshops and the brigades, the poor condition of military vehicles, inadequate preventative treatment of ordnance equipment by the units responsible for them, lack of clarity regarding the authority of the ordnance officers as staff officers in charge of professional coordination" ("The Origins of the Ordnance Corps," the Ordnance Association, May 2004, page 103). During the drills, the Ordnance Corps emphasized equipping the divisions with ammunition and a vehicle and focused on the manner in which supplies were taken from storage bases and then returned to be sorted, packaged, and restored. As for the corps and expectations, nobody really dealt with the issue of the weapons themselves and their relation to the outline of the drill against the enemy, and as a result, no one dealt with the need to upgrade or develop better weapons.

In the early 1950s, the intelligence forces believed that it would be all right to take a risk and minimize the weapons in the IDF because all the countries in the area, Israel as well as the Arab countries, were under the same restrictions imposed by the western great powers regarding the supply of weapons. But later on, we uncovered different agreements, according to which certain western countries, headed by Britain, were planning to give the Arab countries large quantities of weapons that were of a higher quality than the weapons they were permitting Israel to have. Additional intelligence information also served as a warning sign about the war-related intentions of Egypt. The IDF changed its policy and decided to significantly expand the combat divisions and their supplies. On the eve of my acceptance of my new position, Moshe Dayan, as chief of staff, supported the plans to strengthen the army and emphasized the improved role of the Ordnance Corps. He also emphasized the purchasing of weapons via the international market and their technical adaptation to the plan, both in terms of adapting the corps' workshops to restoration and development of existing weapons and weapons that would be newly purchased abroad and in terms of creating a weaponized formation that would be spread out between the field corps in a way that would provide greater firepower and maneuverability.

As part of the plan to strengthen the IDF and its implications for the Ordnance Corps, at the end of 1953, as head of the Ordnance Corps, I participated in a tour of Europe to examine the weapons market. The delegation, also including Colonel Emanuel Pratt and including high-ranking officers, visited and collected open and secret information from the militaries of a few weapons-manufacturing western European countries. We concentrated on the examination of possibilities for purchasing old armored combat vehicles for a cheap price and then upgrading them. The head ordnance officer focused most of his attention on acquiring knowledge as to how to upgrade wrecked Sherman tanks in large numbers in a military workshop.

Colonel Pratt did not have time to complete the main parts of the plan to prepare the Ordnance Corps in this new age of the IDF. His relationships with the staff, mainly the new chief of staff, Moshe Dayan, held his progress back. When I stepped into the position, the foundations and plans that Pratt had created were already there. As the Arab countries were restoring their strength, I ran headfirst into the challenge before me, feeling that I had all the tools I needed: experience as a combat soldier in the field and as a commander in the Palmach; participation in the headquarters of the southern front; the planner of the combat of all the brigades in the IDF until the end of the War of Independence; theoretical technological knowledge from the most advanced at that time; the fact that I grew up next to a father who's curious and gifted in technological developments, in some of which I was an active participant. Using all of these resources, I made my way through the command of the Ordnance Corps at a critical time, preparing the IDF for the threats and wars that were already knocking on our doors.

Between the end of the War of Independence and 1954, we made very few purchases. We were so poor, even if anybody had wanted to sell us anything we couldn't have afforded it. When I arrived at the Ordnance Corps, there were only seventy-six tanks in the entire IDF, lesser machines with short, 75 mm canons. By the Six-Day War, thirteen years later, the armored corps had 1,115 tanks, more than nine hundred of which that came out of the factories of the Ordnance Corps and had the ability to deal with the Soviet tanks.

Helped by a Tailwind—Systemic Changes

Beginning in 1954, the year I took on my new role, the pressure to make drastic changes in ordnance was growing, which enabled me to bring my plans and abilities to fruition. There were three main components: first, the unwavering support of the chief of staff, Moshe Dayan, who gave me a great deal of independence. Under his command, the Ordnance Corps accomplished the achievements that won me the support of following chiefs of staff, even if there were arguments and struggles at times. Second, the dramatic changes in the assessment of the existing threats from the Arab countries towards the state that had just been established, which led to plans for expanding the IDF's forces in terms of personnel and advanced weaponry. Given these changes, the IDF progressed from frugality to a budgetary expansion, which included the Ordnance Corps. The vital third component had to do with the international arena. On the one hand, France, for its own reasons, opened new avenues for Israel in purchasing almost unlimited technical-military knowledge, and on the other hand, the Soviet countries intensified the arms race for quantity and quality of weapons against the IDF through advanced weapons deals in large quantities with Egypt and other countries in the area.

With this tailwind, I implemented system-wide changes, which, taken together and in the long run, enabled the corps to overcome its weak points and provide the necessary requirements for ordnance in preparation for upcoming military battles. In other words, I viewed the complex connection between ordnance and the combat forces, especially the armored and artillery corps, as a central objective for the upgrading of the Ordinance Corps. I aspired to design a professional corps that, on the one hand, had very clear rules and regulations, and, on the other hand, maintained a certain level of flexibility, which is required to cope with constantly changing situations.

Some of these changes entailed improvement of existing structures, while most required fundamental changes and significant breakthroughs. I am most proud of these.

These changes made their way to every part of the Ordnance Corps: storage bases, on-base workshops, improvement of technological knowledge and professional standards of the personnel in the corps, self-guidance systems, formations in the field, and streamlining the corps' headquarters.

The IDF's weapons were stored in old facilities built by the British army during World War II, and they functioned in ways that were, to say the least, inadequate for our needs. That is why we added storage sites in the existing bases, and we built new bases, partly underground. In addition, we added improvements and developed new ways to maintain the functionality of the weaponry. To control and regulate the stored supplies, we implemented technology that was quite new at that time—a computer.

What had been called on-base workshops essentially became small factories with production lines that operated according to advanced principles of production engineering and pricing systems. This is how factories were built, and later, as decisions were made, this allowed us to manufacture tanks and other vehicles. Until that point, maintenance of the ammunition, which included supply, storage in secure bunkers, and repairs, had been conducted on the bases according to methods dating back to the time the British had been in Israel; these processes also underwent a "face-lift." Among other things, new ammunition bases were built that also included factories for ammunition repairs.

We moved forward with multiple processes to simultaneously raise the level of formal technological knowledge and practically deepen our professional abilities.

When I took up my new position, there were only five officers with engineering qualifications in the whole corps. To quickly change this situation, I recruited Technion alumni who had served in the Palmach. Later, we took in people with varied backgrounds. I appointed them second-in-command to the commanders of the larger bases, thinking that their formal education, along with the experience they would gain, would prepare them to be base commanders. It was very important to me to maintain continuity and at the same time to promote the quality of the personnel, without unceremoniously firing anyone who did their best under the conditions that we faced.

In the corps, I found experienced, qualified professionals who had had military experience in World War II. They were officers but did not enjoy the same status as the engineers. I opened an advanced professional course for them, which allowed us to register them as engineers, and their salaries went up. Anyone who was of the right age was sent to the Technion. There were those whom I sent to get master's degrees at Columbia University, MIT, CalTech, and other serious places. Lieutenant colonels in the corps had to be able to perform at a high technological level and to be able to speak the same language as Elbit, Elscint, and Tadiran. Twelve years later, in 1966, we had 172 academics, 68 of whom were engineers.

The heart of the training program of the corps, which I deemed extremely important, is in Training Camp 20 in Zirifin not far from Rishon Lezion, which had been built for this purpose. Until then, ordnance training had been conducted in different bases, spread out from one another, and this was not suitable for the IDF, not during the initial period of frugality, and even less so during times of military expansion. At Training Camp 20, we were able to really invest in improving the training, in terms of both quantity and quality. At this base we also started educational activities with teenagers who had dropped out of school or were having a hard time in the educational system. We brought them to an on-base boarding school. Along with educational activities, we also provided them with the training they would need in the corps, and they became our future generations of professionals. I grew up in a socialist youth movement, and the books I had read, such as *The Pedagogical Poem* by Makarenko (describing the author's experiences as a director of a colony for juvenile delinquents in the early Soviet Union), definitely influenced my choices within the military system.

The formations in the field, from commanders all the way down the command chain, suffered many deficiencies, mostly due to issues of control and procedures. The Ordnance Corps was only the professional guide, but the command responsibility was divided between different people, and long-lasting painstaking work was required to change the way things were done. The Suez Crisis in 1956 highlighted the problematic situation, which could no longer be ignored, and with improvisation the IDF was able to correct many of its failures—helped along by the fact that the war only lasted seven days.

The Ordnance Corps is a combat-support organization responsible for the development and maintenance of war materiel, combat-support materials, and other systems. When I arrived at the corps, I saw that very little attention was paid to field formation, which remained the responsibility of commanding ordnance officers who lacked authority and did not have the rear-support of headquarters or a staff member to plan doctrine and the modes of action during routine and emergency times. After the Suez Crisis, I really delved into this, and through years of patient work and cooperation with field commanders, headed by the major generals and the commander of the armored corps, by 1960 we had completed a comprehensive reform. The changes were meant to provide for the different needs the combat units faced in different situations while maintaining the flexibility required during times of war. Among other things, we regularized the activity of both the mobile ordnance service battalions, which accompany the forces, and the permanent, stationary ordnance service battalions. We learned from every possible source of knowledge, such as the British and French armies, where I sent people to study.

Managing an advanced and widespread ordnance formation as it was being developed also required making changes in the corps' headquarters, which expanded and became more professional in terms of staff positions and technical, economic, and administrative expertise.

A Technological Affair with the French and the Lesson on the Side

As director general of the Ministry of Defense, Shimon Peres was the architect of the special relationship with France, while Minister of Defense Pinhas Lavon, who was not part of the clique that was close to Ben-Gurion, Dayan, and Peres, was almost entirely excluded from decisions as they were made. Fragments of the lack of trust made their way to me when one day Lavon called me in for a conversation about the French. He didn't believe Moshe Dayan and Shimon Peres, who said that a "Golden Age" with the French was on its way, and suspected that something was going on behind his back. The conversation between us was not pleasant, and I felt as though he was interrogating me. That being said, I told him everything I knew; I didn't keep anything from him.

From 1954 to 1967, I was in charge of communication between the ground forces and the French army, and this technological-industrial relationship developed, intensified, and expanded into fully cooperative research and development. It was a very interesting relationship. The French loved working with us because we were young and daring. Young engineers, officers with spunk—this excited them.

The relationship began in November of 1954, at the beginning of the Algerian Revolution, when the Arabs were our common enemy. This allowed me to really get to know the French army's different weapons. At the beginning, they offered us the AMX13, a light patrol tank with an excellent 75 mm canon and a towable 155 mm howitzer, but we couldn't do much with that.

From the outset, I had a very clear approach. I preferred collaborative work over purchasing, and I wanted our engineers to work in France with the French and to develop weapons together. Engineers from the Ordnance Corps regularly worked from the DEFA offices—the *Direction des études et fabrications d'armement*, the French government agency responsible for the research, development, and production of military equipment—in St. Cloud near Paris, as well as in an arsenal in Bourges. The French did more for us than we expected of them. I had almost unlimited access to the French military technology that applied to the ground forces.

I brought General Carougeo, the head of the DEFA, a photo of the first tank we improved together, the Sherman M50, and he hung it in

The French visit—with General Marest

The French visit—an explanation about the abilities of the Ordnance Corps

The French visit—with General Molineux

his office. It was a time of great creativity, which was free to develop because I had freedom of action, backed up by Moshe Dayan. I can whole-heartedly summarize and say that, thanks to the French, the IDF was starting to change for the better.

The relationships developed so well that I invited French generals to Israel to try and influence Chief of Staff Yitzhak Rabin to approve the collaborative design and manufacture of a primary battle tank. I wanted them to endorse my assumption that we were capable of doing so. I did not succeed in my mission—he did not approve the project. I think that, as I had, Yitzhak had drawn his own conclusions after the War of Independence, during which we were entirely dependent on the grace and good will of other countries. As chief of staff, he vowed that we would never again suffer from the shortages we experienced during the battles for Jerusalem; unlike me, however, he didn't reach the necessary conclusions about our lack of dependence on others. His lack of appreciation for our abilities only strengthened his objections.

The unusual relationship we maintained with the French over thirteen years of learning and deep friendship really helped us. This was the school where everyone could advance—the military and air industries and the Ordnance Corps. When the head of the DEFA invites you to his home while he is sick with the flu, now, that is certainly unusual. Once, when I was in Bourges, I forgot something in the arsenal. General Marest told me to wait, he went inside with his car, and returned with the missing piece. In America, that would not have happened. During the Six-Day War, de Gaulle cut off the relationship with Israel and embargoed us, and the doors to France were closed. The love affair between our two countries was over. The air force was able to get fifty planes out despite the embargo, and the navy was able to recover five Sa'ar 3-class missile boats that had been built in Cherbourg. I transferred everything to local production.

Engineers Build the Force—Getting out of the "Dependency" Trap

From the embargo during the War of Independence, the terrible results of which my friends and I experienced daily in battle, through the next few years, and through the stark change in the relationship with the French military and industry as it transformed from mutual cooperation to embargo, I learned a hard lesson that will never be forgotten. I aspired and acted to minimize our dependency on strangers; in my view, this was our most terrible weakness, politically as well as militarily. Because nothing is free. This understanding shaped my policy, but unfortunately the high-ranking, decision-making officers, who were not interested in logistics and ordnance, did not set a clear policy on this matter.

In the beginning, the Ordnance Corps didn't manufacture from scratch, but rather combined different parts and pieces from many different places. Accordingly, my main effort was devoted to promoting self-manufacturing. The development of weapons entails a number of steps, starting from research, technical development, tactical-operational experiments, all the way to mass production in Israel, be it in the IDF or local industry.

In Matzlach (center for fighting equipment and spare parts), we maintained a permanent exhibition for industrialists, with all the parts we needed, so we could order what we needed from local industries. I wanted the industrialists to do what was called "reverse engineering," that is, to make something new by taking apart and analyzing something that already exists, so that we could make a new design and manufacture the product by ourselves. We repaired spare parts, learned about the different technologies, and when production became massive, I initiated the building of private factories or an additional branch in an existing factory, for whom we would provide sketches and orders. That was how we put four hundred products into production. For example, when we couldn't get tracks for the half-tracks we had bought very cheaply, we initiated building a factory that created tracks, and the Carmel Forge factory manufactured the missing metal parts for us. "Alliance" manufactured tires for us for a Russian tank we took as spoils of war. For the tanks, I initiated a factory to manufacture wheels.

A Network at the Top of the World Military Scrap Market

Given our limited financial situation, the use of spare parts and even scraps from World War II was the only way I could see to build up the IDF. There was no fundamental discussion about this with the staff, so I worked quickly. I was responsible for both the plan and the execution, first as the technology and maintenance officer and then as head of the quartermaster's branch, but I could not have done it without the support of Moshe Dayan, Tzvi Tzur, Yitzhak Rabin, and Haim Barlev, the chiefs of staff under whom I served. I have no doubt that, to a great degree, this support stemmed from our shared backgrounds in the War of Independence, and from the trust, friendship, and mutual appreciation forged during fighting and working together during the toughest times the state had known. Nevertheless, it was not blind support, and I had quite a few difficult arguments with the general staff.

At first, we couldn't purchase new products that were not made of spare parts, but we had a budgetary issue. As the technology and maintenance officer, I received the budget for purchasing from the reparations money we received from Germany. I could purchase spare parts from World War II in the United States and American equipment that was being stored in Germany. The British also sold spare parts. To build the Ordnance Corps, I learned all about the world's military scrap market. I located the main scrap yards. I knew all the scrap traders in the United States—they were, of course, Jews. In 1955, I began to send ordnance people to sit with the Ministry of Defense's purchasing delegations in New York, Paris, and London; when they located a place that could be useful for us, I would go there myself to make a decision. The Ordnance Corps was the professional echelon and was in charge of financial considerations, but negotiations were run by the purchasing delegation. I had the privilege of working with Yaakov "Shefik" Shapira, who was head of the Ministry of Defense delegation in New York, with whom I had a relationship based on trust and a sense of partnership. Shapira's approach influenced the other delegations in different countries, and this was crucial to our success. I stationed my representative, Dov Laor, in New York, not with the delegation of the Ministry of Defense, but at the scrapyard, so he could see what equipment was brought in. His work took him all the way to Canada, where he located the Levi brothers who traded in scrap parts and had engines, weapons, equipment, and spare parts.

From a Small Workshop to a Factory That Upgrades
Tanks out of Scraps and Spare Parts

The project of purchasing scraps and spare parts was the Ordnance Corps' most significant contribution during the period during which the IDF was upgraded. Out of scraps and spare parts, we built an armored corps of about 2,250 tanks and 60 mobile cannons, as well as thousands of half-tracks, mortars, and antitank missile launchers for use against half-tracks. By 1965–66, all tanks had been upgraded by the Ordnance Corps, and the IDF no longer had even one tank that was purchased new from a production line abroad, other than the French AMX13 and the American M60 Patton. From the Suez Crisis to the Six-Day War, over ten and a half years, the Ordnance Corps provided the armored corps with over a thousand tanks. In addition, during the Yom Kippur War, the tanks we manufactured also served in fighting against the Russian-armed forces in the Egyptian, Syrian, and Iraqi armies. Later, after we restored MXs and the Centurions, we sold them to other countries.

We repaired and repurposed the new purchases in a highly advanced industrial process in a factory built on the foundations of a small workshop in Tel HaShomer, which became a restoration and maintenance center with almost three thousand workers, most of them civilians employed by the military. All tank models went through a process of development, upgrading, and manufacturing, including those that were hit in battles and Russian tanks taken as spoils of war. We created a factory similar to the tank factories in the United States. Something specific was done with the tank at every station, and it moved a step forward every single day. The factory was a center for visiting and admiring our innovativeness and the extent of our manufacturing.

The industry generated excitement and the desire to keep going. We purchased advanced equipment. For example, we purchased a manipulator that could catch the tank and turn it around to do

"Scraps"—the American "Sherman" M4 that was purchased by weight

This is what the "Sherman" tank looked like after it was upgraded (M51)

welding work in the chassis. We also purchased automatic welding machines and a giant lathe to engrave the turret ring of a tank that had been hit.

We were prepared to learn in any and all places possible and from any country, with no particular sentiment. That's how I ended up traveling to Germany, to a company in Stuttgart that manufactured the Porsche car and had manufactured tanks during the World War. I don't like the Germans, but they know how to work and how to make high-quality

Centurion (Shot Kal) tanks in action

products. I also traveled to Alabama in the United States with a few officers; we had wanted to mount a 105 mm cannon that had been used by NATO on top of the Patton, instead of the original 90 mm cannon. We also wanted to replace the gasoline engine with a diesel engine. We were the first to upgrade the M48A1 to a M48A3, which we called Centurion "Shot Kal," a tank whose quality matches that of the M60.

When There Is No Other Choice— This Is How We Build Strength

Purchasing a Thousand Tanks by Weight

In 1955, a representative of the Ministry of Defense delegation in New York took me to Chicago to meet with a Jewish scrap trader. It was winter and acres of snow-covered Sherman tanks lay before me. I purchased a thousand Shermans by weight, at three cents a pound, which came to two thousand dollars for a tank of thirty tons, and two million dollars for a thousand tanks. Despite a cover story in which the tanks were intended to be converted into tractors for growing peanuts in Kenya, the tradesman said to me, "We have to demilitarize the tanks." I replied, "Cut off the barrels." We didn't need the barrels because we already had barrels that we had developed with the French and had started assembling in Israel. In the meantime, I got Israel Military Industries into manufacturing cannons. I was assisted by Osher'ke Peled, who was in charge of ordnance in the Defense Ministry. We had an exceptional relationship, and he handled all aspects of the purchase of those thousand tanks.

In Israel, they only found out that I had purchased the thousand tanks after the fact. I was called in for an inquiry. Have you lost your mind? I told to Dayan, "I purchased them so they would serve as spare parts for our Shermans." I told Dayan a myth, but he wanted what I wanted and completely understood me. I told the French that I wanted to mount a long-barreled, 75 mm cannon on our junk Sherman tanks that could penetrate the armor that faced us. Dayan approved it. I sent engineers to an arsenal in Bourges, I brought a Sherman, we mounted the cannon and called the tank the M50. Some very serious machining was required to upgrade the tank turret so that it could hold the French cannon; the only machine in Israel that could do it was located in Efraim Ilin's factory, and they were asking for an outrageous price. I purchased a device that does only that specific type of work. We created a cement pillar and mounted the device on it, and then did the work for all the tanks. One day, I got a call from Pinchas Sapir saying that Efrain Ilin was complaining that he had a machine that does exactly the same thing, and that I was not doing the project through him. I replied to Sapir, "That is correct, but he wants £2,500 a unit, and I'm doing it for £250." At the end of the project, I brought the armored corps soldiers to the shooting range for an experiment that proved the new cannon's ability to penetrate the armor of a Soviet tank, the tank was approved, and we started activating an assembly line to repurpose all the "scraps."

In a secret operation before the Suez Crisis, the French provided us with more advanced Sherman tanks with 76 mm cannons and a

Prime Minister Ben-Gurion at the ceremony for the first series of M50 tanks.
On the left, Amos Horev.

wider continuous track. Nathan Alterman wrote his poem, "It Will be Told," about the night of their arrival in Haifa, a poem that the prime minister chose to read at the Knesset. (The military censor had prohibited the publication of the poem, but the poet sent a copy to Prime Minister Ben-Gurion. When the operation was disclosed to the public on October 15th, Ben-Gurion read the poem over the Knesset stage. The next day, the poem was printed in Alterman's column, "the Seventh Column," under the title "A Night With No Title or Name" and later on under the name "One of These Nights.")

We unloaded about fifty Sherman tanks and provided the IDF with the first twenty-four Sherman tanks manufactured in Israel by the Ordnance Corps. During the Suez Crisis, we already had three active Sherman battalions from France, our "own" M50 tanks and the AMX13.

During an armored drill in the Negev, which also took place before the Suez Crisis, all the tank engines stopped working. After I checked them, it turned out that the oil poured into the engines had been contaminated with sand. This happened because oil barrels had not been properly closed, and the main bearing of the tank was worn down. We worked on them, and the tanks were once again fit for fighting. The Suez Crisis also served as a real-time experiment with the first tank we manufactured (M50) as well as the French Shermans, but I was not happy with the results—the continuous track was too narrow, the rack didn't work, and the continental engine was of poor quality. Immediately after the war, we started looking into any and every way possible to upgrade the tanks.

The Story of the Sherman Tank Engine

We built an engine repair factory in a building in Beit Dagan, where there was once an Arab textile factory called the Golden Spindle. Simultaneously, following the Suez Crisis, I started looking for an engine through my representative in the United States. I went to the Cummins diesel factory in Columbus, Indiana. I found an engine that would work for us. It was being used in a heavy vehicle in a mine in Nevada. I flew out there with officers who were experts in our engines. We drove to the mine. I saw the giant dusty trucks in conditions that were similar to conditions in Sinai. We checked the engine manual book and discovered that the engine would work for us. I then gave the head of the quartermasters branch a proposal for the purchase of one thousand engines. Simultaneously, because of my "obsession" to find any opportunity to minimize our dependency on external sources and to manufacture locally in Israel, I turned to Soltam Systems. I proposed that we purchase the necessary parts for them and that gradually they would develop the ability to manufacture engines. We received a cold shoulder. For lack of any other option, we purchased one thousand complete engines that we had located in America. We bypassed the American military standard (MILSPEC) and were able to lower the cost to $7,000 an engine instead of $10,000. Every month, ten engines would arrive from the Cummins factory, and Lieutenant Colonel Israel Tilan, an excellent engineer, a graduate of the Technion and head of the tank branch in the technology and maintenance corps, was able to build the engines into the Sherman.

How to Beat the Advanced Soviet Weaponry That had been Sent to Egypt—A Difficult Situation That Demanded Thinking Outside the Box

In September of 1995, the arms deal between Czechoslovakia and Egypt provided Egypt with massive quantities of Soviet weaponry, including 230 T34 tanks with an excellent, long 85 mm cannon that had proven their ability to fight against the German armed forces during World War II. Later, they also received T54 and T55 tanks. The balance of power is like a spiral: The enemy improves, you improve; the enemy improves, you improve; and there is no end. Suddenly, we needed tanks that were better than the ones we had had until that point. We wanted a better cannon to fight against the Russian armored forces. The French developed and sold us 105 mm cannons with an antitank shell with a hollow charge that could penetrate Soviet armor. We put the cannons on the Shermans. And thus, we could fire hollow, tank-penetrating charges from old tanks. That was the M51. Our engineers worked on attaching the cannon from the arsenal in Bourges, and we were in fact the first to fire these charges in battle—and did so successfully. Alongside the M51, we continued with the M50 while improving the engine and rack and control settings. Motke Ben Porat, commander of the armored division, fought in the Golan Heights with these tanks during the Yom Kippur War, and they pierced the Soviet armor easily.

A Step Up in the Development of the Tank Factory, but Not Without Confrontations

In 1964, when I became Chief Ordnance Officer again after three years of studying for my third degree at MIT, I found out that Talik,

Israel Tal, commander of the armored forces, wanted to improve the M48A1 in the British Ordnance Corps factory in Leeds and turn it into an M48A3 with a 150 mm cannon and an M60 diesel engine.

I had many arguments with Talik over the years about almost every topic. Now we began another argument. I asked Lieutenant Colonel Ronis, head of the project branch in the Ordnance Corps, to do the financial calculation. When it turned out that local manufacturing was cheaper, I convinced Deputy Minister of Defense Shimon Peres, who backed me up, and I improved the tank in our factory in Tel HaShomer. Peres's decision was significant, because the budget that had been intended for the British was given to me, and that provided the factory with great momentum. I could purchase equipment that we could not buy before because it had been too expensive for us. It was a giant step up in the development of the tank factory.

The Story of the Centurions—Imagination, Technological Capabilities, and Audacity

We started purchasing large numbers of tanks before the Six-Day War from the British and the Germans, excess Centurions with an ordnance QF 17- or 20-pounder, for £3,000 per tank. It was a new and advanced model with preferred armor and an electronic stabilizer for the cannon, whose manufacture began after World War II, so it hadn't actually been tested in real combat.

We brought one Centurion to the factory in Tel HaShomer. We learned all about it and upgraded it. We attached a 150 mm cannon, which was widely available since the NATO forces had it. Later, we manufactured the cannon in Israel and didn't need to import them anymore.

The Centurion started working in Sinai, but the British gasoline engine with the water-cooling system was problematic, and the logistical range was short. I expected that. We had purchased the tanks as is, as an immediate solution. We created detachable gas tanks that could be removed when entering the battlefield. It was clear that we could not avoid replacing the entire engine. And where could we find a suitable engine? To succeed, we needed a lot of imagination, technological abilities, and audacity.

We went—Dov Lior, Shefik Shapira, Talik (the commander of the armored forces), and I—to the Continental factory in Michigan, which manufactured engines for the M60 tank. The giant factory had been built prior to World War II and spread out over ten acres, but large parts of it remained full of machines for the manufacturing of engines, which were covered in plastic.

At the entrance to the factory there was a model of the M60 engine, and I heard Talik say, "Put that in the Centurion? No way." Before I left, I asked Lieutenant Colonel Tilan to prepare a 1:1 drawing of the engine compartment in the Centurion: "Ignore the top part, put the American M60 engine inside" Before we completed our visit to the factory, I told the manager, "I want to present a project to you." I laid the 1:1 drawing on the table and showed that the M60 engine could fit inside. I also told him I would send the engine compartment and our own engineers, and together they could put the engine into the Centurion. That is what we did, and the engine fit inside. The Americans taught us the craft of repurposing. They enabled us to use their engine and gearbox in British Centurions. But the journey did not end there. We went to the Ordan (Industries Metal Casting) factory in Netanya. There, they cast the upper armor of the engine compartment. We started the experiments. Suddenly, Tilan approached me, looking panicked. He said he hadn't noticed that the direction of rotation of the motor in the original Centurion is opposite from the rotation of the M60, and instead of driving forward it was driving the tank backwards. I said, "Don't panic, the tank has a final drive, we will remove a gear wheel and change the direction." We went to the Ashot factory in Ashkelon, which manufactured gears, and, working together, they manufactured gears that fit, and our tank started driving forward.

We started to repurpose all the Centurions to become what we called "Shot Kal" Shot, Continental, diesel. An exceptional upgraded tank, valued at $250,000. All the tanks that we repurposed proved their worth during the Six-Day War and in the upcoming days of battle in the Yom Kippur War.

During the War of Attrition, when I was already head of the quartermaster's branch, we purchased new Centurions, but not from the manufacturers in Leeds, because the British refused to allow their government factory to manufacture things for us. That is why we purchased the tanks from the Vickers-Armstrong factory, a private British company, and then we upgraded them. They manufactured seven–eight new tanks, with a NATO 150 mm cannon. It was Britain's first official sale. They demanded discretion and commended Israel for keeping the secret. Unlike the French, from whom we learned a lot, the British did not share knowledge. Granted, the French did not have main battle tanks, which the British did. We didn't stop looking at new tanks such as the British Chieftain, but at the same time we continued upgrading the excess Centurions. We purchased and upgraded a total of about 665 Centurions.

The artillery's pursuit of the forces on the move—the story of the development of a self-propelled cannon and mortar on the Half-Track

During the Suez Crisis, I learned that by the time the artillery forces spread out and positioned themselves, the enemy units were no longer in range. We had thirty-six owitzers with French towable 155 mm cannons. For that reason, I decided to build a mobile cannon, which we did not yet have in the IDF because no one would sell it to us. I went to France with a few of the corps' engineers, and we decided to make the cannon mobile by mounting it on the body of the tank. It was suggested that we move the tank's engine forward to clear the body for the cannon. It was not possible to install a pivoting turret, however, so we were satisfied with the option of limited movement. To prevent the tank from moving as a result of recoil, we stopped the recoil with triangular heavy wood pieces that we placed under the half-tracks, and that was how we designed the mobile 155 mm cannon that we started to manufacture. To do so, we had to purchase 125 new towable cannons from American spare parts, which were actually purchased from France, but we didn't use them. I had a budget intended for spare parts for the thirty-six howitzer towable cannons, and I used this budget to manufacture sixty mobile cannons at the price of 160,000 Israeli Lira per unit.

A mobile 155 mm cannon with the fighting forces

Later on, we developed a 120 mm mortar on a half-track, with a special development to balance the barrel while firing—"Model D." When you fire a mortar, the barrel sends recoil to the base, which then sinks into the ground a little and requires recalibrating after every shot, which slows the firing pace. We used the half-track as a recoil system, and indeed, after firing, it returned to the original calibration. I was

very proud when lieutenant colonel David Benor from the Ordnance
Corps, head of the planning team, received the 1961 Israel Defense
Prize for this development. Later, this infrastructure enabled us to
mobilize SS11 antitank missiles on half-tracks.

Fighting and Staying Alive—the Story of the Armored Personnel Carriers

I wanted to change things to save soldiers' lives. In the half-tracks, the
gas tank was under the seats. During one of the discussions we had with
Yitzhak Rabin, I brought up the half-tracks, their inferiority, and the
risk they posed when they carried forces. In the heat of the discussion
I said to Yitzhak, "Don't you understand that these half-tracks, when
they hit a mine, are the equivalent to coffins?" He did not like what I
said and did not respond. We created the fuel tanks and moved them
out of the tank chassis with the possibility of replacing them.

I told Yitzhak Rabin, while he was still head of operations, that
within the framework of the priorities for self-manufacturing, the
personnel carriers—from within which you could fight—were more
important than the tanks we had. I suggested that we take the French
VTT, a fighting machine designed to carry personnel, and manufacture
them in Israel. The French agreed. Rabin didn't believe we had the
ability to do it. He believed in purchasing. A lot of time passed until
he started believing in our science and technology. This bothered me
because I saw self-manufacturing as a nationally important issue. For
me, the idea of not being dependent on anyone was one of the most
important principles.

The Americans had an excellent personnel carrier, the M113
or "Zelda," made from aluminum. It was a transport vehicle, not
intended for fighting, but its automotive parts were excellent. In the
future, as head of the Quartermaster's Branch, in cooperation with
Avraham Adan (Bren), who was commander of the armored forces,
and Haim Domi, commander of the Ordnance Corps factory in

Haifa, we tried to build an armored body for the American "Zelda," so it could also be a fighting machine—a combat armored personnel carrier. We were not able to get the decision-makers to take an interest in this development. This was also true for the idea of an armored personnel carrier on wheels instead of chains. It was called the "Sho'et" (Galloper) and was developed on the basis of Russian spoils from the Six-Day War. Instead, we inserted the high-quality "Zelda" engines into the many thousands of the Israeli half-tracks. Since we needed thousands of engines, I tried to convince the government to create a factory for diesel engines, but I did not succeed in that either. I changed the entire armored corps from diesel to gasoline. According to an annual calculation, the savings on the cost of gas provided the funds required to purchase all the engines for the half-tracks.

More and more issues came up, and if any significant changes needed to be made, we did not give up. That is how we handled that issue of small arms, because there were many different types of guns in the IDF, and each one required different ammunition. The first step was to try and standardize the weapons as much as possible, and we continued searching for small arms that would be suitable in changing weather conditions, in dust, and for the fighting requirements of the IDF. This search produced the Uzi, which was developed by an officer in the Ordnance Corps named Uzi (Uziel) Gal, who received the Israel Defense Prize for this development in 1958. The Uzi was produced by Israel Military Industries, which also exported it in very large quantities.

A Greenhouse for Research and Development

I looked for a person with whom I could break ahead and develop new fields, more advanced than what already existed. In the Palmach, I had known Uzi Sharon from Givat HaShlosha, who was very talented when it came to technical fields, and we formed a very close friendship.

My late father had helped Uzi with development for the Palmach naval company and, subsequently, the navy. To hit British deportation ships he designed a floating missile that could be calibrated from afar. The missile was tested in the fish pools in Maoz Haim. In the navy, he dealt with, among other things, the development of a personal submarine. I convinced him to join the Ordnance Corps and created a research and development branch of which he was in charge. Together we were a laboratory for ideas and attempts at implementation. It was a focal point for scientific work, a center for laboratories, and a testing center for all sorts of topics, focusing on three main aspects: technological, military, and economic. The branch dealt with many different developments, and as is the way with research and development, we only succeeded in some of them, and those were brought into the IDF. The branch dealt with many different topics, such as:

- How do you extend the shelf life of ammunition? We discovered that if you store the ammunition at a constant, regulated temperature, it can last twenty-five years instead of only the previously thought twelve years.
- Developing a missile that can hit a tank's weak spot—the large surface on the top of the tank and the upper armor are thin and thus more vulnerable. We looked for a way to develop the French SS11 cruise missile, which we had, so that it would explode when it was above the tank. Under the leadership of Uzi Sharon, we attached hollow charges to the missile, so that they were facing downwards, and using a joystick on a cord, we blew up the charge and it pierced the tank even from a height of two meters. After the development stage, we needed a sensor that would identify the missile's location and blow it up directly above the tank. I asked for budget approval. I went with the idea to Rafael: to create a hollow charge with a magnetic sensor that could penetrate a tank from above. I asked them to develop that sensor, but they were unsuccessful at the time.

- Developing a dust-stopper to minimize the tank's exposure while firing.
- Using active infrared equipment for night-vision, at a time when there was no starlight-based technology. There was an exceptional engineer and optician named Plaut in the Ordnance Corps, and with him we developed and manufactured driving goggles for night vision and used infrared to aim the non-recoil cannon. At the time, the Americans were unwilling to sell infrared light enhancers, but they did allow us to purchase five thousand defective devices. Among those defective devices, we found about five hundred that were in working order. With the establishment of the electro-optics industries and the founding of the "Elop" company, Moshe Kashti, the director general of the Ministry of Defense, tasked me with transferring all the knowledge we had on infrared. I did it willingly, because it was right and proper that the IDF should not compete with civilian industries.
- Using massive smoke as a way to hide and as a weapon directed at enemy targets, such as snipers. I discovered that, before the Yom Kippur War, not enough ammunition for the smoke canisters on the tanks, intended to conceal the tank during battle, had been purchased or manufactured. I have no doubt in my mind that if this efficient method had been used, fewer tanks would have been hit.

CHAPTER 15

A Break for Studies and a Quick Return to the Position of Chief Ordnance Officer

After eight years as chief ordnance officer and unsuccessful attempts to plan and manufacture a tank, and despite unpleasant political dynamics. Tzvi Tzur, the chief of staff, wanted to promote me to major general. I asked to take a step back and take a break (from the army) to get my PhD at MIT.

In September 1962, I went back to MIT again with my family. This time was much easier, more comfortable, and over-all much better than before. I had time to study in the pre-doctoral program for two years. I passed the exams and started to plan the dissertation for my doctorate. There, just like in Israel, the subject of designing a tank was on my mind, and my doctorate proposal could have been implemented in the development of the tank. The proposal was accepted by MIT in 1964, eight years before the creation of the Merkava tank, and dealt with optimization of designing large engineering systems.

But Yitzhak Rabin, who became chief of staff at the end of December 1963, asked me to come back to Israel, and I never completed my doctorate.

The story of the next period is complex and filled with pressure, anger, and bitterness. After he was appointed chief of staff, Rabin came to New York, and when we met, he said to me, "Amos, come back to Israel, be a major general in the position of head of the quartermaster's branch." I didn't accept his offer and asked to be allowed to finish my doctorate and then to return as the head of a new branch that would focus on research and development. Rabin agreed, but Shimon Peres, who was deputy minister of defense at the time, refused. Rabin wrote to me from Israel, telling me that Peres would not change his mind, and he asked me to come and try to convince him. Why did he think I would be able to convince him? Was it because of our cooperation during the French issue? Or maybe because of Shimon's appreciation of science? Either way, Rabin thought that I would know how to convince Peres better than he did. I stopped my studies and met with Peres three times, to no avail. Peres told me in simple words, "The army will not dictate what I develop."

Dealing with my next position cut my studies short and I never returned to MIT, while in Israel I was left with no position, although I had a salary and a driver. After a short while, Rabin appointed me, again, to be chief ordnance officer, with the personal rank of major general. I put my bitterness aside and once again was working on the apple of my eye—manufacturing an Israeli tank. I knew about the development of the Ordnance Corps' professional abilities, I was familiar with the infrastructure, and I was convinced that we could make a technological leap and manufacture an Israeli tank. The waning of the market for war scraps and spare parts only strengthened my belief that we needed to move toward local manufacturing.

A Glance into the Decision-Making—the Merkava Tank and the Separation of Powers in the Army

The First Israeli-Made Primary Battle Tank

At the beginning of the '60s, when I was chief ordnance officer, there was a piece of paper on my desk: a model of a non-existent Israeli tank that matched my vision: small, low, with a very strong engine, and a cannon with automatic reload and a floating turret—the cannon and the turret were one unit. And this is what I wrote on the page:

a. Weight 32 tons, height 160–170 cm, because the smaller the contour of the tank, the less vulnerable it is. There is no need to create a monster because it will be hit more easily.
b. A small and fast tank needs a smaller but more powerful engine, with a very high ratio of horsepower to weight—and the engine needs to be in the back.
c. An excellent cannon with an automatic reload option. The crew, three people, would not be in the turret, but in a less vulnerable place, at the bottom.

Self-manufacturing required that certain conditions would fall into place, and in the meantime, we were in contact with the French, who wanted to design the AMX30 primary battle tank and were willing for us to take part in the design and then to manufacture it in Israel. I appointed a committee of ordnance personnel, headed by my second-in-command, Lieutenant Colonel Inon Ezroni. That committee did the economic math and recommended manufacturing the tank in Israel. During my second period in the Ordnance Corps, from 1965 to 1966, I invited high-ranking officers from the French army's directorate of development and manufacturing for a visit in order to convince Rabin that we had the ability to develop and manufacture a tank. They gave their opinions and recommendations, but Rabin did not change his mind. In my opinion, during this time Rabin did not have faith in our abilities—and in general, in science. In the heat of one of our many conversations, he accidentally said, "You and your professors are worth . . ." I didn't speak to him for six months after that. Only later did he change his mind. Despite being concerned about the possibility of an embargo, he didn't trust research, development, and self-manufacturing. But that was his right, he was the chief of staff.

The British suggested that we manufacture the Chieftain in Israel since it was their advanced tank. We brought a tank, the ordnance and armored corps conducted an experiment, and we made a list of changes without which we would not want the tank. I had an argument with Talik about the Chieftain's cannon. I claimed that we could get the existing 105 mm cannon to perform in a way that wouldn't require us to get the 120 mm cannon. In the end, neither we nor the British followed through with the plan.

The time had come to manufacture a tank that met our needs.

In the army I was considered "the enemy of the Merkava." From the 1960s to 1985, I was strongly and vocally opposed to Talik's approach. I worked closely with Bren, who took Talik's place as commander of the armored corps (1969–1974), and together we defined the parameters of the tank that the IDF required. We marked a new milestone on the path to manufacturing the tank in 1972, when Talik was appointed deputy chief of staff and began to promote the development of a tank according to his approach, which was different than our recommendation. Bren and I were not able to influence his opinion. And that is how the Merkava tank came to be, a seventy-ton tank with an engine in the front.

Talik and I were acquaintances and even friends as long as we didn't argue about professional matters. During the War of Independence, when the residents of Be'er Tuvia were evacuated to Ne'taim, where I lived, Talik's sister and her kids lived in our home. Talik had been drafted and was living in Rehovot, which was close to Ne'taim, so we would meet quite often, and we had friendly conversations.

I filled my role as chief ordnance officer according to the instructions of the higher command, and I also had my own rules, which were based on many years of experience. An example was my approach to standardization, which affected the entire system. I wasn't willing for any changes to be made to a tank, cannon, or vehicle unless they were made to all units across the board. You want to change something? Okay, but make that change to all the units of that kind. I was opposed to anyone taking a welding machine and adding even a hook to a tank only because the head of the armored corps liked it. I gave instructions to remove anything that had been added on in that way. That's how the disagreement between Talik and myself began. I explained to him that I wanted the mechanic who moves from one tank to the next to remember that whatever he sees, he has already seen in the previous tank. If a certain change is important, then it must be done to all units. They knew I was coming to visit the emergency storage spaces, and that I would be very strict about any work anomalies that had not been supervised by me and authorized by the Ordnance Corps. Talik, who also considered himself a technological person, got involved in these matters, and we argued over changes that he made that had not been approved by the Ordnance Corps.

I'm not completely rejecting the Merkava tank. I was opposed to its features and to the main parts of its design, mostly in terms of the location of the engine. I only know of one tank whose engine is in the front. The AMX13 light tank, which is not a primary battle tank, which we purchased from the French because it was light and short, due to the front placement of the engine, making it possible to fly it in cargo planes. We installed an engine in the front using different tools that we developed—mobile cannons and ambulances. During the War of Attrition, when I built an armored ambulance out of a Sherman tank, the entrance, just like in the personnel carriers, was in the back. Unlike these vehicles, in a primary battle tank the engine has to be in the back. In light of my critique, Talik invited to me share my opinions in a meeting with the commanders of the armored brigades. I thanked him and explained my main objections to the Merkava design, which related, above all, to the location of the engine and the gears at the front of the tank, which was different than its location in the back of the tank where it is in every primary battle tank in the world (the United States, Russia, Germany, France, etc.) which was no coincidence.

The Merkava designers argued that putting the engine and the gears at the front of the tank added mass to the armor, enabled the tank to handle impact from armor-piercing weapons, and provided significant additional protection to the tank crew. Unlike this approach, I argued that the tank and crew's protection was dependent on three things—firepower, armor and structure, and mobility. With regard to everything having to do with the engine and the gearbox, which are the tank's most vulnerable parts, all it takes is a little bit of damage, a hole or a crack, and they stop working. One mortar hit to the front of the tank and the engine is out of commission. In battle, the second a tank loses its mobility it becomes a standing target and soon a corpse, and the fate of its crew is sealed.

In my opinion, to protect the tank and its crew, and to increase the chances of survival, the engine and the gears must be in the rear end of the tank, the less vulnerable side.

Arrows of ridicule were sent my way at every opportunity. During our conversations, Talik used to use demeaning language, "Who am I to understand this, you are the engineer after all," he would say. Years after all of that, when I was president of the Technion, Training Camp 20 held an ordnance convention to which I was invited. I watched as Talik became the main authority of the corps. The corps took him in. Talik was supposed to talk about the corps, the technology, etc., but he chose to start his speech by addressing me nastily, and said, "This is a convention about the storms and floods in the world, and I would just like to warn you that Noah is sitting in the crowd." I really did not appreciate that.

When I was head of the quartermaster's branch, Talik approached me and suggested that we develop and design a tank together, based on his idea of what the tank should be, and that we could "share the glory." I refused, but I told him that as head of the quartermaster's branch I would manufacture the tank that the IDF designated as its primary tank. And in fact, I built the factory that manufactured the Merkava tank based on Talik's idea.

The Decision-Making Process and the Conspiracy of Silence

The decision-making process surrounding the Merkava was convoluted, so my voice and considerations did not find expression in the higher-ranking forums in which decisions were being made. It was not discussed in the full staff forum of which I was a member, only with the chief of staff. I was not invited, and as far as I am aware there was no record of the meeting. The matter was brought before the Knesset's committee of security and foreign affairs. I was summoned to a committee with Talik. He was not willing to speak in my presence. For him, the Merkava was a very personal matter, perhaps even the essence of his life. I explained my opinions, at length, to the committee.

In August 1970, a report stated:

At the end of three months of studying, the Minister of Finance (Pinchas Sapir) convened the critical discussion in which it was decided to proceed with the project of the first Israeli tank. The following people participated in the meeting: Minister of Defense Moshe Dayan, Chief of Staff Haim Bar Lev, personnel from the ministry of defense, and members of the general staff. In addition, there were experts from the ministry of finance. All participants agreed unanimously, and announced at the end of the meeting, "The State of Israel will develop a tank and build up a tank industry to manufacture tanks for the IDF, and in the future will even export them.

Did the members of the general staff actually take part? I, as a member of the general staff, was not invited. That is how history is rewritten.

The decision was made although my objections were not brought before those who dedicated the "three months to learning" on which they based their decision. I heard about the decisive meeting after the fact, when everyone in the defense system was talking about it. Those who needed to know about my opinion definitely knew, and they made sure it was not heard or presented at the meeting. To this day, I am not sure what the prime minister or what Pinchas Sapir, the finance minister, knew.

To this day, I have a feeling that there was a conspiracy of silence surrounding me, related to challenging dynamics and lack of professional integrity, but I put it all aside and built the factory in Tel HaShomer that manufactured the Merkava. In 1978, after a few years of development, this factory began manufacturing Merkava tanks and has done so for over forty years.

At the same time, and even before the Merkava tanks were on the battlefield, I continued to deal with this matter and question the assumptions that led to my objections to the structure and the tank's vulnerability, reliability, and safety for the crew.

Colonel Dr. Menachem Dishon, a very reliable scientist, was head of the testing branch of the Ordnance Corps. Since I was chief scientist in the ministry of defense, I worked closely with him and with Professor George H. Weiss from the United States, an expert on performance research, to check the question of the location of the tank engine. Both these scientists summarized their conclusions in very detailed articles, basing them on the data gathered from the testing of two thousand tanks from the IDF as well as enemy tanks that had participated and been hit during the Six-Day War and during the Yom Kippur War. One of their main findings indicated that the number of tanks hit in the front was more than double the number of tanks hit in the back. These findings supported my claim that if advanced mortars that can pierce a tank's armor on the battlefield, even if they are just close enough to reach the engine and put it out of commission, the tank will become a standing target, and the chances of the crew's survival are minimized. Since in an armored battle there are clearly more hits to the front than to the back, placing the engine in the front does not improve the crew's defense or its ability to survive.

These findings were kept at bay by Talik and by the security forces comptroller, using ridiculous claims, such as "these articles don't meet the expected scientific criteria . . . the numbers brought as examples [in both models] are not and cannot be real . . . the claim in the article [that placing the engine in the front makes the tank more vulnerable] is presented as a given fact, and is planted in such a way that both critics did not notice that it is in fact an arbitrary assumption and not fort:207

a fact." I understood that there was no way that I would be able to bring this comprehensive and thorough test of two thousand tanks and its conclusions to the discussion. None of this can make it past a man who is not willing to let facts distract him.

I continued to study the Merkava topic in depth for years, and started checking data from the Lebanon War, in which Merkava tanks were also hit. I summarized my conclusions but deep down I understood, with a sense of pain and of a missed opportunity, that I no longer had the ability to influence or change this decision.

Looking to the future, I believe that in the development of tanks, certain crucial aspects need to be considered. True, there are advantages to a more advanced computerized system inside the tank, but it must be taken into account that there are also advantages to a less sophisticated tank. Another consideration pertains to the financial aspect, as it is more expensive to manufacture one Merkava tank than to manufacture a larger number of tanks for a cheaper price, and sometimes quantity does create quality. Another crucial aspect about future decisions is ensuring suitability for the terrain the tanks are expected to fight on. The Merkava was designed in the '70s for large armored battles, but had yet to be tested in the field. The attitude was, and still is to a certain degree, that the Merkava would solve all our problems, and that we don't need anything else. That being said, we need to ask ourselves what kind of future war are we expecting? With ISIS? In the latest wars, tanks destroyed homes. You don't need the Merkava's massive cannon to destroy a house, if you want to turn the tank in a dense urban area, it is not possible. For that kind of fighting a different tank is required, and a different weapon system is needed for combat fighting.

Separation of Powers in the Army—a Complex Hierarchy

While I was chief ordnance officer, at the same time as the fight about the right tank structure for the IDF was raging, another conflict developed regarding different approaches to the question of the ranking between the professional guidance and coordinating part of the staff and the operational parts of the army.

According to the system in place at the time, the quartermaster's branch was considered to be the staff that coordinated between the chief of staff and the heads of the professional corps, the logistics belonged to the communications corps and the medical corps, and everyone was under the command of the chief of staff. As chief ordnance officer, the head of the quartermaster's branch gave me instructions and guidelines according to which I worked, and there was also someone in charge of supervision and inspection of the corps. I had the right to express my opinion and to try to convince others, but in the end, when there was an argument between the coordination and operational parts of the army, the chief of staff would make the final decision.

But for Matti Peled, this did not seem like the right structure. He suggested making a change. That was his right. According to this change, the corps would be under his command—not the chief of staff's. In this new structure, he wanted to be the commander of all the heads of the professional corps, a super-major general. I objected. It sounded like a matter of semantics, but it wasn't. It was a fundamental issue. In the discussion, I told Yitzhak Rabin, the chief of staff, "If you want to destroy the professional corps, that is your right. But then do what the American army did: create a logistical headquarters that brings the corps together, coordinated by the head of the quartermaster's branch, directly under your command. That is the right thing organizationally. What you are doing is turning the staff part of the army into the operational part, and that creates an inherent conflict of interest." In every industrial organization, the staff sets the objectives, and the operational structure executes them or convinces the staff that it cannot do so and asks to have the objectives changed. Separation of powers is a basic principle in an organizational structure. For a year, 1964–1965, Matti Peled worked tirelessly to convince the chief of staff and eventually succeeded in doing so, and the reform that he wanted passed.

In my opinion, the struggle to change the structure stems from the fact that while I was in the Ordnance Corps, the corps' powerful and dominant strength could not be ignored. I was also a major general, with the same rank as Matti Peled as the head of the quartermaster's branch. This situation was unacceptable to him and prevented him from establishing his position and strength as a super-major general, the head of all the professional corps. He received massive support from Talik, who for his own reasons and following the argument about the manufacturing of the Israeli Merkava tank, collaborated with Matti against me in the discussions in the chief of staff's office.

It was an argument between two intelligent major generals, both of whom were very opinionated and tended to try to force their opinions on others. During one of the discussions with Rabin, the chief of staff, I said harsh things to Matti. I drove him mad. During an argument, they were both swept up in a great storm of emotions, while I remained calm and serene. They were probably used to dealing with people who were not as strong, opinionated, and stubborn as they themselves were. Yitzhak seemed to be at a loss. The two of them dedicated much time and effort to convince the chief of staff and were not opposed to being manipulative. In the end, Rabin accepted Matti Peled's claim. As I have written, as chief of staff, it was his right and obligation to make decisions.

Following the decision, Rabin sent me to talk to Levi Eshkol, the prime minister and minister of defense. What did Rabin expect of Eshkol? Maybe he thought that the issue was important enough to present it to the minister of defense. Eshkol listened, asked questions, but did not intervene. I wondered if Rabin's decision indicated that he was unable to stand the pressure of these two major generals. And maybe the opposite was true; maybe they were just closer to him than I was and he trusted them more than he trusted me professionally? I don't know. One day, as we returned together from a meeting at the Holy Land Hotel in Jerusalem, Rabin tried to convince me to accept the decision about the structural change, but I refused and told him I was resigning. I told him, "I'm leaving. They just might end up blaming me if this logistical structure fails. You made a mistake. This negates every logical structure in an industrial organization. You made a decision, and I respect your decision. Appoint someone else as chief ordnance officer." And so, in 1966, a year and a half after I returned, I resigned.

This tense argument was essentially a professional one, but it became more complicated when personal issues and interpersonal relationships were brought into it.

On both these matters, the tank and the structure of the quartermaster's branch in relation to the logistical corps, I was unable to convince others, but fortunately and throughout most of my professional career, for the most part I have been given a free hand to act as I saw fit. There were very talented people working beside me, and together we could think, consult, and make the right decision. However, a shared background doesn't always help to create a shared language and understanding in times of disagreement. And so, the argument between me and Matti Peled became a bitter rivalry as his extreme personality clashed with my stubbornness over things I believed were crucial. He joined the Palmach with me and we were together in Kfar Giladi. He was "Canaanite," joined the "Am Lochem" (fighting nation) movement, and was forced to resign from the Palmach. He fought in Givati during the War of Independence and was an excellent soldier. He went from one extreme to another. He was very right-wing in the beginning, and ended up as an extreme leftist. I knew him in the general staff as a man with extreme opinions that manifested themselves in discussions with Eshkol during the waiting period before the Six-Day War, when he demanded "nothing less than conquering Cairo." That was a different Matti than the one who had left the army.

Since we were not able to have open and candid conversations, I was left with questions as to what was personal and what was professional in our conflict. Of course, there was a professional basis, because Matti was an intelligent, thoughtful man with opinions that he formed on his own and for which he fought with all his might, but I have no doubt that the personal aspect carried some serious weight as well.

It was the end of an era, and today, when I sum up those years in the Ordnance Corps, even my humility cannot hide my achievements. To my understanding and after analyzing the results, I come to the conclusion that I was the right person for the right job at the right time. I combined my experience from home, military combat experience, and knowledge of engineering with vision and resourcefulness. A massive corps was built up from nearly nothing. Our contribution to the IDF's strength during the wars was crucial. The tough situations in which the IDF found itself forced us to think outside the box, to dare, and to take risks. My head was brimming with ideas. Some were implemented, some were not. From my perspective, the "esprit de corps"—the spirit of the corps—of the Ordnance Corps reached incredible heights. This was the experience of the engineers who built the IDF's strength.

The matter of large-scale manufacturing was discussed over the years but never leaked out. The big secret was the number. The enemy did not know how many armored vehicles we had. Our enemies knew about every single tank we purchased on the free market. But they didn't know anything about the tanks that we had built from scraps. During the Six-Day War and the Yom Kippur War, the enemy was surprised by the number of tanks we had. They hadn't imagined that we had built, with our own hands, machines whose quality could handle their armored forces.

I was relatively discreet and hid things from my supervisors, with the resourcefulness of an underground force. I created undisputable facts on the ground. I didn't ask to do many things, I just did them, and if somebody asked questions in the aftermath, I could explain everything. The successes spoke for themselves. However, over the years, the technological field was not viewed with the importance it deserved in terms of the thought process and the general staff's priorities.

Something about this attitude trickled down to the Ordnance Corps, which is supposed to perpetuate and teach about its history and the people who built it. Next to the tank display it said "upgraded in Israel," "repurposed," "had installed in it," "improvements made," and other general statements. I didn't see any sign of the fact that in the ordnance base at Tel HaShomer there was a tank factory that we had built, or that if we hadn't restored and improved about 2,250 working tanks from spare parts, during a long period in which the countries of the world refused to sell us new tanks, Israel would not exist today. The armored forces fought with these "junk machines," and won.

CHAPTER 16

With Professor Katzir as Deputy to the Chief Scientist of the Ministry of Defense

With Rabin's approval I left the army, and after a short while I accepted an offer from Ephraim Katzir, chief scientist of the Ministry of Defense, who really wanted me to be his deputy—and I obliged. We worked together excellently. A major general working under a civilian. We did things that it is better not to speak about to this day. I can't expand on my time as deputy to the chief scientist (1966–1968) or about my time as chief scientist. We supervised the military's plans for technological development. Very serious topics. I can't ignore the problems with the military personnel, who made Ephraim and me miserable.

We had known Ephraim Katzir for a very long time, from our home in Jerusalem, when he and his brother, Aharon, were students, and in later years, they would come to our house to meet my dad to discuss the development of weapons as part of "Hemed." Our friendship became closer in America, during my first period of studies at MIT, when Aharon was on sabbatical at Harvard and his brother joined him. When they went away, we watched over their three kids, and after a while, when they left America, we moved into their attic apartment in Cambridge. Our good relationship lasted for years, even after Ephraim became president.

In May 1967, Ephraim and I had an interesting visit to the research and development facilities that belonged to the British military forces as well as the Swedish and the Norwegian military forces. We were graciously welcomed. Maybe thanks to Ephraim, who was well known. At the time, there had been articles published that were of interest to us, but they spoke to us specifically about confidential topics, such as the meaning of chemical warfare. We were impressed by their humility and how close we felt to them, especially when the head of the Swedish research team hosted us in his home and not in a restaurant, as was customary.

Towards June 1967, when the tension in Israel began, we cut our visit short. Because of my new job, I was not formally part of the general staff, but they included me. I was part of a difficult conversation between the major generals and Levi Eshkol. Rabin was not present for that meeting. The problem was how long we had to wait. We were hoping that the United States would resolve the crisis. I said something, which Ezer Weizman mentions in his book, about the one good thing that could come from waiting: that the Jordanian king would make a mistake and join the war. Then we could finally complete all the objectives of the War of Independence.

On May 25, I approached Yitzhak Rabin during one of the hardest times before the war and I told him that I was at his service. Despite the many disagreements, the friendship between us hadn't been shaken. During the war, Deputy Chief of Staff Haim Bar Lev sent me on a number of missions, such as checking on Mevaseret during the Jordanian bombing. Later, I joined Uzi Narkiss in Jerusalem and was with him at the police academy before and after the battles of Ammunition Hill, Sheikh Jarrah, and the Rockefeller Museum. I followed the paratroopers into the Old City, to the Temple Mount, and the Western Wall. Alongside the historical achievements, I painfully remember the hours spent with Major General Meir Zorea, "Zarro," knowing that his son, a pilot, had died in the Golan Heights and that he still hadn't been notified about it. Everyone was a friend of mine from the Palmach, and I had even fought with Zarro in the War of Independence, and there we were, meeting once again in another war.

CHAPTER 17

Head of the Quartermaster's Branch during the War of Attrition and Looking Ahead at the Next War

In 1968, Matti Peled retired from the army and Haim Bar Lev, the chief of staff, appointed me Matti's successor. I put aside my conflict over the reform, to which I strongly objected, and fully engrossed myself in promoting the branch at a turning point in the IDF, when it needed to arrange itself in spaces it had never known before and simultaneously maintain an ongoing war in Sinai for a number of years—the War of Attrition.

A terrible bombing all along the canal welcomed me into my new position on September 8, 1968. Ten of our soldiers were killed. In fact, by the end of the war in August 1970, we were managing two different arenas. The first, supplying logistical support to a widespread area that was at war, with constant bombing and shooting. It is difficult to understand what it means to drive and provide logistical support along the entire canal, from Port Sa'id to Isma'iliyya, under fire. The second, which was happening at the same time, was preparing the Sinai for the next war, which was imminent. I don't want to imagine what would have happened to the IDF during the Yom Kippur War if we hadn't made all the logistical preparations. I knew what needed to be done, I knew what was important. I was given a free hand, no one intervened in my decision-making, and I had a budget.

In Sinai, we set up an entire logistical system that dealt with all the army's needs during war. We paved and restored 1,840 kilometers of roads, built dozens of camps, and set up semi-underground operation rooms. We moved the ammunition storage units forward.

The Egyptians solved the water issue in Sinai when they set up a water-supply system and a water reservoir. When they stopped the flow of water from Egypt, all we had to do was connect a waterline from Israel to the already existing pipe system. The quartermaster's branch did it, and later we installed an additional water system 650 kilometers long. Water was brought to Sharm el-Sheikh in barrels from Eilat until the boat hit rocks. There were two water-purification facilities in Tel Baruch, each providing one thousand cubic meters of water per day, which we purchased and moved to Sharm el-Sheikh to purify water from a seawater well we had dug. There was no longer any need to transfer water from Eilat in barrels on a ship. The first massive water-purification in this country was done by us.

The Challenge of Logistical Service to the IDF after June 1967

Until June 1967, the IDF was spread out over a territory of about eight thousand square miles, and after the war, within a few days, it found itself spread out over more than twenty-seven thousand square miles. The quartermaster's branch had to provide the IDF with logistical support from the northeastern part of the Golan all the way to the Suez Canal and the Gulf of Sharm-el-Sheikh, which we renamed the Gulf of Solomon. The budget was doubled, and we worked with massive numbers and quantities that the IDF had never before witnessed. For example, the number of items that the quartermaster dealt with increased from 165,000 to 453,000. Food quality checks went up by 445%. The water tank number went up so high that in one water cycle you could transport a million liters.

I didn't think it was my right to cancel the reform, but I imagined that I could function without its flaws, and so I worked with the officers of the corps that were under my command. While working in the general staff, I formed relationships that strengthened the commanding authority of every person in their corps. As a member of

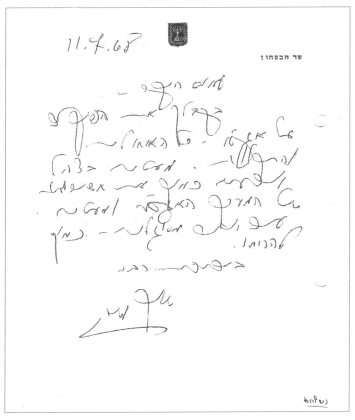

When I received the command over the quartermaster's branch—a letter from Minister of Defense Moshe Dayan

Dear Amos
As you receive the Command
of Quartermaster's Branch (AGA) all wishes
and hopes. Only a few in the IDF
know like you the importance
of the alignment of the Command
Quartermaster's Branch (AGA)
and fewer are capable like you to elevate it.
With great friendship,
Yours,
Moshe

the staff, I determined what the plans would be while consulting with every corps in its own area of expertise. Minister of Defense Moshe Dayan continued to support me and to believe in my abilities, and he even expressed this in writing.

With one of the biggest budgets in the IDF, a lot of leeway, and corps in charge of executing everything, I could do a lot—and I could allow myself not to ask for permission. The branch staff comprised about two hundred people, and some of them filled positions that represented all the components of the quartermaster's branch to the different corps. We made a clear connection between the ranking officers of the quartermaster's branch and the parallel officers in the different corps.

Since we were the largest organizational structure in Israel, we could dictate what products we would purchase and at what prices. I set up an expert division that dealt solely with the research of economic profitability, to ensure that every product and service would be analyzed in terms of its economic validity. We didn't skip the cost of doing laundry in the army or that of manufacturing clothes in the army. As a structure of that magnitude, I was under a lot of pressure and also under pressure to obtain contracts in less-than-legal ways, and I made sure to cover all my bases so neither I nor any of my people failed. For example, I made sure never to meet with businesspeople without the presence of a representative from the Defense Ministry.

One day, when we were taking care of paving the road to Sharm el-Sheikh, I was driving with one of the contractors to New York for a consultation. At the hotel, when I went to pay, I was told that "It has already been paid." I called the contractor over and asked, "Do you want to get on my bad side? Take the money." There were other attempts at influence, for example, some with that same Jew, a very wealthy man named Bruce Rappaport. When he was just getting started, he was a ghaffir (a Jewish guard nominated by the British during the British Mandate) in Nahalal and emigrated to Switzerland where he built a factory that manufactured prepared meals. There was an event in Tzahala, at the offices of the Director General of the

Ministry of Defense, Yeshayahu Levi. Present at that meeting were Minister of Defense Moshe Dayan and Bruce Rappaport. Dayan turned to me and said, "Why don't you buy food from Bruce Rappaport?" I said, "First of all, I don't know this company or its products. But I want to remind you that yesterday you approved a budget to purchase sixteen hundred spare trucks, and now you want me to waste money on prepared food? We will do thorough work, conduct trials on five thousand soldiers, see what their reactions are, check the price, and only then make a decision." After checking all of these, I approached Dayan and said to him, "It's not worth the money, forget about it."

Fighting equipment of all shapes and sizes was the main priority on my list. The most important and advanced combat issues were what interested me most, the rest of it was support. As a result of the massive growth of the IDF, we set up dozens of new emergency storage units, and I made sure to strictly supervise everything and to make sure that despite the increase in quantity, we would not experience a decrease in the quality of the ammunition or other equipment. There was not a single place that I did not visit personally, sometimes as a surprise visit, and everything having to do with logistics was checked: food, shoes, socks, tents, ammunition, weapons—everything. During one of the visits to a battalion in the Golan, the battalion commander claimed that there was not enough food and that the soldiers were hungry. I went to the dumpster area with him, lifted up the lids, and saw food that had been thrown away. I said to him, "You're hungry? You received enough food. Here, look. There is a lack of organization, and this is wasteful." I couldn't stand wastefulness. He got an earful from me. I had a reputation as someone who not only dealt with the macro aspect of things, but also checked everything to the very last detail. People knew that when I visited a workshop, I didn't only check whether the walkways were painted and clean, I opened the toolbox, took out the pliers, and checked that they closed properly.

When officers of mine from lieutenant colonel and up finished serving in a certain position, I would ask them for a report that summarized and indicated the problems, complaints, and other issues they thought needed to be improved. I wanted to understand and learn, in depth, from each person's personal experience. During the many conversations I had, I felt that I had brought into the IDF something from the soldier-commander relationship that had existed in the Palmach. It was a relationship that combined equality, which enabled people to express, argue, object, and make suggestions, with a very clear hierarchy in which the highest-ranking commander ultimately makes the final decision.

The Ordnance Corp—Withstanding the Challenges in the IDF Following the Six-Day War

The Ordnance Corps under my command was different from all the other corps, and as part of my position as head of the quartermaster's branch, they were once again under my command.

I started to manage the Ordnance Corps again and dealt intensively with the issue of manufacturing a tank. Not a year had gone by, and in 1969 Talik was appointed head of an independent tank administration in the Ministry of Defense. Everything went to him. In his opinion, the tank was the center of everything. He believed, "With a tank, we conquer the world." During the War of Attrition, when he was deputy chief of staff, we paid a very heavy price for his views and his stubbornness.

The Ordnance Corps expanded and improved. The number of people who went to study in the Technion as part of the Ordnance Corps had tripled. To encourage people to sign on for extra service time, we sent hundreds of soldiers to short professional-development sessions abroad. The number of developmental assignments in the corps increased from a few dozen a year to hundreds.

Alongside ongoing maintenance, the corps faced unprecedented challenges in managing and purchasing and the enormous amount of spoils of war we obtained during the Six-Day War. It is no coincidence that in 1970 the Kaplan Award (for work productivity) was given to the restoration and storage facility number 7200, in Haifa, for using manufacturing methods that were based on innovative techniques and advanced knowledge.

The magnitude of the spoils we collected during the Six-Day War was humongous, almost the size of the IDF before 1967. The ordnance corps collected it, sorted it, determined the viability of restoring or repurposing it, and restored most of it.

The spoils included 513 tanks from seven different models, more than half of them Soviet tanks. After repurposing and restoration, the IDF received 355 tanks and created brigades comprised of excellent Soviet tanks named "Tiran." Hundreds of armored personnel carriers (APCs) were also seized, along with over eight thousand motorized vehicles of all kinds, thousands of different types of cannons, massive quantities of light weapons, and ammunition.

The scope of purchasing was also quite large at the time. We bought about 900 tanks of different kinds, most of them for the purpose of repurposing, 60 mobile cannons, 450 APCs, about 3,400 trucks for restoration, and twelve M60 mobile bridging tanks vehicle-launched bridges (which we nicknamed "Tamshach"). At the time, about 1,600 tanks and mobile cannons, 2,900 half-tracks, about 700 APCs and 1,000 communications vehicles were restored and repurposed. These numbers were unprecedented.

The Supply Corps — Striving for Expertise, Professionalism, and Quality Even in Things That Don't Shoot

I had no training in food or cooking, in sewing clothes, or in shoemaking, but I developed an approach that pertained to every aspect of supply, and it shaped the improvements that we made for the benefit of the soldiers, while also making production, supply, and savings more efficient.

Nutrition in the army was also an issue that was on my mind, in terms of budget and quality. There were no high-level professionals in the corps, and we didn't have a food lab. During one of the first meetings, I almost screamed, "Are you crazy? You're feeding one, two, three hundred thousand people a day without any knowledge about food?" I was looking for professionalism and quality that would lead to the establishment of a high-level functioning system.

We sent officers from the supply corps to academic institutions abroad to specialize in food and two academic officers to get doctorates in America. And so, a generation was trained in the manufacture of food; when they finished their service, these people improved the quality of civilian factories such as "Osem."

A food lab center was built. I demanded that the corps commander gather comprehensive information about the costs of food products so that suppliers wouldn't tell us tall tales and so that we could bargain with them. We imported coffee beans from Africa, roasted them, and packaged coffee for the IDF. When we got even smarter, we approached the local industry with the required quantities because we didn't want to compete with it. On the contrary, I wanted to give Jews jobs. Yes, I am a Zionist.

We needed to make significant changes in the meat and its by-products to prevent the food from spoiling and rotting and to improve its nutritional value. It was common to purchase kosher meat from meat suppliers in Israel who imported it frozen and then defrosted it. After the meat had defrosted, it looked like a wet rag. I remember an unusual case when sixty tons of meat was thrown out because the meat had defrosted and smelled rancid. We had experts come and check it—we destroyed it all. I didn't pay the suppliers. They came to my house and yelled. I told them to leave. Are you crazy? You sent the army bad meat? Don't you know how to check your meat? Of course, they didn't do it on purpose, but that is not how you sell meat.

I said to Rabbi Goren, "Why don't we kasher the meat when it's soft, after the slaughtering?" He agreed, and the procedure of purchasing meat was modified. Of course, the meat suppliers objected, and then I started importing meat directly from slaughterhouses in Argentina and Ireland, meat in any size I wanted, kosher, and sliced for whatever purpose we needed.

Along with the factory in Arad that manufactured schnitzels made of soy, we developed, according to doctors' recommendations, a hamburger that was a mixture of meat and soy to improve the nutritional value by lowering the amounts of fat.

We went to J. Lyons & Co., in London, to learn how they operated their network of restaurants, and to the Birds Eye frozen food company factories in New York. We asked to gain knowledge so that we could build a central kitchen in Tzrifin with first-class cooks and then provide food to the rest of the IDF's bases. I didn't succeed in that endeavor because the commanders wanted the kitchen and the cook close to them, "to make an omelet when they're hungry."

We checked the quality of the bakeries with which we had supply contracts and continued with only two of them. To reduce the quantity of bread that was thrown out, we changed the packaging. Instead of 1 kg unpacked, unsliced loaves of bread, we switched to 750 grams of sliced, packaged white bread.

We discovered that ice transported from Ashkelon to Sinai doesn't really make it, so we purchased an ice factory, with its operator, and set it up at the Rephidim air base—called Bir Gifgafa by the Egyptians when they build the air base in 1956—in the western Sinai.

Other Products

Bullet-proof vests. The War of Attrition in the Suez Canal area, in which many were wounded from bombing and snipers, raised the imminent need for personal protective gear. We purchased five hundred American bullet-proof vests and sent them into the canal. We discovered that they successfully stopped the shrapnel. The positive outcome helped convince the general staff to self-manufacture vests.

We purchased raw materials and the ordnance corps sewed bullet-proof vests, and later on we exported the manufacturing to an external factory.

Sleeping bags instead of blankets. I was tired of seeing the blankets tied to the tanks. Can you really imagine the IDF moving around with blankets instead of sleeping bags? There were no sleeping bags in the IDF until the Ordnance Corps designed and issued them.

Uniforms and bras. Issuing uniforms was the responsibility of the Ordnance Corps. I went to the military induction center to check what they were giving the women in the induction process and saw that they received a bra and underwear, and by the time they reached the end of the hallway the new recruits would throw them in the trash. I suggested to the head officer of the female corps, Colonel Deborah Tomer, that we give the female soldiers vouchers to buy the bras and underwear they wanted at the canteen. Until 1968, there were no long pants for women in the IDF, only skirts. The fact that female soldiers now wear pants is a result of my decision.

Shoes. The head supply officer was responsible for the largest shoemaking workshop in the Middle East. I was astounded to see the enormous building in which dozens of shoemakers worked. The average age of the workers was sixty-five to seventy. When I was done touring the factory, I asked the head supply officer: "Do you think we will continue fixing shoes in the future?" We developed a vulcanized shoe that could not be fixed, red for the paratroopers, the rest in black, and we let the shoemaking workshop die out on its own as the workers slowly retired.

The Medical Corps—instead of flying the wounded out we built operating rooms in Sinai. The medical equipment that the quartermaster's branch was in charge of went through inspection and was fixed, and new inspection rules were issued, pertaining to everything from the thickness of the needles to the quality of the band aids to the equipment in the field hospitals. The medical logistics system's approach in the army included decisions pertaining to the treatment of soldiers injured during war. I made the final decision about this, in contradiction to the head medical officer's opinion, who had planned to fly the injured soldiers out of Sinai to hospitals in Israel in war time. I ordered him to set up semi-underground operation rooms in Sinai, away from the airport area, to shorten the time it took to get soldiers to the hospital. I have no doubt that thanks to this decision, we saved the lives of hundreds of injured soldiers.

The Engineering Corps—Lessons Learned and Building during the War

At the end of the Six-Day War, we were told to immediately build bases in Sinai, especially after an entire base had been destroyed during the War of Attrition. I asked myself what we should do. Do I bring construction workers from the center of Israel to build in Sinai? I remembered that on their drilling sites, the Americans would use structures that were built on a frame, allowing them to move the buildings from place to place. I drove with the head engineering officers to a company in Florida that built structures from isolated aluminum plates, which enabled them to put the structures together very quickly. We purchased a few structures for a trial run, and we put them together, like LEGO sets, in the Sinai. But pretty quickly it became clear that the structures couldn't handle the dry, hot Sinai climate.

Together with the Ashtrom building company, we developed a cement structure shaped like a room with several openings, a slanted roof, and four hooks to enable it to be lifted by a crane. The structures, which we called "ashkubit" (a prefabricated cube-like building), were built in a factory near Holon and transported in very large quantities to Sinai on tank transporters. When we cleared out of Sinai, we took everything with us, and the "ashkubiyot" were transported to the settlements.

Another field I was deeply involved in was the unification of the measurements of all the components in the building process from doors to walls. When I was a student in Boston, I found an apartment that was missing doors. I went to a woodshop to buy a door, and discovered that, by law, there were three sizes, and when I wanted to hang a picture, I found out that in the drywall there is a designated spot where a nail could be hammered in. This too, was according to the law: "It is a drywall. If you measure one foot from the door you will reach a beam on which you can hang a picture." I learned that standardization has serious, significant implications, but I saw that here, every person does as he pleases. That is why I created a branch that dealt with the standardization of building methods, which led to a significant decrease in prices and improvement in the quality of the building.

What do you make a fortification sandbag out of? Out of jute. If you create fortifications with sandbags, then the cost of a bag that rips is not just the bag itself, seventeen cents, but also everything around it. I implemented the use of Polyethylene sandbags, which were a little more expensive, but in the overall calculation were the cheapest, because these bags didn't rip.

Four Years as Head of the Quartermaster's Branch Came to an End

With Dado (David Elazar), the chief of staff, I had a monthly meeting. We would sit for half an hour, and the meeting would be over. I didn't feel that he was interested in the logistical issues. On the one hand, I remained independent, and that's a good thing. On the other hand, it's a shame he didn't really take an interest. Despite the fact that I did everything that was required of me, I think he had his own reasons for notifying me that I would be ending my job, for reasons that had nothing to do with my performance as head of the quartermaster's branch. Another chapter in my professional life had come to an end.

The quartermaster's branch is responsible for a field that didn't particularly interest the high-ranking commanding officers in the army, even though it is an extremely crucial component in the entire army's abilities, both during routine times and during emergencies. In fact, I had managed the largest technological-logistical operation in the country. This position enabled me to deal with and learn a lot about fields I had never known before, to make significant changes, and to develop an approach and work principles about how to do logistics properly. It was very satisfying. So it was on the staff level, but alongside that there was an entire system that identified commanding and management in the quartermaster's branch differently. Brigadier General Dov Laor, my second-in-command, said during my goodbye party:

It was a pleasure working for you, Amos. You gave us the feeling that each of us is a meaningful part of the machine and not just a small screw. We were given independence at work, personal responsibility, and the feeling that each of us could achieve the goals set before them . . . from the lowest rank to the high-ranking commanding officers, you gave us the feeling that we were all working for the important issues—and you directed us . . . I would like to dedicate a few words to your accomplishments in the areas of engineering, ordnance, and the development of weaponry in the IDF. Most of the people here won't believe it, but 92% of the tanks in the IDF went through you, and the craft of restoring, repurposing, and modernizing them was planned by you, and they became first grade tanks, recognized around the world as excellent tanks. You are the one who started the tradition of repurposing scrap tanks as modern tanks. 85% of the mobile artillery in the IDF was designed by you and built in facilities that were under your command as head ordnance officer in the past and as head of the quartermaster's branch in the present. The development of all these machines and methods are, almost entirely, an original Israeli development. (Dov Laor, pers. comm.)

I could have continued for another four years. I was used to filling long-term positions. I wanted to leave my mark in the logistics department. I didn't leave the army because I had had enough, but rather because the chief of staff decided not to extend my service.

My service ended with a tough conversation with Dado that included my harsh words about the importance of the position and the choice for my replacement, Nehemia Kain, which was strange to say the least, especially with regard to politics. In my opinion, then and now, Dado did not see the true importance of the logistical aspects. My replacement chose to establish his authority by trying to hurt me and my achievements, by establishing two inquiry committees against me, to investigate the purchasing of ammunition and replacement parts that he thought had been much greater than was necessary. "Amos asked for a budget for 25,000 mortars, and purchased, without permission, a much larger quantity." I was proud that two years before the Yom Kippur War, after the War of Attrition was over, I increased our stock—which had been very minimal—and instead of purchasing 25,000 mortars for $500 dollars per mortar, I purchased 200,000 mortars for about $10 dollars per mortar.

If that wasn't enough, it was also said that "Amos hoarded shelves full of spare parts and engine parts from the 'cannibalization' of tanks." I had no qualms about this either, and I was certain it was the right way to deal with the need to restore every damaged tank to full functionality after a war or after the engine had been working for five hundred hours, and much of this required a full restoration. I also knew, that if I asked for replacement parts for routine maintenance of the engine, and then later also asked for spare parts for a full restoration, I would find myself in unnecessary arguments that would ultimately hurt the main cause—equipping the army.

Both committees found no incriminating evidence against me.

CHAPTER 18

From October to October — Terrible Neglect

In October 1972, when I finished my position as head of the quartermaster's branch, the Sinai was prepared for war. As part of my position in the quartermaster's branch, I did everything logistically necessary. We also took care of the Golan and the West Bank, but all that was very simple compared to the Sinai. And yet, in my opinion, what happened from the moment I left in 1972 until October 1973 is the worst thing that could have happened.

I was angry when the horrible war broke out in October 1973, because it was the result of an inflated sense of security and confidence and an approach that a tank can do everything, a thesis that did not hold up to reality. This approach caused a dismissal of the importance of artillery, because, of course, "the tank has a cannon." Due to arrogance and complacence, people ignored information gathered by the intelligence stating the massive number of personal anti-tank missiles, the "Sagger missiles," that the Egyptians and Syrians had purchased.

In his book, Zvika (Zvi) Zamir writes:

[T]he extent to which the Egyptian and Syrian armies grew and strengthened was not properly addressed [by the IDF]. *The Egyptians and the Syrians received thousands of Sagger missiles. These missiles caused grave damage. So what? The armored forces thought that a shaped charge is nothing. They said to me: "Zvi, you weren't here for the Six Day War. What does a missile with a shaped charge do? It only makes a hole. Sometimes you don't*

229

even know it, and it's already been in and out." The fact of the matter is that the armored forces developed no strategy to defend themselves against these missiles, even though they had hit and caused damage during the Six Day War. (Zvi Zamir and Efrat Mass, With Eyes Wide Open, Kinneret Zmora-Bitan Publishing House,2011, pages 166–167)

A half-track carrying guided anti-tank missile number 11

I can't find any justification for the fact that no one gave any consideration to the Russian Sagger missiles when we had almost identical French ss10/ss11 missiles.

Regarding the terrible failure on the Egyptian front on October 8, the chief of staff, Dado Elazar, himself testified before the Agranat Commission (established to investigate the lead up to and initial stages of the Yom Kippur War):

One of the reasons for this failure, was the fact that we did not consider them [the Sagger missiles] to be of importance before the war. (The Agranat Commission report, volume 1, page 38 April 1, 1974)

The Agranat Commission did not really get into the depths of the logistical aspects, even though they had a huge impact on the awful results of the first days of the war and even though they were the result of wrong decisions and severe neglect.

I am filled with terrible anger and disappointment when I recall what happened between the time I left in October 1972 and when the war broke out in October 1973. The failures that were the greatest obstacles in the logistical field, were:

- Severe neglect of the systems and equipment that had been prepared for war.
- Lack of tank transporters to spread out the forces.
- Inadequate amounts of ammunition in stock.
- Failures of the roller bridges intended for use in crossing the Suez Canal.

I have chosen to expound a little bit upon some of the issues relating to this, if only to enlighten those who wish to learn from the terrible disaster that befell us.

A Smoke Screen—Canister Launchers and Shells

The smoke canister launcher's job is to conceal the tank from direct fire, including from joystick-guided missiles. You shoot smoke shells all around you, the tank is concealed inside a smoke screen ten times larger than the tank itself, and it is completely hidden from the eye; in that way the chances of getting hit decrease significantly. As head ordnance officer, we adopted the French smoke canister launcher. We installed it on every armored vehicle—tanks, half-tracks, and others. In addition, we developed "model D," which was a 120 mm mortar mounted on half-tracks. The mortar had three types of shells— explosive, lighting, and massive smoke—that covered and blinded the enemy. When they didn't mount the smoke launchers on the tanks, and the shells of the "model D" mortar weren't even taken out of storage, the efficiency of the anti-tank missiles, particularly the Saggers, which the Egyptian and Syrian soldiers had in abundance, increased, and many armored forces soldiers and tanks were hurt. That was the hardest hit we took.

Emergency Storage Facilities

As head ordnance officer, I was also responsible for the war reserve unit storage warehouses. In 1964, I visited the Swedish and Norwegian armies, just to get a sense how they handled storage and equipment maintenance in their war reserves. We learned about the dry storage method. We adopted some of that method, so thousands of vehicles, tanks, and cannons would always be functional for an immediate war. After the reform in the quartermaster's branch's structure, the emergency storage units came under the responsibility of the head of the quartermaster's branch, and they were not properly taken care of. And so, when I started my position, this area required much work. A system that specialized in testing and inspecting the war reserves unit stores was built. It is true that it was very expensive, but it was also very effective. Our method of inspecting the emergency storage units was draconian. I really gave the people in charge a hard time. In October 1972, I left the emergency storage units to the person who would take my place, and they were in perfect condition. Only a year went by and their condition deteriorated, and when the Yom Kippur War broke out there were terrible malfunctions that caused a delay in the deployment of the forces and the quality of the equipment they had with them. From the lessons learned from this war, I understood how much supervision and inspection were lacking, the required equipment had been misplaced and was not properly covered, and along with all of these failings, some commanders didn't make sure everything and everyone was properly equipped. They took equipment, probably for training, and then just didn't put it back.

Tank Transporters

As head of the quartermaster's branch, I was responsible for the distribution of the forces in preparation for war and during actual war. This was a situation which we called "the everything event," an all-inclusive war. We were required to figure out and plan how to mobilize the armored divisions from the storage facilities in the center of Israel to the Sinai and the Golan, mounted on carriers carrying heavy tanks. Turns out, we were missing transporters, and in the staff meeting on August 21, 1972, I presented a number of plans for preparations during war, and I said:

> We have a computer program that we use when working on transportation issues. I tried checking what the meaning and effect would be of buying additional carriers for the armored forces in the Sinai. We ran a simple simulation of what would happen if we purchased 60 additional fast carriers . . . the difference would be 24 hours . . . 60 carriers cost about what 15–18 tanks cost. And so, according to the Ofek plan, the augmentation of carriers [will enable] our strategic flexibility, which is dependent on our ability to be mobile. I don't think the issue of tracks [that a tank would move on the tracks and not mounted on a carrier] is a good idea. About the tracks, we spend so much money that also makes the storage more expensive— and there are also technical difficulties along the way. There is no reason that a tank, before war, will drive 300 km on its tracks.

I asked for permission to purchase about two hundred transporters. Moshe Dayan asked me, "Amos, what about the money?" I said to him, "[We'll have] fifty tanks less, but we'll have more tanks on the frontline." He agreed with me but didn't support the decision. Behind Dayan's objection stood Talik, the deputy chief of staff. Talik didn't want to financially detract from the development of the Merkava. Dado Elazar, the chief of staff, also objected.

We paid a heavy price for this miserable decision. Tanks drove on tracks all the way to the Golan Heights, and all the way to the frontline in the Sinai. Tens of kilometers on tracks, and quite a few got stuck along the way and needed to be fixed. Those that did make it arrived crucially late, and, in addition, the teams were exhausted. It should not have happened.

Ammunition and Inventory Levels

There was harsh criticism about the fact that I had too many supplies in inventory, while I claimed that the inventory of spare parts for tanks must be sufficient for war—and for repairs of the tanks immediately after the war. The levels of inventory were determined according to a calculation of the needs for "an engine hour" and "a day of fighting," two terms with logistical meaning that I brought into the system in order to base our calculations on calculations as objective as possible.

To my dismay, the person who took my position changed the policy, and the inventories—including that of ammunition—started to shrink; in addition, the inventory in the emergency storage facilities also decreased because it was being used for training and not returned.

During the war, there was panic because there was a shortage of ammunition, and to my understanding it was a little over the top, but the management of the inventory was flawed, and the Americans felt, rightly so, that they are the ones who saved us. I don't know what price we paid for that after the war, but obviously we paid some price (because, as we know, there's no such thing as a free meal).

"The True Heroes of the Crossing Battle— the amphibious tank-carrier"

After the Six-Day War, when the IDF was spread out along the Suez Canal, a crossing unit was formed. As head of the quartermaster's branch, I dealt with that. In the beginning, we purchased various types

Ready to cross—an amphibious tank-carrier attached to a tank.
Mobilizing the tank-carrier to the waterline.

of equipment to be prepared immediately if crossing the canal were required. We purchased parts of a British bridge, floating elements called "Unifloat," each of which had an engine that enabled it to move in the water. We filled the floating devices with polyurethane, and so, even if they were hit, they would continue to float. Lieutenant Colonel Zvi Orbach, an excellent engineer and head of the vehicle branch in the ordnance corps, came up with the idea, and based on this, we put tires on the towed part, and every towed part had a piece of the bridge on it. A tank could easily tow a three-ton load, even in difficult conditions. The ground conditions were not even an issue. The tank reaches the canal, turns around, and slides the piece into the water. That way we don't have to mobilize a bridge, but rather put it together in the water. Engineering people on rubber boats did the task, and we successfully practiced connecting the different pieces in the Abu-Agila dam.

Following the idea and the experiments we did with a trailer on wheels, we took another step, on the recommendation of Shaika Gavish and with my approval the Koor Industries purchased from the French factory sixty surplus vehicles in poor condition named Jiloa (Gillois) at a cost $5,000 per unit. The Jiloa are amphibious vehicles that connect to each other to form a bridge. We called them "Hatmasach." With military funding, Yeshayahu, then at Koor, repaired them in the "Merkavim" factory. The Hatmasach was equipped with wheels and an engine and could carry tanks to cross water.

In his book, Shaika (Yeshayahu) Gavish writes:

From Jiloa in poor condition to an amphibious bridge tank—"Hatmasach"

While repairing the vehicles I received a call from Israel Tal, the deputy Chief of Staff, who told me that he was reducing the order to only 20 units. This was because he developed the roller bridge, so we don't need the Jiloa.

I told him he was wrong, that the Jiloa is a wonderful tool, an excellent solution for crossing, and it should not be tied to the roller bridge, or rafts, or to bridges that are put together on the water. Talik would not budge. The manufacturing stopped after 20 units. The rest is already known. . . . the first tanks crossed using the crocodiles. Those that we had had time to repair before Talik asked us to stop. That was how Talik saved a few thousand dollars, but lost equipment that could have gotten more tanks to the west bank of the canal and would have saved the loss of many lives and equipment. Thanks to the crocodiles, the IDF was able to reinforce, with tanks, the paratroopers' brigade that had managed to cross the canal. If it hadn't been for these tools, it could have been that the paratroopers would have received an order to return to the east bank. (*Yeshayahu Gavish,* in his autobiographical book , "Red Sheet," published by Kinneret Zamora-Beitan, page 265, 2016)

Unfortunately, Talik's position as deputy chief of staff allowed him to stop the repair work on the Jiloas and to focus on the development of the roller bridge, which he thought of as the jewel in the crown. I objected to the roller bridge. The army was busy experimenting with crossing over the Abu-Agila lake. I told Talik: "This won't work. To get a bridge like this through you need a flat soccer field." "No," he responded, and he was completely confident. It was very painful to once again reach the conclusion that at a certain point the weight of the objective considerations, the technological advantages and disadvantages, were not what led the decision-making process. We paid a heavy price in lost lives, and it could have been done differently.

Oded Megiddo, a lieutenant colonel in the reserves, served in the battalion that towed the roller bridge to the canal. In his article, which is based on a journal that he kept during the war and interviews with commanders, and after checking data, he examined the "myths and slander" as to the responsibility of the armored units in the delay of the roller bridge. He describes in detail the chain of events leading to the towing and the malfunctions, and he proves that the armored units did the best they could. He concludes:

> The roller bridge, the development of which, as well as the development of its usage doctrine, were not completed before the war broke out, was not intended, was not designed, and was not built for towing in the conditions that battalion 257 confronted, and could not bring it to the waterline. . . . And so, the bridge, which had received the Israel Security award in 1972 and was the diamond in the jewel of the engineering corps crossing set up, became irrelevant to the crucial moves of transferring most of the armored forces of the Southern Command across the canal. (Oded Megiddo, "In the Armored Forces" June 2012)

In addition, major general in the reserves Jacob Even and colonel in the reserves Simcha Maoz, write in their book,

. . . the real heroes of the crossing battle—the crocodiles. If these "second hand" tools were made of pure gold and lined with diamonds, their value still wouldn't amount to a thousandth of their contribution to the success of the crossing battle and defeating the Egyptians. (At the point of gravity—sentinels on the trench front in the Yom Kippur War, Moden Systems Publishing 2012)

A Time of Distress

On October 1, 1973, I started my position as president of the Technion, and six days later, the war broke out. I was called, like many other commanders of my generation, to return to the army, not to my position in the logistical units, but rather as assistant to the deputy chief of staff, Israel Tal. There was great tension between us. Everyone knew about the fight we had had surrounding the Merkava.

It's not clear to me why they deployed me to that particular position, but I accepted it. I came to do a job, and in the difficult situation that we faced, neither of us allowed himself to bring up our past tensions.

The Failures of the Intelligence Branch, the Tank and the Sagger Missile in the Center of a Personal Disaster

Only a few days had gone by and the systematic failures painfully made their way into my family—Moishe'le Yoffe, our daughter Nira's husband, was killed on October 8, 1973, on the Hamutal Ridge, about 8.5 miles east of the canal, when a Sagger hit the tank he was commanding.

Moshe'le had served on the canal before the war broke out. About a week before the battles started, when he was home for a break, he told me they saw Egyptian tanks—the Russian-made T62s, T55s, and T54s—moving without their reserve fuel tanks. This was significant because reserve fuel tanks, which are connected to the outside of the tanks for use during logistical movements, are removed for battle because they are not protected and endanger the crew's lives if hit. They also saw Egyptian soldiers measuring the depth of the water in the canal. These were all signs that a war was going to break out. He saw this and understood, but the head of intelligence did not understand.

The war broke out, and contact with Moishe'le was cut off. We didn't know where he was. We were shown pictures of captive soldiers. I checked, but I didn't see him. I went with Nira to look at photos taken from the air to try and recognize the damaged tanks. We couldn't find his tank.

During a lull in the fighting, I took Assi, Moishe'le's dad, and we rushed to the Rephidim air base in the western Sinai. The Egyptian field army was surrounded, but the war was not over. The fact that I was a major general helped a lot. A jeep was waiting for me, and I received a lot of assistance. They told me they saw him in the Bren Division. We crossed the canal, but Bren didn't know anything. I met with a few people who were involved in the battle for the Hamutal Ridge, and that was how we located the tank driver, who was under Moishe'le's command. From him, we learned that the tank had been hit. The driver had been pulled out, he climbed onto a different tank and fought in Isma'iliya. From additional encounters with company commanders who fought on the Hamutal Ridge, it became clear to me that the damaged tank had been there.

Assi went back to Nahalal and I continued with Eliezer, Moishe'le's brother, commander of an armored company. We drove to the unit closest to Hamutal Ridge, a brigade of Soviet tanks that had been upgraded by the ordnance corps. The brigade's commander, Yoel Gonen, brother of Major General Shmuel "Gorodish" Gonen, was very helpful to us. Using massive binoculars, we saw two tanks in the no man's land between us and the Egyptian army. As someone who had been head ordnance officer, I knew what emergency storage units they came from, and using the tank serial numbers, I was able to locate Moishe'le's tank. It hadn't gone up in flames. We worked quickly to get the tank from the demilitarized zone. Soldiers under the command of brigade commander Gonen crawled with a cable and attached it to the tank. I wanted to crawl with them, but Gonen said, "a major general doesn't risk his life that way. You never know, maybe there are mines, and that's dangerous." They dragged the tank back to our side during the night. When we opened the turret door, Eliezer and I wore masks and lowered ourselves into the tank. We found Moishe'le, sprawled out, a month after he was killed. We immediately recognized him. His watch had been taken. I don't know if it was looting. The gunman was also killed. He was the one who took the hit from the Sagger. We took him out of the tank as well. I watched with unending appreciation as the burial society (Hevrah Kadisha) took care of the corpses. The next day, we buried Moishe'le in Nahalal. The first casualty of war to be buried in the Yishuv, on November 9, 1973. My personal family was starting the long and difficult road of dealing with grief, and I was moving between our grief and the grief felt by the entire State of Israel.

The War Has Ended. I Am Responsible for Assessing the Damage to the IDF, and I Return to the Technion

Moshe Dayan appointed me to be responsible for assessing the damage caused by the war and for the connections with the American generals in the field of ground forces. I received reports from the generals and lists of losses in tanks, ammunition, and other equipment. It is very difficult to fly heavy tanks, but it is possible to restore them, and we did restore them, the Americans gave us spare parts for their tanks—Pattons, trucks, and small arms. The Air Force was hit very hard and quickly received American planes. This what the Air Force personnel dealt with. I sat with the Americans in the Kirya, (military headquarters in Tel-Aviv) and presented them with the damages, they provided us with everything we needed, and it was clear that they cared about our safety. Maybe because they thought that this wasn't a done deal yet.

I completed this job, and in November I returned to manage the Technion. My feelings were so much more difficult than I had felt before or during the war, and these feelings are with me to this day. I can't leave the IDF behind me, and it is alive within me at all times, as if I were still in the service.

CHAPTER 19

President of the Technion—Starting during a time of National Distress and Personal Grief

I knew how the Technion had begun; I could sense the vision of its founders, and I felt responsibility and privilege to continue their work. The Technion was founded because Jews couldn't study exact sciences and engineering in Europe, where the discrimination against Jews had been horrible. In 1902, a committee of three young people— Haim Weizmann, Martin Buber, and Berthold Feiwel—made a comprehensive proposal to the Zionist Congress to establish a Jewish university that would also teach scientific-technical subjects. Not in Europe, but here, in the Ottoman Empire, in Haifa. Why specifically in Haifa, which was just a small city at the time? Because Jerusalem was too religious. And there was talk of expanding the port in Haifa, which would broaden connections with the outer world. The local center of the Ottoman Empire was in Akko (Acre), from where the Hijazi train departed. And so began a huge start-up for the Jewish people. An incredible story. The execution of the plan began in 1908, when initial funding was provided by a Jewish-Russian tea tradesman named Zev Wisotsky, who donated $62,000, and was joined by Jacob Schiff, a German-born, American Jewish investment banker and philanthropist who was a major supporter of Zionism, who donated another $100,000. The Jewish-German "Ezra" Association was a crucial part of the initial process. The cornerstone of the "Technicom" was laid in 1912. Studies began in 1924, with seventeen students, who demanded that Hebrew, rather than German, be the language of instruction. They succeeded.

In the spring of 1947, I left my studies at the Technion, just six weeks after I had started. For many months, the War of Independence took all I had to give, and I did not return to my studies after it ended. Twenty-six years later, I returned as president.

Academia was not foreign to me, thanks to my dad's connections to academia and to the leading scientists who frequented our house. When the war ended, I had gone to study mechanical engineering at MIT, at the time the best such institution in the world. It was at MIT that I set the bar for the achievements that, as head of the Technion, I worked very hard to reach.

During my service in the IDF, I had had different contacts with the Technion. One of my main missions in the Ordnance Corps had been to create a crew of engineers. To that end, I built long-lasting relationships with the Technion and pressured them to offer elective courses in various subjects, specifically ones that the ordnance corps was interested in. When I was appointed head of the Technion, I was already at the height of my second period as chief scientist of the Ministry of Defense, and, as part of that position, I also maintained working relationships and cooperation with the metal institute and with the faculties of electricity and electronics.

After I was elected, and before assuming my position, I went to the Technion every Friday, still in uniform, and visited a single faculty, with pen and notebook in hand. I listened, asked questions, asked the deans for materials. In October 1973, I finished my military service in the IDF and was on my way to becoming president of the Technion. A ceremony welcoming me into my position took place on October 1, in the presence of Yigal Allon, the then-minister of education. On October 6, the Yom Kippur War broke out. I immediately returned to the army.

Immediately after the war, I came back to the Technion. I looked at everything from the perspective of a major general who had led and influenced the military foundations until just a year before the war broke out, and as a father whose daughter had lost her husband and who had retrieved his body from the tank with his bare hands.

The acceptance ceremony for the position of the Technion presidency

In my inaugural speech, the content and words were shaped by my anger, rage, disappointment, and terrifying pain. Yet, like a tree that had burned down and is starting to bloom again, I started my new position with renewed strength and a clear policy. That policy became more valid and more urgent as I became aware of the lessons I had learned in the Yom Kippur War with regard to scientific-technological topics, to which the Technion could contribute. Yesha'yahu Ben Porat wrote in the *Yedioth Ahronoth* newspaper:

> *Instead of a poetic speech—for the opening of the academic year—the president of the Technion chose to give a harsh critique about things that are happening in Israel today. Two days ago, the president of the Technion, Major General (Res.) Amos Horev, did something that should never be done: at the opening ceremony, when everyone expected him, as is customary on such a joyous occasion, to give a poetic and somewhat empty speech, he chose to*

speak the truth. Perhaps it marred the joyousness of the occasion
and surprised the listeners . . . the purpose of Mr. Horev's words at
this occasion was to make it clear to the public that in his opinion
"we won't do and have not done a thing" since the Yom Kippur
War. "We should have learned our lessons, reached new conclusions
and implemented them . . . but despite everything—we didn't do
a thing, and because of the failure of our own hands we are losing
the independence of this country, the incredible privilege we have
to stand tall and not be beggars." (Yesha'yahu Ben Porat, [excerpt
from Amos Horev's speech, title unknown] [Yedioth Ahronoth
(newspaper), October 21, 1973])

In the following meetings in various forums, I said things that
pertained to values and the loss of those values, the need to minimize
our dependency, the low morale, the lack of education, and the need
to fix it. I talked about lessons learned not from a military perspective,
but from the seeds of arrogance and complacency that followed the
Six-Day War and sprouted during the Yom Kippur War. These were the
basis for everything else that I led in the nine years that I was president
of the Technion, and then over the next thirty-two years as head of the
Friends of the Technion Association in Israel.

From the time that I was able to form my own opinions, it had
been clear to me that we must minimize our dependency and create
a strong base for our own independent abilities here, in the Land of
Israel. This opinion was reinforced during the War of Independence
when I served as fighter and commander. The embargo on arms
shipments imposed on our country that had just been established
and was fighting for its survival was etched deep into my mind.

If we had had a more developed industry, we could have at least
minimized our dependency, if not completely eliminated it. During
the Yom Kippur War, our industry still couldn't properly handle all
the needs of protracted war. We had to depend on storage supplies
for just about everything, since a massive part of our equipment was

not manufactured locally. In my different positions, mainly as head ordnance officer and as head of the quartermaster's branch, I worked to increase and expand the local production through knowledge and procurement from local industry.

As part of my position at the Technion, I could once again work to strengthen and improve the quality of local industry, with the help of Technion alumni and initiatives that would get the expansion started. The Technion began to offer consultation services, tests, and research, all requested by industry, in order to advance production knowledge levels. During conversations with a number of the heads of industry, some of whom I had known since my time in the Ordnance Corps and the quartermaster's branch, I expounded upon our aspiration to educate and shape a thinking engineer, one who knows how to adapt to what the industry really needs, and I emphasized that the industry must invest in that engineer so that they will derive the maximum benefit from their studies.

Eight Objectives and the Many Activities to Fulfill Them

In my view, the Technion is supposed to serve long-term objectives based on a broad view of the country's economic, security, and social needs, which I translated into eight areas, all of which I was personally involved in during my nine years as president.

- Providing high-level training to influence the quality of industry.
- Creating an organizational structure to ensure mutual influence among different professions, leading to cooperation in research and development, which requires multidisciplinary perspectives and knowledge.
- Expanding the populations eligible for acceptance into the Technion, but only through preparatory programs and not through reduced admission standards.

- Exposing exceptional young Jews and Arabs to the Technion and providing them with financial support.
- Providing massive support for signs of excellence and initiative through fundraising and use of the Technion's scientific base.
- Putting students in the center of our focus and investing in their wellbeing in a variety of ways.
- Ensuring that the Technion serves as a foundation and steppingstone for developments regarding security needs, through the facilities and professional manpower of the Technion and collaborations with the security system.
- Maintaining the Technion's high level of excellence and unique character for many years to come, and, accordingly, setting rules for receiving tenure, salary levels, resolution of conflicts, and the structure of forums that manage the different divisions.

To Be Israel's MIT

I was very interested in excellence. From my first day, I wanted the Technion to be the best institution in the world. I said that there was no reason that we shouldn't be number one—in other words, to be Israel's MIT. It was possible, but it would be difficult if the state did not prioritize this.

To this day, I claim that excellence needs to be nurtured, first and foremost, among approximately fifteen hundred Technion graduates a year. Instead of investing a fortune in bringing old Israeli professors back from abroad, we should subsidize people who go abroad to do a post-doctorate with the amount of $100,000 dollars a year, and not $30,000 as it is today. Students could aspire to attend the best universities and could entirely commit themselves to their research, without needing to find a paying job just so they could live. They will return to us as experts at the beginning of their scientific careers.

At the faculty senate meeting, I said, "Let's stop giving ourselves grades, let other people check our work," and an international committee was formed to investigate and evaluate the faculties. The people I chose for the committee, all from abroad, were the best of the best. I would notify a certain faculty, a year in advance, that it was up for evaluation and that it was required to create a report, going five years back and looking at the prospects for the next five years. The reports were passed on to the members of the committee before they arrived in Israel. The committee produced two reports. One was personal, received only by the dean and the president. The second report was financial and it presented the faculty in an international context. It was a serious instrument devoid of politics and personal interests.

Multidisciplinary Schools—the Struggle That Was Unable to Break Down the Walls between the Faculties

I arrived at an institution that had nineteen academic units, and a Chinese wall surrounded each one. According to my basic approach, there is a connection between different fields of knowledge, and eventually everything needs to come together, which is why the organizational structure that separated the units was wrong.

My first step was to relocate all the faculties that had been spread out around the city to the Carmel campus so they could all be in one place. I had a difficult struggle with an architecture professor, one of the important ones, who claimed that the architecture faculty needed to stay in Haifa's urban center and backed his stand with opinions from the professional field. In contrast, I claimed that there is great importance to the connection between the building designed by architects and the fields that complete the architect's work and are studied in the rest of the faculties. That is why it is important to be located in one complex.

For the second phase, I wanted to take the nineteen academic units and combine them into three or four schools. For example, an engineering school, whose director would be in charge of agricultural engineering, mechanical engineering, electrical engineering, materials science, and aerospace engineering. I proposed that the president give that person some of the authority of both the president and the faculty senate. I submitted my proposal to the senate. I knew that everyone was looking for their own little piece of heaven, but I didn't realize just how tall the walls were, and so my proposal was rejected. I waited a year and submitted it again, and again it was rejected. From then on, I tried to promote my idea in more roundabout ways.

In collaboration with Jacob Ziv, a leading computer scientist who served as Dean of the Faculty of Engineering and Vice President for Academic Affairs, we created labs and research institutes in fields that require integration. When we founded the school of medicine, we invested a lot of money in creating an institute for bio-medical engineering, which was run by people from the fields of mechanical and electric engineering. An institute for medical research is an independent research center, and, theoretically, every faculty member in the Technion who wants to deal with that subject is welcome to. A faculty member belongs to a particular faculty and has responsibilities and duties—for example, they must teach—but research can be done outside that faculty's walls.

After I quit my job as president of the Technion, as part of my position on the managing committee and the directorate, I pressured the new president of the Technion to establish the schools I had been talking about. At the beginning of 2017, I was asked once again to present my opinion as to the reorganization of the Technion before a number of senior people in the field. My opinion was accepted and was passed on for approval by the senate and maybe even the board of governors. It was possible that after almost forty-five years, the Technion would finally transition to the format of schools. My stubbornness paid off, at least in this instance.

The School of Medicine

Back in 1948, Professor David Ehrlich, head of the surgical department at Rambam Hospital, had already thought about establishing a school of medicine in Haifa, and he worked on it for years. In 1969, it became a reality and the process began. A few years later, he was integrated into the Technion, and, based on his approach, the technological and medical studies related to a doctor's work were given a more significant place in the curriculum.

Professor David Ehrlich, the first dean of the school, and Dr. David Barzilai, his deputy and eventual successor, contacted Bruce Rappaport, who had donated 13.5 million dollars for a building for the school of medicine. The finance minister, Pinchas Sapir, added $27 million. I decided to have the building built next to Rambam, the main hospital in the area, because during the clinical phase the students need to be at the hospital. The student dorms were also built near Rambam.

I didn't want a university hospital. Such a model would have filled the senate with professors from the hospital, and the balance would have been ruined. I convinced the Technion to affiliate certain departments in the nearby hospitals with the university. Each department was examined to see if it was suitable for teaching, in terms of faculty and equipment. If a department successfully passed the inspection, we signed a five-year contract.

No to affirmative discrimination, yes to remedial correcting

I had been in education for many years—in fact, since I was a company commander—and one of the things that there was a law about is that there is no affirmative discrimination. I did want affirmative action for acceptance into the preparatory program, but to be accepted into the first year of regular studies, all students had to meet the same requirements. To parents of friends who asked me to use my connections I would say, "If you want to save your kid, send him to the preparatory program. It will take an additional eight months, and he will be accepted on his own merit and not because of a connection, which is also a form of discrimination." But I also had another rule at the Technion: under no circumstances would a student be unable to complete their studies because of financial need. Indeed, that situation never arose. Not so many years ago, while I was still head of the Friends of the Technion Association, I met with an important donor who asked to donate money towards scholarships in the Technion that would be given only to "Sephardim." I told her I don't give out scholarships based on origin—and I refused to accept the donation.

When I was president of the Technion, kibbutz high-school education did not provide a graduate diploma. I called up the educators in the kibbutz movement and told them, "I assume that the kibbutz movement cannot exist without industry, and so I am doing something that is against the rules; I will accept your high-school graduates without a graduation diploma and based only on the admissions exams. But that is only under the condition that you commit to starting, within a few years, to make the graduation exams mandatory." I accepted kibbutz graduates into the Technion, and the results justified the decision.

Not long ago, we allowed Ultra-Orthodox students into the Technion without a graduation diploma, under the condition that they would partake in a pre-academic preparatory program and then successfully pass the admissions exams. They arrived not knowing the basics of a secular, scientific education, but they did know how to sit for hours and study. After a sixteen-month special preparatory program for the Ultra-Orthodox, half successfully passed the admissions exams for the Technion. That being said, I objected to the trend developing today of separate classes for Ultra-Orthodox men and women.

Exposure and Preparing Teenagers

Within the Technion are many programs for teenagers—Jews, Arabs, and Druze—who study sciences in small classes and labs built for them. The instructors are excellent and achieve wonderful results.

Later, a businessman named Arie Carasso donated a special wing for pre-academic activities for teenagers. Avihu Ben-Nun, former commander of the air force, established something called "First," to which he is completely committed; it is a wonderful initiative to advance robotics among children and serves as an engine to create excellence. As head of the Friends of Technion Association, we agreed with Avihu that this activity would be part of the Technion, and that is what happened.

The National Museum for Science and Technology in Haifa

The natural next step of building a museum of science and technology next to the Technion went through a few phases. It started with a committee for the establishment of the museum that received one acre of land in Neve Sha'anan; however, the museum was not built immediately because it turned out that the land, which I had thought belonged to the Technion, had been sold during a time of need to the Jewish National Fund for 3,000 Egyptian pounds. It was a special building used by the architecture faculty before I moved them to the new campus in the Carmel, and that was where the museum was built. I also had to do more fundraising, at the end of which an interactive museum was established for kids, teens, and anyone interested in science. It was named after Danny Recanati and his wife, Matilda, whose son Leon was one of the biggest donors to the museum.

Studies and Leisure in the Center—but Politics Only Outside of the Technion

At the end of the Yom Kippur War, students still hadn't been released from the army and remained on the front lines, cut off from their studies. The head of the teaching department, Professor Arie Perlberg, approached me with an idea: Let's videotape the lessons and send them to the soldiers. I approached the finance minister, Pinchas Sapir, who approved the budget for purchase of a tax-free video system. We purchased, we recorded, and we sent it. But it turned out it wasn't professional enough, and with the donation of Arie Carasso, which included a maintenance fund, we built a center for self-learning with two studio classrooms equipped for videotaping. We filmed eighty courses. A student who was on reserve duty for a week or two and missed a course could come to the center, get the recording of the course from the librarian, and watch it in a private booth. Students who were actively studying and wanted to review the lesson and study with a buddy also used the tapes. We moved from tapes to discs and created a disc machine. You took a disc and went to study in a room.

My policy towards the students was led by my attention to the quality of their lives and my refusal to compromise on the level of their studies. I tried to always have respectful conversations, to avoid conflict, and mainly to explain. For example, when there was a budget issue and they asked for help, we explained the financial situation, and I suggested that all the service and cleaning jobs would be given to the students, for pay. The students agreed.

The dorms made up an important component in the quality of life in the Technion. I started with four to five hundred places for students, and with momentum we built about thirty-five hundred places.

For students who experienced emotional distress, and there were quite a few of them, my wife, Shoshana, who was the first to incorporate the position of a guidance counselor in high schools, raised $160,000, and we built a place to discretely and privately meet with advisors in the Technion. Recently, another million dollars were dedicated to expanding this center.

We built a facility for leisure activities for students, faculty members, and employees from all fields and their families. It included an indoor, heated Olympic-sized swimming pool, a jacuzzi for thirty people, and a cafeteria. This also allowed me to break the barriers between students, faculty, and employees.

I did everything I could for the students in terms of their professional development, but at the same time I also worked to prevent political issues from taking over the conversation and affecting the relations between the people, both as faculty and as future scientists. That's why I didn't allow the creation of separate student unions for Jews and Arabs, even though Arabs make up about 20% of the students. I wasn't willing to bring a political atmosphere into the Technion. I was concerned that creation of a separate union would exacerbate the already existing extreme nationalism. When I spoke, I said more than once, "Sit together in the student union meeting. Sit together because you are forced to, because you have a shared interest." My concern was not baseless, and the fact is that a fight broke out between Jewish and Arab nationalists. I punished them severely. In addition, I did not allow politicians to operate inside the Technion. You want to speak— speak from the other side of the fence, not inside.

Tuition—Enable People to Develop Themselves, Help Them

For many years I tried, unsuccessfully, to promote the tuition model used at MIT. In Israel, the state decides on the tuition rate for all universities, with no correlation to the actual costs, which differ between faculties. At the Technion, students pay about 14,000 shekels a year (in 2023, a little under $4,000). The actual cost of a student at the Technion is almost 50,000 shekels a year. A student pays the university the agreed-upon tuition rate, and the state pays the difference—which means that the state subsidizes the academic institution.

Based on the suggestion I was trying to promote, the state would not subsidize the Technion, but rather the students themselves. That is, every student who had served in the army and was accepted to a university would receive 50,000 shekels a year and would pay full tuition. According to the economic calculation, when someone starts working in a profession that they've studied, they pay taxes until the day they retire, and thus would pay back within five or six years the subsidy that they had received. This calculation was made in America and was the basis for the structure of tuition.

A person who had served in the army for three years and is committed to twenty years of reserve duty deserves a little bit more from the state. For those who did not serve in the army, I suggested that they take a loan and start paying it back when they completed their studies.

In 1975, I went to the Finance Ministry with a proposal, and they weren't even willing to consider it. I did not give up and went to Minister of Education Zevelun Hammer, to Prime Minister Ehud Barak, and finally also to Netanyahu, but I could not convince them. At the end of 2017, I asked to meet with Minister of Education Naftali Bennett, who is a hi-tech man. Months went by and I did not get to meet him.

The issue of tuition troubles me. The way I see it, based on my many years of experience, it's best to give people the freedom to develop themselves, plan for themselves, and build themselves up. They only need guidance, a little push. That is what will drive the growth of the entire economy. The model in place today does not provide adequate leverage for growth, not for the student and not for the academic institution.

The Technion as a Leverage for the Seeds of Excellence and Entrepreneurship

Special initiatives could be leveraged using the Technion's existing infrastructure, which is why I have often tried to make a connection between entrepreneurs or anyone with excellent skills and the options the Technion has to offer in terms of knowledge or fundraising.

I brought in a military officer who had been a robotics professor at the school of marine engineering in France, and he became a leading lecturer in the field of robotics and established an important lab. I raised money and incorporated the field of computer-aided design. That is, the use of computerization technology as a tool for planning, designing, and manufacturing products, which has been vital to the advancement and development of industry.

I deemed it important to open the Technion to high-ranking officers in the IDF, who arrived with extensive knowledge in certain areas and so received credit for this knowledge while completing the material in other fields.

Professor Michael Pore was working on wind tunnels, which allow the mobilization of model planes in different wind conditions and are also necessary for the development of air-to-air missiles. I came and saw what he was doing and I asked him, how much? He said, "$170,000." A week later, I had the funding from a donation. The wind tunnel in the Technion has served Rafael Advanced Defense Systems many times in the development of missiles.

In addition, I recognized the lack of electronic microscopes, and so I concentrated all the electric microscopes in a single space open to all researchers. Dan Shechtman's research, which won a Nobel Prize, was, in many ways, made possible thanks to the electronic microscope. I found a place for Professor Peretz Lavie, the current president of the Technion and an important expert on sleep, to set up a lab for research in that field.

I also thought that relationships and research collaborations with universities abroad and with excellent research institutes that would provide a place for sabbatical years for the academic faculty were very important. An example is the relationship with Ecole Polytechnique and Génie Maritime in France. I was looking for a way to create a connection with universities and research institutes in Germany, as well. It wasn't easy for me to get over my reservations, and I remember how hard it was in the '50s, when the only budget for military purchases came from German reparations payments. I took my time until I received the moral approval of Justice Moshe Landau, a former president of the Supreme Court, who was a member of the Technion's Presidential Committee. Formally, I didn't need his approval, but he was my moral compass, and I didn't want to act against his opinions.

The Rhine-Westphalia Technical University in Aachen, Germany, was the only place to have already incorporated technology in the study of medicine, and their growing experience helped me make a decision to establish a school of medicine as part of a technological institute and as a basis from which to improve the quality of doctors, simply through the knowledge and understanding of these systems and their uses. There, I was painfully reminded of the complex reality in which we live. When I gave an open lecture about the Technion, technology and science, Maoist students demonstrated against me. The atmosphere was so tense that police officers had to protect me.

The Technion as a Foundation and as Leverage for Security Developments

The proximity of the Technion to Rafael Advanced Defense Systems served us well. As a result of our close collaboration, many of our alumni found work at Rafael. We created service institutes for the security services and an infra-red laboratory used only by the security forces. Jacob Ziv and Moshe Zakai, two renowned professors in the fields of electrical engineering and electronics, came to us from Rafael and were part of a combined team of the Technion and Rafael. This team worked on ground-to-air missiles, the SA6, which had brought down many air force planes and had restricted the IDF's freedom of action during the Yom Kippur War. Professor Ziv and Professor Lempel developed the algorithm for data compression, which led to a world revolution in the world of media. If we had patented it, the Technion would no longer have had any financial issues.

Some of the collaborations, which could only be made with the Technion, had strategic significance. When developing air-to-air missiles, we needed a heat-seeking sensor to identify the target and activate the missile's system. No country would sell us this crucial element. The Solid State Institute (part of the Technion) developed this sensor under the direction of Professor Yitzhak Kidron, and it provided us with strategic abilities, that is, freedom from dependency. When William Perry, then America's deputy secretary of defense, visited the Technion, I took him to the Solid State Institute and showed him what I was talking about. When people from the Ministry of Defense asked us to build a factory for infra-red sensors at the Technion, I told them I don't compete with industry, but I do give it knowledge. We gave this knowledge to Tadiran (TTL) and Rafael, who built a company in Karmiel. That company provided Israel with everything it needed in the field of the Dark-Sky Reserve (optical devices for night vision, based on light from the moon). There were fields in which the company provided 30% of the needs of the global market. In retrospect, thinking about the future and a more business-like approach, maybe it would have been smart to have asked for payments and commissions for the Technion, since it had funded at least some of the developments.

I Didn't Ask for "Peace and Quiet" or for Anybody to Like Me

As president of the Technion, I was required to handle several issues that were seemingly in the grey area and had nothing to do with technology or any kind of future vision. But, as in every matter, I took a stand and proceeded to act from a place of wide perspective and long-term thinking. In my mind, I sometimes thought that maybe I engaged in a few unnecessary arguments, but I couldn't be someone I am not; I didn't ask for peace and quiet nor for anybody to like me. I did want to maintain the uniqueness and excellence of the Technion over the long run.

Up against the Demands of the Workers' Committee

It was the same with the conflicts with the Technion's workers' committee. While we were writing the collective bargaining agreement, I said to the committee, let's sit on this day and night for the next two weeks, but no more. The children of Technion employees don't pay tuition. The workers asked that we fund studies for their children anywhere in Israel—I refused. I also wanted to cancel some twisted decisions made in terms of salaries and working conditions, things that had been decided during the time of my predecessor, and a riot broke out. Yitzhak Schneersohn, head of human resources, called me and said that the workers' committee had broken the main electric board in the faculty for civilian engineering. I replied, "call the police." A police officer showed up and took the committee members to the police station. Fingerprints were taken and that was that. What the committee did was criminal, and I didn't have a choice. A weekly Haifa newspaper ran with the headline, "Technion teachers and workers accuse the president of the Technion of calling the police— Horev is destroying working relations."

Up against the Council of Higher Education—the Struggle for the Technion's Independence

One of the critical issues that kept me busy was dealing with negative directions in which the Council for Higher Education was leading the Technion. The council started to intervene in inappropriate ways, and I viewed this as a development that put academic freedom, which is incredibly vital to institutions of higher education, at risk.

For example, the council created a committee to examine academic structure. One of the decisions was that an institution whose ongoing budget is subsidized by more than 50% would be considered "a public fund," and would therefore be directly under the Civil and Financial Service Commission. The state abused its authority. Under the previous structure of the regulations and the Technion constitution, the board of governors was above the president. That was the correct structure, because the people involved are experienced and responsible, and you can't take away from their status or disregard their opinion, especially when their money is always accepted. The decision made by the Council for Higher Education destroyed, to some degree, the international board of governors.

Another strange and misguided decision, in which there was an unnecessarily aggressive intervention, was the law according to which the faculty senate cannot consist of more than seventy-two members. According to section 15 in the Council for Higher Education's legislation, the institute had complete liberty for management within the budget it was given. This caused a huge uproar in the academic world, especially in the Technion, because in the Technion every professor was also a member of the senate. What does the state care how many people are in the senate? You want real inspection, check the quality. Maybe the academic management is better with three hundred senate members? Years after I left my position as president of the Technion, the struggle between the Council of Higher Education and the Technion continued over various issues. In 2008, the president, Yitzhak Apeloig, appointed a serious internal committee to examine implementation of decisions made by the Council for Higher Education starting in June of that year, including every foreseeable implication and consequence. The academic faculty was in an uproar and intended to cast a vote of no confidence against the president. A moment before the vote, the president asked me to speak before the senate, something that was not acceptable at the time. I studied the topic and reached the conclusion that there was no justification for any extreme measures. And indeed, I spoke to the senate and was able to convince its members that there was no need to destroy the relationship with the Council for Higher Education over topics that the committee dealt with, since these things are not the most important topics on the agenda. Before I spoke to the senate, most of them were against the president. When I was finished, most of them supported him.

The Best to the Teaching Faculty and the Relationship to Questions of Tenure, Professorship, and Pensions

When I entered the Technion, there were about nine thousand five hundred students. In 1980, the student-faculty ratio, which is an indicator of the quality of an institute, was about 13 students per faculty member. Today the ratio is about 25 students per faculty member. This means that the classes are larger, making excellence harder to achieve. In the elite universities in the United States, the ratio is only about 8 students per faculty member.

Addressing the numerical ratio between students and lecturers is only one crucial component needed in the improvement of the quality of the Technion. We also need a foundation of rules and a budget, which together create a system that helps its people grow, promotes the exceptional ones, and guarantees their continued work in research and teaching. To reach exceptional people, we must broaden the selection process, so that approximately three times the number of lecturers would start the process, and from this group, we would cultivate the exceptional ones. The smaller the faculty, the smaller the number of lecturers we would want to keep with us as quality leaders.

Unfortunately, I failed in changing the tenure process and in my attempt to get budgets that could compete with universities and research facilities abroad, where I found many of the exceptional Technion alumni.

Another failure of mine was a forced retirement at the age of sixty-eight. I see no reason why, as life expectancy grows, people shouldn't retire at the age of seventy-two, allowing professors to contribute their knowledge and experience for longer periods of time.

Connected to the Technion with my soul—
After finishing my position as president

I was president of the Technion for nine years. A wonderful time. I enjoyed the revolution we brought along. I could have stayed for a third term, but as I was fifty-eight I wanted to have time to fill one more significant position directly related to the committees I had been a part of. I especially aspired to implement the decisions made by the nuclear energy committee and to build a nuclear power plant for electricity and water purification. Unfortunately, I could not convince anyone to implement the in-depth practicability test performed by the committee that I had headed, and so I found myself in the medical start-up field for a few years.

When I completed my position, I still felt very connected to the Technion with all my heart, and I continued volunteering as deputy to the chairperson of the board of governors and as a member of different committees, and to this day I am still a member of the governing council. The highlight as far as I am concerned, after my presidency, was as chairman of the Friends of Technion Association, a position which I filled for thirty-two years. I dealt with topics that I loved so much and knew how to do: fundraising in Israel and abroad and building relationships with society and industry in Israel.

CHAPTER 20

Leading changes in Rafael Advanced Defense Systems—From collapsing to a leading government company

Prime Minister Yitzhak Rabin asked me to come to Rafael because of the crisis that the company was going through. I agreed and in 1993 I started serving as the chairman of its advisory committee, a little more than three years later I was appointed chairman of the company, a position I held until 2001.

I had known Rafael since before the establishment of the State of Israel, when it was still called HEMED—the Hebrew acronym for "science corps." Since then, the company had developed into a national laboratory, developed products, and passed the manufacturing on to Israel Military Industries Ltd. (IMI) and the Israel Aerospace Industry Ltd. (IAI). If Rafael had remained a national laboratory, everything would have been simple. A team of researchers develops a product, then the company checks it for economic viability. And the profitability of the execution factor, the state knew that the profit should finance the development.

A crucial expansion of Rafael's activities to include manufacturing and selling was led by Yeshayahu Levi, the company's CEO from 1968 to 1970. This expansion beyond Rafael's historic expertise in development led to heavy financial losses. Although the company had ingenious developments and excellent products, the price for the consumer was too high. With massive annual losses deep and wide cuts became necessary.

In collaboration between a large team with the CEO, Yitzhak Gat, and the governing council, which included Amos Lapidot,

Oded Messer, ex-military intelligence people, and two wonderful women, Ruth Lowental and Shoshana Weinshall, and with the help of additional professionals, most of them from the field of economics, we designed a new structure. We received crucial support for this change, which took a few years, from the director generals of the Ministry of Defense: Menachem Meron, David Ivry, and, after him, Ilan Biran. The challenge was to crucially change the terms of employment of about seven thousand employees, two thousand of whom were engineers, without causing any riots or commotions that could destroy the system. We chose a model of gradual change, and the "trick" was moving forward with a "no turning back" policy. Everything we did was irreversible. Some of the employees strongly objected. That's fine, at least they weren't burning tires.

I needed all the experience I had accumulated from previous positions to successfully choose the way to implement the process that would help bring change to this special organization. The CEO, Giora Shalgi, who replaced Yitzhak Gat, sent me excerpts from a book he is writing about Rafael, in which he summarized, from his perspective, the initial period, when I was chairman of the advisory committee:

Some of the successes need to be attributed to the advisory committee in the directorate during the time when we were an auxiliary unit. Major General (Res.) Amos Horev, as head of the committee, filled his position with wisdom, humility, and patience. A great example of quiet leadership.

The beginning of the process of transitioning from an auxiliary unit under the Ministry of Defense to a government-owned company was building a workforce company, "Rafael, Inc." and only at the end, when all the workers were working for Rafael, Inc., did we unite everybody under Rafael, the government company.

The technicians were the first to transition to Rafael, Inc. They didn't care. We had lent them to Rafael. After them, we brought in the practical engineers, and finally we dealt with the "top of the pyramid," the engineers and the researchers, a tough, somewhat combative group. The engineers joined because they benefited from the new collective agreement that we wrote up at the same time. It was the best collective agreement in the hi-tech industries in Israel.

The opposition was challenging because nobody likes drastic change. The CEO, Yitzhak Gat, was the target of the anger of most of the employees. To my great dismay he resigned in 1998, despite my requests that he stay, because he didn't believe the change would be approved. A few months after he resigned, the change was approved.

The treasury strongly objected. They wanted control, to place reviewers in the administration. We were able to work it out with other people who objected—including ministers, who didn't know, didn't understand, and weren't interested. The final approval was given to me by the prime minister and minister of defense, Ehud Barak, when I approached him with agreements on all sides. This is how Rafael functions today. Economic thinking in the fields of research and defense development was a revolutionary thing for researchers and the implementers of their developments, who have been in the field for decades. Development and manufacturing took on new meaning from the moment that there was no one who would automatically cover any deficits. We are talking about people who are exceptionally smart in their profession, people with a sense of purpose who know how to problem-solve. And there was plenty of knowledge on the shelves. You don't have to recreate the wheel every time. It exists, you just keep on developing it. Rafael works according to an economic model, and that makes it a unique company. It has fields that don't follow the calculations of an economic company, and I made sure it would stay that way. Changing the structure, like changing the way of thinking, turned Rafael into a profitable company, yet it also remained a national laboratory. The profits funded the extra projects that were executed without financial considerations. In those cases, the state, as a client, funds certain projects—and that is how it should be. There are some products that Rafael should not be allowed to sell abroad due to very clear security reasons.

Today, Rafael is a profitable government company with seven thousand employees. In my opinion, it is the best hi-tech company in Israel. I don't know any other company that could develop the "Iron Dome" in two years, a project that has the accumulated knowledge of sixty years, without having made an "exit." To my understanding, part of the company's strength comes from the fact that, unlike many other government companies, it was very strict about not hiring people based on their political affiliation. I hope that is how it still is today.

CHAPTER 21

Maybe I'm Not a Good Fit for the Private Market?

In 1981, a year before I completed my position in the Technion, for the first time in my life I started to get to know the world of private entrepreneurship as a member of the Bank Leumi directorate under the management of Ernst Yeffet. This period in my life ended after three years with a bitter taste of failure, alongside the beginnings of successes that, to my dismay, didn't survive the budget issues and the struggles of the private market. Ernst Yeffet formed a committee to examine whether it was logical and worthwhile for the bank to take part in industrial development and manufacturing, in the manner of Bank Discount. The committee, which I headed, decided in favor, and when I completed my position as president of the Technion, Yeffet appointed me chairman of the investment committee and of Bank Leumi Investment.

We formed four start-up companies in the medical field, and then the bank-stock crisis of 1983 hit. By my estimation, if Yeffet had remained in his position, and if the state hadn't forced the banks to step back from all non-bank-related activities, the businesses might have succeeded. The bank would have funded the development phase until we received approval from the FDA, and we can assume that at least two of the four start-ups would have been successful.

When the crisis hit and the bank was forced to step back from non-bank-related activities, I did something called a "Management Buyout," which means that the company management buys the company. As chairman, I raised a million dollars and we called the company "Atidan" (Futurologist). At the beginning, money came in

269

from shareholders and the investments of each and every one of us. We believed the medical field to be a pretty safe investment because people tend to care about their health even when their financial situation isn't great. We dealt with the development of prostate cancer treatment, a pacemaker, a mitral valve, and artificial skin. The company was a promising combination of both medicine and engineering. This turned out to be crucial, because doctors alone cannot develop the world of medicine.

The company failed, however, because we didn't understand that a million dollars will get you nowhere. A process that includes the approval of the FDA is an entire world of its own. For that stage alone, we needed three million dollars. We were very naïve. It turned out, unfortunately, that my experience from previous positions did not prepare me for this chapter, and events that are well-known to people in the private market were a painful surprise to me. For example, a Japanese company bought and marketed our prostate-cancer treatment, until one day its management was sent to prison for embezzling money from the bank that was their parent company. We lost the money they owed us and had to stop production. I was also naïve to think that we would make money in at least one area, and with that we could fund the rest. I was deluding myself. Eventually, we decided to close down the company, we sold everything, including all the knowledge, and returned the money to our investors.

I saw myself as responsible for this failure and was left with the feeling that maybe I am not a good fit for private entrepreneurship.

CHAPTER 22

I Never Imagined This Is What I Would Do – the Great Philanthropy

At the age of twenty-seven, when I was still a student in the United States, I began giving lectures about Israel. I spoke in the Dorchester and Roxbury sections of Boston, which at the time were some of the biggest Jewish neighborhoods in the world. I spoke about the War of Independence while everything was still fresh, and my words came from my heart and soul. Years later, I started lecturing in the United States again, this time as an emissary of the IDF, when officers were asked to represent the army at meetings with Jewish congregations and to raise money for the United Jewish Appeal. That is how I was introduced to the world of philanthropy, which I later used as an important tool in realizing the plans for the civil and security systems in which I was involved.

I discovered that the ability to speak and raise money came naturally to me, but I never imagined that it would be something I would do regularly and professionally for decades. It is rare to find projects that I believe in for which I couldn't raise money.

After the Yom Kippur War, I arrived in the United States as a major general in reserves, and there, in contrast to the atmosphere prevalent in Israel, the war had an aura of success because, in the end, Israel came out victorious. True, we found ourselves in a very challenging situation, but we were able to turn it around. This also caused American Jews a little bit of fear—what would have happened if Israel had been defeated?

I went to every fundraising mission knowing the relevant details that would determine the worthwhileness of the investment.

In conversations, I would find the "twist" that would make the investment appealing to the specific people I was speaking to. I found a path to all those who chose to donate, wanted to feel part of the work, and really wanted to take part in the development of the state. The various positions I had held in my life had created an extensive network of connections and acquaintances with people in Israel and abroad to whom I could turn. It's easy for me to create a direct connection to people, whether in a one-on-one conversation or when speaking to an entire room of people, and I was able to influence them without manipulating them or telling them half-truths. It is very important to tell the truth as it is and not sugar-coat it. I never forgot the contributors and their rights. I am their watchdog. I signed an agreement with the donor and demanded that it remain unchanged. That's how everyone knew me: by my and the Technion's trustworthiness towards our donors.

People have different reasons to give away some of their fortune, and they usually have some personal aspects, such as a worldview, together with financial reasons. Connecting these personal reasons to the Technion, on the scale that we needed, required meticulous preparation to get to know the person and their world. People's personal stories, including how they made their fortune and why they wanted to donate specifically to Israel, were of extreme interest to me. My ability to reach people, my willingness to tell the truth, and the proper and loyal handling of the donations created credibility— and credibility creates friendship. The philanthropy chapter of my life expanded my circle of friends in the United States. Everyone is connected to the Technion and to the Land of Israel. I had the privilege of knowing people, with some of whom a long-lasting personal friendship developed, filled with mutual appreciation. When I travel to the United States, I still meet with them. Many, unfortunately, are no longer with us.

The philanthropy work focused mainly on fundraising for the Technion, and then expanded to companies, and then included extensive involvement in different philanthropic funds, such as the Beracha Foundation (Keren Beracha), founded by Caroline and Joseph Gruss, which focused on the environment, education, and culture; the Rashi Foundation; the Gutwirth Foundation; and philanthropical gatherings such the Harvey Award.

Fundraising for the Technion was part of my work when I was still president of the Technion, and I dedicated my vacation time to it, too. When I completed my position as president and was appointed chairman of the Friends of the Technion Association in Israel and deputy chairman of the Technion's international board of governors, I continued fundraising even more intensively. For thirty-two years, until the age of ninety, this was part of my life. By the end of these years, I had raised over 1.2 billion shekels for the Technion.

To demonstrate the feel of philanthropy and how a donation of millions makes its way into the world, I have chosen the stories of two of the dozens of donors, each of whom had a story of their own. I have chosen Isaac Ivanir and Josef Gruss. Ivanir, the son of a Jewish nail and screw factory owner in Romania, survived the Holocaust, the only one from his entire family. All he wanted was to get as far away from Europe as possible. And so, seizing his first opportunity and without any planning, he arrived in Canada, lonely and terribly poor. He continued his father's legacy through the iron factories he built in Canada, and he became very rich. The Friends of Technion Association in Canada, who knew him, connected us. Through the conversations we had, I got to know the man and his entirely understandable aspiration to invest in Israel. I also learned about the traumas that the Holocaust had caused him and that had stayed with him. I saw an extremely rich man collecting leftover food from meals at fancy restaurants. Not a crumb was left on the table.

When I was looking for an appropriate field for him to invest in, I suggested something that would interest Ivanir—metals. And so we developed his investment in the Institute for Metal Research at the Technion. This institute, alongside the research, was also a service center for Israeli industry. The equipment and building were minimal, and we used the money Ivanir donated to build an industrial building suitable for this type of work. Most of the investment was in new, modern equipment that improved the research and application for local industry.

The other story has to do with Josef Gruss and "Keren Beracha." Gruss was a smart Jew from Lviv, Poland, who went with his wife to New York on business in 1939. The war broke out and their way back to Poland was blocked, while their son had been left with his caretaker at home, as was customary among rich people. The war ended—and the son did not survive the Holocaust. In the United States, Josef rebuilt his life, and he and his wife Caroline, a lawyer, had two children. He was very successful in his business and became one of America's richest people. In 1971, he and his wife created the "Beracha Foundation" in Switzerland. Gruss, in German, means a blessing of peace, which is how the foundation got its name. He was very connected to Israel throughout his entire life, and he especially admired Menachem Begin, and was even buried next to him on the Mount of Olives.

While I was president of the Technion, I received a telex from Gruss, whom I didn't know at the time, offering to donate a complex of buildings in the Bayit VeGan neighborhood in Jerusalem to the Technion. To this day, I don't know who referred him to me, but I am certain it was a result of the connections and acquaintances I had made over the years.

Two weeks after I received the telex, he told me he was coming to Jerusalem and wanted to meet. I went together with Shoshana to the King David Hotel, entered his room, and Teddy Kollek, the mayor of Jerusalem, was already sitting there. Thanking Josef Gruss for the good will, I said I can't accept the donation, but I could give him the names of five organizations that could use the property. He was shocked by my response and immediately asked me what I could use. "A heated Olympic pool for the students of the Technion," I responded. He asked its cost; I said a million dollars. We got the donation from him, and the pool was built.

My connection with Gruss did not end there, and after building the pool and leaving my position as president, he asked me to manage Keren Beracha in Israel and to make a list of projects to present to the advisory committee for approval. This appointment allowed me to make a difference and to help many different causes. From 1982 until 1993–1994, I managed the projects and presented them to the foundation's committee for approval. Most of the proposals I made were approved. I chose projects based on my own view of the world, my experience, my familiarity with the society in Israel and its needs, and my understanding that a donation can be of great help to a wide range of populations.

CHAPTER 23

Committees on Topics of National Security—Continuing to Make a Difference

The Committee for the Investigation of the Events at Ma'alot—an Unbiased Investigation

On May 14-15, 1974, terrorists commandeered a school in Ma'alot, near the Lebanese border, in which students from nearby Tsfat were sleeping. During the rescue attempt by Sayeret Matkal (IDF elite forces), twenty-two of the students were murdered by the terrorists and dozens of civilians and soldiers were injured. Sayeret Matkal's attempt to breach the school failed. Golda Meir appointed me chairman of the investigation committee, with the participation of lawyer Irvin Shimron and member of the Knesset Moshe Unna. For three weeks, eighteen hours a day, we spoke to forty witnesses, including the minister of defense, Moshe Dayan, and at the end of these weeks we submitted a report.

We wrote the truth, completely unbiased. Moshe Dayan was very upset with me after we found fault with his actions during the event. Most of the criticism towards Dayan was related to letters that the terrorists had delivered to him, in which they wrote their terms for releasing the hostages. In the committee, we reached the conclusion that, "It is understandable that he saw no importance in these letters . . . the Chief of Staff also ignored them and saw no importance in them . . . to begin with, the emphasis was on the conversations with the terrorists, not the letters they sent, because according to the Minister of Defense and the Chief of Staff, those letters, which had been written in Beirut, could not have accurately described that situation that had developed in Ma'alot." (The committee's report on the examination of the events that took place in Ma'alot, June 18, 1974, pages 21–22.) That was a grave mistake.

Dayan never showed the letter to Prime Minister Golda Meir, and the government didn't know what was actually going on. Lieutenant Colonel Avner Shalev, the chief of staff's military secretary, who was sent to report to the government, also didn't bring the letter with him and just gave the main points, without mentioning the terrorists' terms:

From the examination of government meeting protocols, it would appear that the 6:00 pm ultimatum was presented to the government as nothing but an abstract concept . . . if the letters or their precise content had been presented to the government at an earlier time, the government could have developed their own first-hand impressions regarding the conditions of the terrorists' and terms for the release of the students and would have reached a conclusion at an earlier stage regarding the options in front of them . . . as a result, and since the government did not receive all the information, there was a lack of clarity as to the terrorists' terms, and the government believed that there was a decent chance of reaching a reasonable agreement with the terrorists that would ensure the safety of the children and the release of the terrorists.

This was how precious time was wasted; indeed, so much time was wasted that, from a certain point on, there was no way to meet the terrorists' demands before the expiration of the ultimatum. During the negotiations, no clear decision was made. The attempt to enter the school was made at the last minute, and the tragic results are known.

Dayan trusted his intuition. That was the man's personality. He was certain that he could understand and do everything alone, something along the lines of "I don't care about your stories." A complex man.

The two most important systemic conclusions the committee reached included the need for organization and clarification of the division of responsibility between the IDF, the police, border patrol, and the General Security Services (Shabak), and that the police should create a professional unit to deal with terrorism. In accordance with these recommendations, that year the government ordered the creation of "Yamam" (also known as National Counter-Terrorism Unit, one of four special units of the Israel Border Police).

Aliya and Integration—Canceling the Ministry of Integration

As a result of public criticism towards the Jewish Agency regarding the process of the aliya, the absorption and integration of Olim (immigrants), Prime Minister Yitzhak Rabin decided in 1976 to establish a commission to examine the issue. He appointed me to chair the Commission, along with Shimon Clear, Avraham Shochat, Aharon Doron, and representatives from all the immigrant organizations.

The Commission dealt with a variety of topics related to the issue. Our main recommendation was to eliminate the Office of Absorption and Immigrants and to establish a council to determine policy and oversee its execution. The Jewish agency would continue its work abroad and would appoint a senior representative to every country where emissaries were located. And the government offices would appoint a vice chair to handle all the absorption issues.

I understood that our main recommendation was problematic politically, which is why I went to the prime minister and told him that it would appear that all the bad things were happening due to the existence of a separate government office for the absorption of Olim, and that we might recommend eliminating it. "You can stop the Commission's work right now," I said, but he only said to me, "No, continue." When it was time to submit the report, we met with the prime minister, Jewish Agency Executive Committee Chairman

Yosef Almogi, and Shlomo Rosen, who was the Minister of Aliya and Absorption at the time and from Mapam (the Zionist-Socialist Party). Rabin didn't want to give up a government ministry, but then he withdrew from the government, and the report was given to Menachem Begin, who was elected prime minister. Begin called me in, gave me a whole lot of compliments, and said: "There is a problem, I ask that you take care of it without eliminating the Ministry of Aliya." I said to him, "Sir, everyone's signature is on that report, with no reservations, and I won't do it," and I left.

Nuclear Electricity—Thirty-Eight Years without Success

I saw nuclear energy as a solution to two main dangers: the ease with which Israel could be put under an electric siege and air pollution. Nuclear electricity is the cheapest and the cleanest. For thirty-eight years, I attempted to promote the establishment of nuclear power plants for the production of electricity—and failed.

I was first introduced to the topic in the 1960s when I was deputy to professor Ephraim Katzir, head scientist for the Ministry of Defense, and the Americans suggested building a dual-purpose nuclear plant in Ashdod that would both produce electricity and purify water. I went to examine the proposal with Tzvi Tzur, who had been appointed CEO of Mekorot, Israel's national water company, following his service as IDF chief of staff. Tzur also headed the water-purification committee in the prime minister's office. After the completion of President Johnson's term, the offer was retracted.

Indeed, nuclear power plants are a scary thing. But the disasters that happened in the plants at Chernobyl and Fukushima, and the leaks from plants in France and the United States, did not change my mind, because what happened there could happen at any point in life and in any field if you don't work correctly. In France, none of the malfunctions affected the environment. The malfunction on Three Mile Island in America in 1979 was caused because the operators weren't professional enough. In Japan, the company had been privatized and they started trying to save money at the expense of quality—and the consequences followed soon after. Privatization yields the same results all around the world. A private company cares mostly about profit, and so they "save" when it comes to maintenance and safety.

In Israel, the first problem you think of is the risk that a nuclear reactor will be hit by rockets during a time of war. In the worst-case scenario, the plants would be HTGR (high-temperature, gas-cooled) reactors, the silo would be hit, and tennis-ball-like units of fuel would go flying, nothing else. There would be no nuclear damage. In my opinion, the Middle East is safer when the Arab countries have nuclear reactors, which creates a balance of terror—and they wouldn't bomb our nuclear power plant. This is true, in my opinion, about the Iranians as well. The danger of the ammonia storage tank in Haifa is much greater.

While I was still president of the Technion, in the mid-70s, I wanted to propose to Egypt to work in collaboration through a third party. Together, we would build an area for nuclear power plants that would also purify water near Arish. We would turn the Sinai into a flourishing garden. I asked for permission from the state but was turned down.

The Horev Committee for the Examination and Testing of Nuclear Power Plants

I don't give up easily, and in 1981 I initiated a government committee to examine the building of nuclear power plants for the production of electricity and was appointed head of the committee. The committee worked under ministers Moda'i, Berman, and Shahal until 1984.

There were good people sitting with me in the committee, which later on became the governing council for issues dealing with nuclear power plants in Israel. Among them were Tzvi Tzur, Yitzhak Hofi (former director of the Mossad and, like me, a reserve major general), and Dan Tolkowsky (former commander of the Air Force and one of the leaders of Israeli hi-tech). Amnon Enav, from the Ministry of Energy, was the secretary of the committee and then became manager of nuclear power plant plans. We did very thorough work and laid down the foundations for decision-making on this strategic issue. As explained to the ministers Moda'i and Shahal, this was also an opportunity to create competition in the market for energy and to take down the electric company's monopoly. However, to ensure that a reliable company would operate a nuclear reactor in Israel, the company would have to be governmental, appointed by the committee for atomic energy and not some private company driven by profit that might try to cut expenses—something that has been proven to be very dangerous.

Based on the opinion of the minister of energy, we tried to purchase two nuclear power plants from Framatome, a French company. We developed a good relationship with Abu Deram, a Moroccan Jew who held a high position in the company. But communication with them stopped when the French withdrew in the middle of a meeting in Paris. They claimed that they withdrew because the company was about to sign a deal with Saudi Arabia. But as far as I know, Framatome did not operate at all in Saudi Arabia and was instead pressured to withdraw from the deal due to a large weapons deal between Saudi Arabia and France.

Together with a German company, the Swiss company, Brown Boveri, developed a new technology, HTGR—High Temperature Gas Reactor, which was "meltsafe," that is, safe from a melting of the core, as in Chernobyl and Fukushima. If there is no fission, there is no fear of disaster. The fuel in these reactors is completely different, resembling tennis balls in a silo, through which helium runs and creates steam that activates electricity turbines. Moshe Shahal, the minister of energy, granted me permission to check these reactors.

The foundations for the relationship we had with the Swiss were laid down by the Israeli Casil Federman, the founder of the Dan Hotel

Chain in Israel, and serious working relations developed in joint work teams that were kept secret, per the request of the Swiss. They suggested a facility of five hundred mega-watts. In 1981–1982, Israel used eleven thousand mega-watts. At some point, for a reason I still don't know to this day, the State of Israel did not wish to continue pursuing this matter, and the topic wasn't even brought before the government.

I didn't give up. I went to Shahal and suggested that we build a one-hundred-mega-watt power plant on our own. In Dimona, we could develop the HTGR fuel for the steam maker and create a nuclear island. True, one hundred mega-watts may not be a huge quantity, but it would be a start. Ten years to build it, and we would be deep into the field. We had already planned the training process for the people in the Technion. The head of the Committee for Nuclear Energy, whom I was trying to get on board, supported my suggestion, but the proposal was once again blocked. To the credit of Yitzhak Moda'i and Moshe Shahal, long may he live, I must say, they both thought outside the box and long-term, but they were replaced, and the plans never came to fruition.

I didn't give up on my vision. In Canada, they wanted to sell us the "CANDU," which is based on natural uranium. I saw a power plant of five thousand mega-watts, half of our electricity consumption at the time, spread out over 125 acres, clean and pretty. In 2011, I approached Minister of Energy Uzi Landau to try and revive the topic. I showed him our prediction charts for energy consumption in the future and energy consumption at the time. He looked at it, called his people in, and said, "Look at that, they got it just right." But a decision was never made, and all that was left of the committee's work was the location of an area near Nitzana, where the ground is sturdy enough for our purposes.

We could have lived with a nuclear reactor, maybe even two, which would have securely produced electricity, but there was no longer anyone to speak to about it in the government. The world didn't stop developing ways to use nuclear energy, and there are still HTGR-based reactors, like the one I suggested thirty years ago, in Russia, China, and South Africa.

I was eighty-six, old? And yet a member of the Turkle Commission

In July 2010 the Israeli government established a commission to inquire and investigate the Marmara Affair—a confrontation that developed following the attempt to stop a flotilla of several ships headed for Gaza, who wanted to demonstrate against the Israeli policy in the Gaza Strip. During the encounter between IDF soldiers and the activists on the ships, the soldiers' lives were at risk. Nine of the activists were killed and thirty were injured. Among the IDF soldiers there were wounded but no fatalities. The challenging results and the clear political interest, mainly that of the Turks, among them the militant organization IHH, led to strong pressure by the international community against Israel. I accepted the request of lawyer Yitzhak Molcho, Prime Minister Binyamin Netanyahu's advisor at the time, and agreed to be on the commission. According to the requirements set by the Americans, the head of the commission was to be a Supreme Court justice; former justice Jacob Turkel was appointed. Alongside us sat Shabtai Rosenne, a ninety-three-year-old international professor of law who passed away while the commission was still meeting, and several deputy attorneys general. Later, Reuven Merhav and professor of law Miguel Deutch were added. Turkel recommended adding external observers. I saw that as a very wise move. Winner of the Nobel Peace Prize, Lord David Trimble of Northern Ireland, and Brigadier (Res.) Kenneth Watkins, who was military advocate general of the Canadian army, were also added to the commission and given the right to speak. They signed off on the appendix, but not on the full report.

I was eighty-six and the media attacked my involvement as a man who was too old, alongside other reactions that emphasized my experience and abilities and claimed that it was not a matter of age. I set aside the hurtful comments and focused on the commission's work. The examination of the issue was threefold: the operational aspect, the intelligence aspect, and the aspect of international law. I was the military and security man on the committee, and opposite me was the Canadian military advocate general. We would meet regularly for scheduled meetings in a safe location in Jerusalem, with no cell phones. There were also meetings into which a small number of viewers were allowed. We heard everyone from Israel speak, including human rights defenders. When the chief of staff and representatives from the IDF showed up, the thorough inquiry took place behind closed doors. We got into detail with the Canadian military advocate general, and it was important for us to hear the opinion of an outsider.

In the investigation of the many witnesses we summoned, including the chief of staff, we also dealt with the decision-making process, and with the question of why the commander left the handling to the Navy alone. We tried to summon witnesses who were part of the flotilla, including from Turkey and Europe, but we couldn't. Nevertheless, we had a picture of the other side from the testimony of a third party, who provided us with data.

We dove deep into the international law and the laws used in the IDF regarding the permitted behavior of soldiers. and the activity outside our territorial waters. The picture we unfolded gave the basis to the claim that an attack on a foreign boat outside our territorial waters is legal when it is clear and known that the boat's intentions are to cause a provocation.

We wrote an open and honest report. Two thick books, in Hebrew and in English. As far as Israel was concerned, this was an international success. The secretary-general of the United Nations created his own committee, in which Israel and Turkey were present (the Palmer Committee), and this committee decided that the naval blockade around Gaza is legal, but that Israel used excessive force when trying to stop the flotilla, and so it recommended that Israel express regret to Turkey and compensate the families of the people killed. Our report criticized the behavior of Turkey and the IHH, and the fact that we got a generally positive response from the UN, which rejected the Turkish report, was a huge win.

The report and the UN response led to an Israeli apology and compensation for the families, and this was the end of this issue, although it was used by the Turkish President, Erdoğan, to negatively affect relations between Israel and Turkey. Joseph Ciechanover, who negotiated with Turkey and the UN, mentioned that the thorough work done by the Commission and the report that it sent out were very helpful to him.

Turns out that age isn't necessarily a disadvantage.

CHAPTER 24

To Be with You, with the Wars and the National Representation Abroad

Shoshana Sapir—with whom I fell completely in love

Ever since I came to know that tall, beautiful girl with the braided hair around her head, Shoshana Sapir, our lives have been completely intertwined. At the end of the day, after the wars, after the positions I filled, and after the struggles to promote one issue or another in the difficult country I am so much a part of, I always came back to our private togetherness, to Shanka, my love.

It would have been right to write this chapter together, from each of our perspectives, which have much in common and yet are also quite different, but by the time I was wrote this chapter, Shoshana was no longer alive, and I was left by myself with a treasure of memories, photographs, and journal pages I found among her papers.

A Woman Looking for Her Way between Her Husband's Job and the Fulfillment of the Dream of Having a Family

The violent encounters between Jews and Arabs before and during the War of Independence, of which I was deeply a part, are not fully portrayed in Shoshana's letters and journal, but rather in the prism of our relationship and her feelings, which in her language were called "work." From what she wrote, it is clear that the option of fulfilling her love the way she dreamed and imagined it, and from that love to create a family for both of us, was filled with difficulties, debates, and dilemmas. However, Shoshana fought proudly to fulfill her desires and world view and did not easily accept the compromises that were required of her.

A few months before we married, when Shoshana was twenty-one years old, she wrote the following in her journal:

October 13th, 1946 [a letter from Neta'im]: *Let me tell you, Amos'ke, just a few moments ago I found myself debating over our last few days together, when suddenly I heard your voice saying to me: "You never ask me what the right work for me is because you never think that I might need a break sometimes . . ." and wondered a minute later and found myself thinking the same about you, meaning, it occurred to me that you don't take care of my health, etc. And after that I thought, how can it be that it would cross your mind that I don't care about your physical wellbeing and that I am not interested in your day-to-day life. All this while I spend every minute in my mind, trying to get past the physical distance between us, and I try to guess what you're doing right now, how are you right now, what are you thinking about? So, because of that, I am inclined to believe that, just like me, it is important for you to always know how your girl is. How could I have ever accused you, for even a second, of not caring? I have no intention of revealing to you these secrets, when I say that the reason for these stupid thoughts is our lack of wholeness. Perhaps not that we are actually incomplete, but that we are close to a lack of completion. Forgive me for the "Yachnon" (Hellebore).*

There were also other times, as when Shoshana joined a trip of members of Kibbutz Tze'elim to the little crater in the Negev desert. A trip on which I acted as a scout. We spent the night cuddled in one sleeping bag.

On September 15, 1947, a short time before the War of Independence broke out, Shoshana was only twenty-two years old and pregnant. Three and a half months before the birth of her first child and she was alone in Neta'im, while I was the commander of the Eighth Company, far from home. This is what she wrote to me:

Amos'ke!
. . . Amos! You may not agree with me when I say that I think it is too often that you can't keep your word, but this fact is not enough to make me think that it is okay for a person to break their word. Just so you know, Amos, even if I chose to be more lenient about this matter with every person, obviously with you I intend to be stricter than strict . . . For with you I can't abide by these same rules because with you I am to live, and living, for me—and hopefully for us—means being whole, and not something miserable that leaves room for disregarding, contempt, pity, and even disappointment . . . However, all of these things are but the smallest tests and they are unimportant, as I feel wholeheartedly about your actions, if only I could justify them to myself . . . I don't know how you experience

our "goodbyes and hellos," you just don't tell me. But for me, every time we say goodbye it feels like it is the first time I have to separate myself from you, and every time I wait for you I expect you every moment and am also worried about seeing you, and before you leave the nest again I miss you all over again, and I imagine that I could never fully quench the thirst of expectation. And when I worry about you and wait and wait and feel pain over the different times you are late, I feel like something in me is starting to crack. But when your truck makes the slightest of appearances I feel as if this crack has mended, as if it had never been there. But when I wait once more for you to fulfill your promise and you are late once again and once again you do not come, and my anger engulfs my thoughts . . . and I feel as though the thing that is most important to me—my trust in you—is shaken just a little. And once in a while I make up my mind that I will never again allow you to be late and not come, and I will feel concern because this thing will never happen again, and I would not want to anger the things that always come back around again . . . I know now that you must learn one of the two following things: either make fewer promises than you do or make more of an effort to keep them. But I can't help you with that, and you must educate yourself on this matter . . .

Yours.

"Maybe You Will Remember to Do Something about the Trees"

In October 1947, while Shoshana was pregnant, I asked to go on leave and study engineering at the Technion. That's how the studies started, and during this time Shoshana continued her agricultural studies at the faculty in Rehovot, and we would meet only on weekends. Six weeks of this studying routine went by, then on November 29, I was called back to the Palmach. I thought to myself that within a couple of weeks I would return to my family and my studies. I never imagined it would be years until I returned after the war of "exist or cease to exist." From November 1947 to 1949, at the end of the War of Independence, my whole world was in that war, and I avoided no risk, challenge, or hardship. We were that young couple who had just gotten married and brought a child into the world, Yehiam—"Yamik"—on December 31, 1947, walking on paths that rarely intersected.

The limited media of those days and the dangers of driving from one settlement to the other were like a stumbling block in the way of a young family. When it was time for Shoshana to give birth, I arrived at Neta'im with a convoy and took Shoshana to Rehovot, but not before one of the members of the moshav gave me a grenade "in case we bump into Arabs" near Nes-Ziona. Shoshana gave birth that night, and I slept on a gurney at the Magen David Adom station. When they came to tell me about the birth, they said: "Go tell your father you have a new brother . . ."

In honor of the birth, my mom came to Neta'im with one of the convoys from Jerusalem. It was unusual that a woman would come from Jerusalem during those difficult times, and she brought a basket full of diapers and other things for the baby. She stayed with us for a few days and returned to her husband. My dad also came, and quickly returned to Jerusalem to work. My dad built us a water heater for the washing machine that circulated the hot water, making it easier to wash diapers. He also built a furnace unit, so we could be warm, and a kettle for boiling water. That's how my father was.

A short while after the birth, I came to Jerusalem because of the war, leaving Shoshana and the baby behind in a small room. It was winter, the atmosphere and conditions were rough. People who were evacuated from kibbutzim and moshavim in the south were sent to Neta'im. The Egyptians were close to Be'er Tuvia, a moshav southeast of Ashdod, which had been bombed. Shoshana didn't say a word about the fact that I was leaving her and returning to Palmach business. But her journal and her letters spoke for her, and I only found some of them after her death.

There were long periods of time when there was barely any connection between us, mostly during periods of fighting and attempts to break the siege on Jerusalem and transfer vital supplies to the city. I even needed the help of Gideon Alrom, the pilot who was her young love. Once, when I was already at Ma'ale HaHamisha, deputy to Zvi Zamir, commander of the Sixth Battalion, I asked him— when he drops ammunition, would he throw a note for Shoshana over Neta'im? And he did.

In January 1948, during one of the hard and bitter days of the war, I went to Shoshana in Neta'im when I was leading a convoy from Jerusalem to Tel Aviv via Hulda, Rehovot, and Rishon LeTziyon. During our stop in Rishon LeTziyon, I borrowed a bicycle from a training group in the area and rode to the moshav. "Shanka'le, something awful has happened, there is no message from Danny Mass," I told her. (As mentioned above, Danny, who was deputy commander of the Sixth Battalion, had led the Convoy of the Thirty-five to assist the settlements of Gush Etzion. The platoon was discovered before it made it to the Gush, and all of its people, Danny among them, were killed in battle.) In the minimal communication we had, I remember that it was just about the only update I gave her on what was happening on this other planet that I was living on. The conversations and updates that we had, here and there in Neta'im, had become very thin. It was difficult to lead the convoys, human losses were a daily occurrence, and no one knew if they would return from the battle over the road to Jerusalem. I had a hard time talking about what was happening there, on that planet that was so different from the one on which Shoshana was living her life in the moshav, a young mother to a child. I spoke very little during the few days I was able to stay at our home. I was in so much pain, but I couldn't cry. I had taken the first steps in building a family, slowly finding my way. How to combine this primal love, this newly formed family, with the war that demanded all my attention and mental and emotional commitment? Today, many years later, Shoshana is no longer by my side, and I have to admit that reading her letters and her journal from the beginning of our shared lives, reading those clear, calculated words, has pained me. I asked myself: did she understand the burden that was on my shoulders? Could I really expect her to live her life on the Palmach planet during that war?

During those days I never let go of my love for her, for Shanka'le, as I called her then and to this day, and the beginning of our relationship was rocky. It was a relationship between two very young people, who lived in two completely different worlds of Israel in the '40s, and at the beginning of that relationship, Shoshana wrote to me:

Twenty-four years old—March 4, 1949, Neta'im Turns out there is nothing left for me to do but return to this notebook, as there is no one for me to speak to and share what is in my heart . . . Amos! I think I don't ask as much of you as you should and could give me. I don't ask you to come home more often than you do, I don't want to force you to write to me and I don't want the thoughts about my life or the development of our child to be a hindrance to your work, but there is one thing of which I want more than you have in you—I want your attention, or more accurately, I want some form of expression for the feeling you have for me and for our child. I think this could manifest itself in a small note every once in a while, or buying a toy for Yamik, really paying attention to what our household needs are, noticing and doing one thing or another that I asked of you that would make my day-to-day life easier.

March 16th, 1949, to Amosi!
I miss you very much and want to see you, but not for a passing moment but to see you and live with you, together. . . . Amos'ke, maybe you can really try to do something to get some vacation? And maybe try to take care of that far off and desired future called . . . completing your military service . . . maybe? Please don't be angry at me, but I really think that it's time we started thinking

about ourselves as well, am I wrong? I will stop here because I don't want to drown you in a sea of emotions because it seems to me that its waters are murky and overflowing . . . and how are you my dear . . . ? Be well and hurry back to the one who is always with you—Shoshana.

P.S.

Maybe you'll remember to do something about the trees. Just so you know, they're not doing so great. Maybe? Please try! Kisses to you from me and your Yamik.

Only in 1950, when we went to the United States for my engineering studies at MIT and Shoshana's educational studies at Harvard, did we start to be a real family.

This has been My Home for Sixty Years

After two years, we felt the need to settle down in a house that wasn't close to "parental oversight." We had our eye on a house in the Neve Magen neighborhood of Ramat HaSharon that cost 12,000 Israeli lira in 1954, half as a mortgage, half in cash. The mortgage was arranged through the army, but we didn't have the other half of the money. I sold my car for 3,000 Israeli lira, a large sum at the time. It was a car that I had bought in the United States for $1,000. I was still 3,000 Israeli lira short. I tried to get them by raising a thousand chickens for eggs that Shoshana's father allowed me to raise on his farm in Neta'im. One day, I was visiting the animal farm and saw that they were throwing food into cages, onto a layer of sawdust at the bottom of the cage. I noticed that they don't eat everything and asked if when they clean the cages they could give me what was to be thrown away and put it in the barrels that I brought from the Moshav. Using a sieve, I separated the food from the sawdust, and fed the chickens with it. I minimized my expenses that way and within a year made up the missing 3,000 Israeli Lira and was able to buy a small, single-family

Family in uniform—Yehiam, Amos, and Nira

home, 2583 square feet, on ten acres of land. We moved in at the end of 1954, and from then until today, it has been our home. Over the years we expanded that house, but we always maintained its simplicity.

Ramat HaSharon, and the neighborhood of Neve Magen where we lived, was a small agricultural moshav, and the minimarket was also the bank. Many of us ex- or current military personnel knew each other well and were friends, the adults and the children: Haim Bar Lev, Avraham Yoffe, Aharon Yariv, Ezer Weizmann, Irwin Doron, Josh Palmon, and many more good people.

We all lived a similar lifestyle, standard living for army personnel. None of us was rich. Our cars were all military. It was like a commune, not exactly equal—there were colonels and a few major generals—and the hierarchy was noticeable.

During the time in the army we didn't go abroad every year, and we didn't go out to restaurants. When I became the president of the Technion our financial situation improved, but even then we continued to live a modest lifestyle. After that, some people were killed in the wars, and the atmosphere in the "commune" was shaken, as it was everywhere else in the country.

A few years later, we started going on trips around Israel and the world with three special groups consisting of people who matched our professional and personal worlds. One was called "Chug Tishrei," a group of ex-IDF and Mossad people, founded by Meir Amit. The other was called "The Dana Group," named by the daughter of Yosef Avidar, whose friends were mainly faculty members at the Hebrew University. The third group was essentially a group of people who gathered around one of the best architects I've ever known—Yoram Tsafrir. Every trip was an experience of special friendships and of discovering the world, learning history and culture, and meeting people in their own natural surroundings. Slowly, the trips stopped, too. During the last trip with "Chug Tishrei," we drifted down the Danube from Vienna to the Black Sea. Meir Amit was in a wheelchair, he insisted on doing everything, and we helped him. The group stopped meeting when he died. And then Yoram Tsafrir died, and only "The Dana Group" still lives on.

Everything we did, we did with what we had. We were not tempted to make our house fancier. It is our house. Modest, humane, warm. It has had the same furniture, the same paintings, the same bookcases, the same books, and the same atmosphere for the past few decades. Together, Shoshana and I worked on the garden, which was about half an acre. A small seedling became a tall tree, and when I sat with Shoshana while she was sick, I told her, "Look how pretty, look at these trees that we planted. Now the pecans are in blossom." This house, surrounded by the garden and the fruit trees, has seen our children's weddings and events with many people such as a traditional Channukah event that took place for almost fifty years, from the time we lived in Neta'im. There, at the beginning of our journey, we invited a few military people, and later on, here in Ramat HaSharon, about 120 people would come. Some were from the Palmach, others were people we worked with and developed friendly relationships with. We put up a massive tent, opened up the entire garden. We served latkes, potato patties in a Ukrainian style, with sour cream and apple sauce, cookies made with our pecans (which everyone loved to take home), and punch, of course. It was a serious business that Shoshana created and ran in her own way until she got sick, and then the tent was folded up, and the house was empty.

When I was president of the Technion, I didn't want to host at restaurants; I wanted people to get to know a warm, Israeli home. We hosted high-ranking people from abroad, presidents of large companies, renowned professors, and other VIPs, per the request of Yitzhak Rabin, when he needed it. I had a complicated relationship with Yitzhak Rabin; we were friends and we would fight. We knew each other well and carried with us good memories from childhood. We always told the truth to each other. Yitzhak could talk to me about people in the system, and I shared nothing of what he said. Rabin, as chief of staff, had meetings at our house about the air force with the Minister of Defense and David Ivri, head of the air force, and the president of Pratt & Whitney Company. There is nothing like the two letters we wrote each other a few months before he was assassinated to demonstrate the friendship that was formed in the Palmach, a friendship that lasted until those godforsaken bullets, fired by a loathsome murderer, that ended his life in a single moment.

January 16th, 1995
Hello Yitzhak my friend,
I received two touching letters from you . . . in your second letter you expressed gratitude and respect for my participation [in the ceremony awarding the Nobel Prize for peace], *and I had felt gratitude and respect for you for choosing to include me in the emotional experience of appreciating your work and your courage. During the ceremony, I closed my eyes and thought that when we were in the Palmach tents, even the wildest imagination could not*

*have foreseen our presence in the townhall in Oslo, you receiving
such an honor and me watching, happy for you. Yitzhak, I must say,
my feelings towards you are embedded deep in the beginning of our
journey and our work to establish a state, work that brought terrible
things and camaraderie among soldiers facing turmoil and harm.
Always, for as long as we've known each other, our relationship has
been characterized by practical, open, and free honesty. I am aware
of the fact that an act of peace is complicated, difficult, and long,
and it is filled with bumps along the way. It definitely is not an exact
science, it is the constant challenge of a lack of certainty in a fickle
world, and it is hard to estimate the risks and the opportunities.*

*I give you my blessing, may you succeed in fulfilling your vision
for the completion, security, and success of the State of Israel.*

Sending warm regards from a loyal friend,
Amos Horev.

January 30ᵗʰ, 1995
Hello Amos,
I received and read your letter from January 16ᵗʰ, 1995.

*What does a man have left in life other than a few friends? You
are one of them.*

Thank you,
Yitzhak Rabin.

"I Want to Continue on Being Sand and Sanda"

I called her Shanka and she called me Amos'ke. The partnership, the
friendship, and the love between us held strong through the challenges
of time and routine. Seventy years together. Seventy years in which we
each made our professional way in the world and moved ahead: she in
the field of education; I in the security forces. Together we raised our two
children, Yehiam and Nira. Ours was an unconditional partnership and
a commitment to our personal family, without taking away from the

mutual freedom to delve into and dedicate time to our own personal interests. It could be that some separation in our professional lives strengthened what we had in common when we got back home.

I remember the many hours during which Shoshana, thanks to her remarkable Hebrew, helped me change the style and wording of the work files I had to write. I remember the many conversations when I was debating about one thing or another, and Shoshana would be a wise person to speak to, a true and honest partner in my life. In terms of everything related to the army, I would sometimes tell her what was happening, and sometimes I wouldn't. She knew about my arguments with Haim Laskov and with Talik. She didn't tell me to leave it alone, maybe because most of the time I told her about it after it already happened. There are things I didn't speak to anyone about, not even Shoshana. I told her more than once, "It's better that you don't know." In addition, I made an effort not to bring home the arguments and struggles that I often had with different people.

The Yom Kippur War, which stormed into our personal lives when Moishe'le, Nira's husband, was killed, strongly affected Shoshana and me for many years to come. I, who had seen so much death around me, continued on because there was no other choice. I didn't let myself break down, even during that moment when we found Moishe'le in the damaged tank and retrieved his body.

From letters that remain and from scraps of memories, I know how hard it was for Shoshana to live alongside me, on a path that began with a battle for life and continued to be filled with struggles and long absences from home while I was in the IDF and in positions that followed. Alongside the understanding, appreciation, and acceptance that I received from her during all those years, the difficulty and the desire for things to be different showed themselves here and there. I learned, painfully, from the journal I found after her death, that I didn't know Shoshana as well and as completely as I thought I did.

The sentence she wrote when she was twenty-four, on March 4, 1949, "Turns out there is nothing left for me to do but return to this notebook, as there is no one for me to speak to and share what is in my heart," hit me like a painful arrow. I read the journal four times and felt that she was alive, standing before me, mercilessly laying her hardships before me, from the beginning of our shared life together. I found comfort in knowing that the rest of our lives was different and that many of her needs and aspirations were fulfilled during our shared times. I read and reread that note that I had found:

> *June 6th, 2006*
> *Amos, my love!*
> *My good man, now, when I am not home and I am thinking about you and missing you, I know that you are my best friend. I know that you care about me very much and I ask that we continue to be Sand and Sanda (a wooden pole for supporting and building facilities) and for that I am also grateful to you from the bottom of my loving heart, and I ask to be good for you.*
> *Your always—Shoshana*

Through her writing, I was exposed to hidden parts of her personality, and I was able to walk along the path of her views on relationships, love, her longing to work in education, and her image as a woman and a mother. I wanted our children, grandchildren, and great-grandchildren to know her, and I published "The Journal—A Brief Biography of Shoshana Horev—from the pages of her journal and letters, 1940–1949."

Together as We Separate

When Shoshana fell ill, our lives changed. Fewer family meals on Friday night, fewer walks to art events than in the past, when Shoshana was the leading authority on culture in the house. When Shoshana was alive, we were two. Today, I am alone and need to accept the situation, accept my own reality. The house is no longer a hub for

With my Shanka

social events, and we meet mostly at the Palmach house, at funerals, and at memorial services.

Shoshana was sick for three years and her condition continued to deteriorate. I never stopped taking care of her, and there was not a single expert in Israel and the world whose door I didn't knock on to see if there was any way to cure her or at least improve her condition. Today, I have this annoying thought that perhaps if she were significantly younger, they would have found something they could have done, but I immediately remove that thought from my mind, as I knew the experts and the hospitals with whom I was in contact.

I changed my lifestyle. I was home more. Nadia, who has been a maid in our home for the past sixty years and was also a part of our family, was with me every hour of every day. "Shoshana is my mother," she said to me on more than one occasion, as we were taking care of her together. I shared the responsibility of taking care of Shoshana with our son Yehiam throughout the entire sickness. At first, I would still go to lecture, mostly in the United States, and then I stopped doing that as well and stayed home. I made sure she did all her tests and examinations, I got her out of bed, I fed her, I bathed her. We sat together in front of the television, as her body was deteriorating, but her mind did not betray her, and we talked a lot. Every once in a while, she would say to me, "Amos, I want to die." I responded, "Do you want to see Guy and Dafna, your great-grandchildren? You won't see them if you die." I did everything I could. I was happy for every day that I could get a smile on her face. Her smile was the light and joy of my life. I knew the end would come, but her death was still a surprise. She asked me, "Amos, do you love me?" "From here and to the heavens," I responded, and I meant it. I gave her ice cream and she said, "Amos, I don't feel so good." I took her to bed, and I had a hard time. Yehiam came to help me and she died in both our arms. Five minutes before that, she had been eating ice cream, and then she painlessly died in our arms.

I didn't cry at her funeral, but the tears flow within me constantly and painfully. I read a poem at her funeral, "The Road Not Taken," by Robert Frost. Friends came. Few of them were left, but all those who are came.

Epilogue

I have been very fortunate. First, my generation was born into a very rare event. A generation of the very few who founded the state and protected it from its beginning. I had the great privilege of being among the founders of the State of Israel, using my own two hands, in places we had never been before, and there was no one else to take our places. I was lucky that I also fit in with the atmosphere of those times, or that it shaped me and made me fit in. I experienced the establishment of the State of Israel. There is no way to describe the relief I felt when I reached the top of a certain mountain and saw more land that we conquered. It is ours. And every time I saw that we were making progress and winning, I had the feeling that we were securing our presence here.

The War of Independence opened up the path on which I walk to this day. I had the privilege of being part of a unique group of people from the Palmach. I paid a heavy price in my personal and family life, as during the war there were long periods of time when Shoshana and I spent very little time together. My contemporaries and I were so invested in fighting for the establishment of the state and guaranteeing its safety. We deeply understood the meaning of failure.

I am aware that memories and past experiences affect views and positions in the present and affect the way one sees reality, but I don't dismiss them. To this day, I am convinced that the fundamental reason for the establishment of the state was to create a place in the world that would forever have a solid and secure Jewish majority. In the diaspora we were a minority, and more than once people chose to slaughter us. This starting point is what should shape our policy about the borders of the state. An additional starting point is the understanding that we were, and always will be, a small country in terms of size and population, and that we depend on our good relationships with countries around the world. Financially, we also can't depend solely on the local market. This fact affects the way we act in the "conquered territories" and affects our agreements and treaties with the Palestinians. As a small state, we must understand that excellence in the fields of education, social studies, sciences, industry, and economics is an existential issue, no less than the security forces. We would not survive long as a state in which mediocrity reigns.

The War of Independence was primarily a physical-military one, and there were times when it was not certain that we would be able to establish a state here. Today, when the state is almost taken for granted by a generation that was not there during those moments of doubt, I am noticing certain trends, almost completely invisible, that put our majority status at risk.

I am concerned mostly about two issues that are quickly gaining momentum, and to my understanding are intertwined and mutually reinforcing. The first is the massive growth in the numbers and political power of extreme nationalists. The second is the situation in the conquered territories of Judea and Samaria, where the Jewish settlements are spread out in ways that will no longer enable a distinction between the Jews and the Arabs. If we look at this objectively, without deluding ourselves, even today we are headed towards a binational state. I am fearful of the creation of a critical mass in the settlements and the loss of the Jewish majority. We will cease to be a state. We simply will not be.

From the outset, I thought some of the settlements were dangerous. Wild settlements in areas of high Palestinian population density. We see the results today. Messianism has taken over the settlers. In a state that is fighting for its democratic, social, and educational soul, I recognize the beginnings of fascism, with a growing population that believes that the land they are on is connected to the divine promise given to the Jewish People, and "the Greater Israel" is more important to them than having a chance at reaching an agreement with our neighbors. The government must acknowledge this danger and act against this foreign, utterly false ideology that is spreading among the extreme right wing and already affecting our reality.

Bringing religious arguments into the conflict only strengthens the motive of a religious war between Judaism and Islam. As far as the Muslims are concerned, we are a hindrance, a foreign culture situated in the Muslim east, and they want to spit us out. And so, both sides, together, add fuel to this flame of hatred. However, it is important to know how to compromise and maybe even to try to reconcile. Not through meaningless talk, but through real action, through cooperation, perhaps on economic and educational issues.

As I understand it, the condition under which we can exist as a Jewish state with minorities living among us is that we maintain a massive Jewish majority. The extreme right is creating an unsustainable situation, at the end of which, demography will destroy Israel. In today's world you can't have apartheid. Israel will turn into a binational state, with everything that entails, including the loss of the Jewish majority.

Immediately after the positive ending of the Six-Day War, Yigal Allon—a wise and experienced leader—presented his well-known plan, known as "the Allon plan." To this day, I remain convinced that this is the right way to solve the Israeli-Palestinian conflict. We must separate from the Palestinians and let them be rulers beyond our borders in their own demilitarized, sovereign country. Israel will be situated in the Jordan Valley to ensure that we are safe from attacks from the east. I hope that this way there will be room for collaboration, which will allow Israel to aid the Palestinian state to develop and succeed.

Furthermore, the plans for "Greater Jerusalem" are folly because they will create a situation in which there is no solid Jewish majority. The Arabs aren't going anywhere, and they will have equal rights and duties as all minority citizens in Israel do—no funny business, because this is not something to mess around with. I don't see a practical possibility for a joint municipality, and for Palestinian government offices to be in the suburbs of the city. It just won't work.

I'm not so concerned about the situation that my innate optimism has been affected. In the long term, I see processes that will have a positive effect: it is all part of a process, everything is in flux. More than once, as I said in the United States, I never saw a stuck pendulum. That is the basis of my optimism. No matter what I am dealing with, I ask myself: what is the size of the critical mass, that, once it has been formed, will create a new, irreversible situation.

I am here, I have no other country that is mine, and I don't want to live in another country. I love my land, the land of the Land of Israel. I "plowed" it with my own two feet. But what about my grandchildren and great-grandchildren? Will they still be able to be here? Yes, I tell myself, they will.

Since I stood my ground, my life has been inseparably intertwined with the affairs of the Jewish people and the state. I have been a public emissary since my youth. In January 2008, when I received the Caesarea Forum award for National Economic Policies, I said, "We didn't just follow our youthful dreams, we did what we thought Zionism needed." Shoshana wanted to study education, and instead studied agriculture, and only got around to education at a later stage in her life. Yitzhak Rabin wanted to be a hydraulic engineer, and instead he spent his entire life dealing with security. I wanted to be an engineer, but I went to the Palmach and the army. It was what was needed at the time. Eventually, and extremely late in my life, the current needs lined up with my youthful dreams. The army gave me an amazing opportunity to go study and implement everything I had learned.

Today, nine decades later, it's not easy to make peace with the fact that I can no longer make a difference and that I am no longer in the circle of the decision-makers, but the thoughts and the plans break into my mind as though I am still holding a position. I find my thoughts about the future of this country and its people occupy my mind no less than my personal issues, old age, and goodbyes.

That being said, I didn't always follow the rules—even within the system—and I didn't always wait to get permission. I never aspired to be chief of staff and went down a technological path. As a member of the general staff, I held a position in the logistic-technologic field, because of everything I had done and thanks to the support of my chief of staff friends.

Most of the time, my world view is the force that drives me. I never searched through the gallery of all possible activities to find the one that would ensure success. But when I took upon myself something that I believed was important, I strived to do the best that I could and to succeed. I wanted to excel at everything I did, not to be mediocre. I felt that people liked to hear my opinion and listened intently. Maybe because they knew that what I say I also do. And indeed, I successfully completed most of the tasks I took upon myself.

In the Palmach, our motivation was the creation of an army and a state. But we had another motive—to conquer all the Land of Israel. We had to fully exhaust all the options laid before us in an unstable world. The War of Independence ended with a ceasefire that invited more wars—the Suez Crisis and the Six-Day War. War is in fact a terrible thing, but I have never forgotten what would have happened if we had lost. Where we would be today, if at all.

"I Will Not Lie to Myself"

I have dealt with my struggles without fear. To this day, for example, I am certain that I was right about developing and manufacturing the Israeli Merkava tank. Today people are already saying "Amos was right." People in the army knew that I was a challenging opponent for Talik, and that my opinion wasn't accepted. There are a lot of things about which my opinion was not accepted. However, the attitude that guided me throughout my life was that if at the end of an argument, heated and long as it may be, my opinion is not accepted, I must move on to other things. On to new challenges.

I never acted in ways that significantly contradicted my views. It is unacceptable for a major general to get up and resign from their position. I quit, and they did not like it in the IDF. Despite quitting, I was made head of the quartermaster's branch. That was a form of acknowledgement of my being right. In addition, my professional attitude about the logistic field and the base that I created for technological thinking were accepted.

From 1955, when the IDF didn't have tanks, until 1972, the Ordnance Corps, under my command, manufactured series of tanks, about 2,250 in total. I was proud of everything we did. I received the formal and respectful acknowledgement only in 2011, when I received the Israel Defense Prize for life work. And still, completing the mission I took upon myself was the biggest prize I could ever receive. It seems that that was the price I paid for my way of fighting during a disagreement.

I have never accepted a position as a springboard to something else. Looking back, I am at peace with this. I wouldn't have gotten as far as I did if I had taken shortcuts. You can't be superficial when it comes to long-term processes. It takes time to build anything with people, and once it is built I am in no rush to leave, because I also enjoy myself, so why should I give up this pleasure? Also, my relationships with my friends are long-term, despite the differences in opinion.

The amount of time I stayed at a position in the IDF was not standard. I was chief ordnance officer for twelve years. When I was head of the quartermaster's branch, people and groups would come to me and offer high-up positions in the economy and academia. I was very much in demand—I guess I had a good reputation—but I refused everything. I wanted to continue in the quartermaster's branch, to leave my mark. Dado—Chief of Staff David Elazar—surprised me when he ended my time in that position after only four years. I am certain, without any modesty, that if I had stayed in the position, the IDF would have been better prepared for the Yom Kippur War, and we would have been able to avoid at least some of the failures that were the result of the terrible condition of the emergency storage units, the ammunition inventory, and the neglected defensive supplies.

I was president of the Technion for nine years, and I could have stayed longer. I was president of the Israel Friends of the Technion for thirty-two years, and during these years I was able to raise over a billion shekels! That's dozens of years that I have been involved in large foundations that helped me then, and to this day help me with everything having to do with Israel.

"If I Had Lived in the Wild West"

I am a short-tempered person by nature. There were times when I reacted harshly out of anger. I raised my voice at people, and very easily could have found myself in a fight on the street.

More than once I regretted something I said. It happened with soldiers, with officers. There was a time in my life during which, if I had lived in the Wild West, I would have been quick to draw my gun. I was considered a tough character in the army.

Over the years, I learned from my mistakes. I learned to control myself. I got over the violent part. I decided I must not act out of anger. I learned to shut up, calm down, and only then respond. People knew that I no longer raised my voice, but that it's still worth listening to what I have to say. I separated between my anger and my reaction, but it never stopped me from saying everything I thought.

And Where Are the Tears?

Human beings are complicated creatures. There is something that to this day has yet to be fully understood: what are feelings, how exactly do emotions work in the brain? Why is there a certain song that causes a lump to form in your throat and brings tears to your eyes? I didn't cry during the War of Independence, but there were times when I felt that lump in my throat. For example, when we buried Moishe'le, my daughter Nira's husband. I had this feeling that if I were to press on a certain spot on my throat, the tears would just come pouring out.

I Am a Jew in My Soul, but I Am Not a Believer

I belong to a generation that was raised on the values of socialism, reading Karl Marx, A. D. Gordon, *The Forty Days of Musa Dagh* by Franz Werfel, and loving Russian poetry and reading Russian literature. Ideologically, I am completely secular. I believe in friendship, respect for people, and values. I love Judaism, the Bible, and history. I do not scorn the religious and the Ultra-Orthodox, but there are people among them who are no different in my eyes than members of the Taliban. I went to synagogue only for my Bar Mitzvah. I remember the neighborhood of Mea Sh'arim, mixed and entirely different from its current extreme inhabitants, some of whom are anti-Zionists. I am concerned about the large population that has no actual interest in the State of Israel, and the zealousness with which they fulfill the religious commandments only grows. That being said, to my understanding the problem will gradually be resolved. The Ultra-Orthodox are fighting a rearguard battle from the front. One of the biggest revolutions in the world was breaking the walls of blindness. Information is available to everyone in an unprecedented way. I assume that curiosity is ingrained in my grandson just as it is in the grandson of an Ultra-Orthodox rabbi's baby. Curiosity is something you are born with. In the long term, the fact that information is making its way to the younger Ultra-Orthodox kids, via the electronic devices they will one day own, will create a situation in which they are gradually less closed off and hostile to the modern world around them. That will also open them up to studying, which will allow them to integrate into the Israeli economy, alongside the secular people.

I am a Jew in my body and my soul, but I am not a believer. I accept the universal values that stem from Judaism. I loved my Bible studies, but to me they had nothing to do with believing in God. I don't believe in any kind of force that created us, but I am curious about the process, how it all began, when the first cell was formed, how many billions of years passed until humans evolved and became thinking beings.

As the Time Left Grows Shorter

We invented God to deal with our fears, and death is our leading fear. To escape this crippling fear, religions invented the afterlife, reincarnation, and other strange and unusual solutions.

I think about death. I have witnessed a lot of death around me—war, old age, disease, and suicides. The way I see it, our entire purpose as human beings is to ensure humanity's continuity. But that is just the primeval work. With age, this project disappears, but thanks to the mind, other projects take its place. You sing, play, research, write, invent, and then you've brought something to life once again.

When can a person decide to put an end to their lives with a clear mind? It's very difficult. When you have an incurable disease, logic holds fast to the possibility that a cure will be found and that it is still worth living. Today we sit, old-aged friends, dinosaurs with a lot of experience, and we see how forgetfulness is affecting us on different levels. But does that mean you should wake up one morning and hang yourself?

Shoshana told me she wanted to die. In her condition, maybe it was the right thing to want. I slept next to her until the day she died. I thought sleeping together helped her, that it helped her that I held her hand, that love could have some sort of effect. But she lost her liveliness. She just wanted it to be over.

I am not afraid of death. In the meantime, I try to make the best of what I have left in life. I drink fancy whiskey with a friend, write my life story, and they move before me, the waters of memory start to rise. I still remember but know that it will end. As we progress with our age, so the time left grows shorter.

Father and Son, Two Generations Seemingly Emerging from the same Tree Trunk

My father—Eliyahu (Elec) Sochaczewer

My dad, Eliyahu (Elec) Sochaczewer, was born in Warsaw—his last name was given in memory of the name of the town Sochaczewr—and I was born in Jerusalem. Today, looking back on the various stages of my life, the positions I've filled, and the choices I've made at the different crossroads in my life, I can clearly see my father's footsteps. Of course, our reality, terminology, knowledge, and souls were completely different, but beyond them, our paths were similar. A father and son, two intertwined generations, seemingly emerging from the same tree trunk. My dad was a professional in mechanical engineering, electricity, and chemistry. His ability to invent things was incredible. He didn't belong to the digital age. He didn't have a computer. He worked with a slide rule. That way he learned, that way he knew what to do. He was not a good fit for the electrical engineering faculty during my time as president of the Technion. He was a perfect example of an outstanding engineer from a different time. He belonged to a generation that saw the different types of engineering in a more holistic way. Today, everything is divided into sub-fields, and who can even see the whole picture? I liked doing a lot of things the way he did. He knew how to work with his hands. I, too, worked with my hands, and to them I added the knowledge required to create production factories. My dad, and I in his footsteps, never stopped, even for a moment, going through every piece of information that existed in the technological world. We tried, each of us on his own path and in his own time, to gain new knowledge, to understand it, and to implement it according to the needs of the People of Israel. My dad, at the university workshop, and in his private home, developed and created almost from nothing—and I in the IDF, as chief ordnance officer and head of the quartermaster's branch, upgraded scraps and provided tanks in numbers that changed the balance of power and the IDF's abilities, using technology my dad could not have even dreamt of. I continued on this path as president of the Technion and in Rafael. But although his life and mine moved on different axes, we were alike in our dedication to technology, the establishment of the State of Israel, and our country's security.

I chose to sketch my father's image while incorporating excerpts from an interview he gave to Ezra Greenboim in 1987, as part of a project to preserve original testimonies. The interview took place at the Yigal Allon Center (*Beit Yigal Allon*).

He Was Very Mischievous

My dad, Eliyahu (Elec) Sochaczewer, was born in 1901 and was orphaned from his mom when he was only ten or eleven years old. He was very mischievous.

When World War I broke out, I went with two other gentiles, friends from school, and we drove to the battlefield . . . [war between Russia and Germany] *and I sat there, emptying the bullets of the gunpowder. . . and we found a key that takes apart the shells* [that hadn't exploded] *and they had an aluminum fuse with some kind of clock inside, with gears . . . and I found a Jew, I remember his name, Bron, from Warsaw, who would buy these clocks and gears from us. My dad believed that a good education could have a crucial importance in life and took me to a preparatory class in the Russian private Reali School. Why a Russian school? Because Polish high-school diplomas had no value. These diplomas were not accepted at the University or the Technion.*

Later, he was accepted to an excellent technical school where he studied building, mechanics, and electricity. At the end of his first year of studies when he was seventeen, he was summoned to join the Polish army but was exempted because of an eye problem. Nevertheless, he didn't return to his studies.

I tell my father: I am going on vacation to Palestine. I don't want to suffer being called a "filthy Jew," being beaten up and spat on.

Even before he made aliya to Israel, he was a part of HaShomer Hatzair ("the Young Guard", a socialist Zionist youth movement and later pre-State political party), but he chose not to go with them to Kibbutz Mishmar HaEmek, and went to Port Sa'id, in Egypt, on his own, making his way to Israel from there. While waiting for arrangements to be made through He-Halutz ("the Pioneer", an organization for preparing Zionist youth to settle on the land), he got himself an electrical engineering certificate, even though he never completed his studies. Later, thanks to his knowledge and abilities in the field of mechanical engineering, he was officially recognized as an engineer and was even added to the list of certified engineers.

In 1919, only eighteen years old, he arrived in the city of Jaffa by boat from Alexandria, in Egypt, with his toolbox (I still have some of these tools). He was a little sick, a little hungry, and he was looking for work. Here and there he would find a temporary job on the roof of the Anglo Palestine Company Bank (later to be the Leumi Bank):

I put together a small American engine, and a 32-volt battery, and eight batteries on each side of a room on the roof—and I created electricity in the building. After that I got money from him (from Hillel Levontin, who pretended to be an electrical engineer and was the bank manager's son). And later I walked around, I didn't have a job, you could yell, but there was no one to yell at, and there was nobody's desk to bang on. I also wasn't the type to bang on desks, I didn't know how.

One day, after almost a year, there was an announcement that there were jobs at the British military base at Sarafand (later known as Tzrifin), about eleven miles southwest of Jaffa. Arriving on foot, he told the guard at the entrance that he wanted to work, was asked what he knew how to do, and responded that he knows how to fix the electricity in cars. And then, a British officer, probably an Oxford graduate, came out to him, led him to the garage and took down twenty broken ignition magnetos from a shelf. Those were the part that creates the spark in the engine. He said, "Fix." Three hours later, he came back. My dad had fixed ten of them. The officer immediately led him to the sergeants' dining hall.

And I hadn't eaten a pretzel, a pita, in three days. They gave me a
plate with a piece of meat and vegetables. There was a large, whole
piece of cheese on the table, jam, and they gave me bread. I was
careful to eat in a way that wouldn't let them know I was hungry.

They gave him a contract as a type A engineer. He worked and
made a good salary. Until he had enough. "First of all, I was tired of
not doing anything. I built power stations, I built magnetos, and I built
different devices." Together with another friend, he left for Jerusalem
and Gdud HaAvoda, a socialist Zionist organization founded in the
fall of 1920 for labor and defense. He stayed for about a year and
fixed cars that the organization purchased from the British Mandate
Government. Because of a crisis and division in Gdud HaAvoda, he
left and worked in a car garage under the employment of a Jew who
was a contractor for the British army and made transport vehicles
useable, while finding creative solutions to different technological
problems. He would fix magnetos for him. Back then, he was probably
the only one in the Land of Israel, maybe even the Near East, who
dealt with magnetos.

He went from a magneto fixer to head engineer in the British
Commissioner's residence, operating water pumps to Jerusalem, and
head engineer at the Hebrew University:

One time, this young guy on a bicycle approached me and said:
"Pinhas Rutenberg wants to speak to you." A moment later . . . I
walked in to speak to him. He said the following: "Look, in about
a month or two you can come work for us. But there is something
here of national importance. We have a new High-Commissioner,
a British Jew, his name is Herbert Samuel, and he lives in a house
in Mount Scopus. In this house, there is a power plant and there are
batteries and there are water pumps. There are all sorts of things
necessary for a solitary house. And he has a mechanic, and this
mechanic is publicly antisemitic." I can help with that, I said.

And so, my dad worked as head engineer in the British Commissioner's residence, for Commissioner Herbert Samuel, the new high commissioner. This was a place in which he met people who led him into the world of the security industry and behind the scenes of the civilian work for the high commissioner, and later at the Hebrew University at Mount Scopus. While he was working for the high commissioner, around 1925, the following happened:

David Fisch, who was a member of HaShomer Hatazir in Kfar Giladi, came to me and said: "Elek, we need you." "What do you need me for?" He said: "We are opening a weapons factory . . . We can't keep depending on weapons that we steal from the army, from the police, or on broken, rusty weapons that the Arabs have." So, I quit.

And then my dad went with his little family—my mom and me, a one-year-old baby—to Afula, to build a weapons-manufacturing factory. It was called "Haroshet Ha'Emek" (the Valley Factory), and my dad was meant to be the technologist who would design the devices and the machines. The factory failed, I had a fever, and the doctor warned, "If you don't take the child away from here, you will not have a child." So my parents returned to the Jerusalem area and lived in the Arab village of Anatot. There, as part of the Mandatory company for public works, my dad built and operated the factory that pumps water from the springs around Anatot, in Ein Fa'ra. Water was pumped from this factory to Jerusalem. At that time, there was no running water in the city. In the summer, after the water in the wells dried out, water was sold in cans. The connection to the beginnings of weapons manufacturing was not cut off for long, however. After a while, my father was invited to fill the position of head mechanic at the Hebrew University in Mount Scopus and to live with his family in the Bukharan neighborhood. The university was, in practice, a springboard for his unique talents that would help the security of the Yishuv and the public infrastructure of the young state. But the salary was lower:

I received 18 pounds a month from the municipality when I worked at Anatot, and at the university I received 16 pounds at the beginning . . .] but the main thing was that he gave me a free hand, and I built labs. It was audacious of me, but I had an open mind and a good understanding of many things. And we built. That was in the year 1927.

In 1934–35, from his position in Mount Scopus, he built the Ziv Institute lab in Rehovot that preceded the Weizmann Institute. He received an award for excellence and was the most beloved man in the institute.

During World War II, many of the faculty members of the Hebrew University, my father among them, took part in the British military efforts. And it truly was an effort, because from a technological perspective the British military was physically very distant from Britain and was incurring supply issues in all areas.

I found a document, a summary of the Hebrew University's contribution to the war. A few professors and my late father were present at the concluding meeting. If statistics were to measure the contributions of practical ideas and their execution, then obviously the largest part of the entire contribution would be attributed to him. My father describes the execution of technology specifically in the field of chemistry, and not mechanical and electrical engineering. He was very multidisciplinary, and a man of action. And what a phenomenal memory he had!

Yes, I got everything I wanted at the university, and not only was I constantly learning, I had keys to all the libraries, I was head electrician, something was happening, you need to know how to get into it. This allowed me to look for information in books . . . and I was curious. If there was something I didn't know, I searched for material on it. And there were science people you could ask. There were those who gave me on point responses, and those who

did not. Afterwards books arrived . . . at the technical school in
Poland, I only studied for three quarters of a year, and all my
technical knowledge is from here, from Israel, from self-teaching
and curiosity.

A man whose life was filled with technology from morning to evening. Alongside his work at Mount Scopus, he also did private jobs. He installed the first air conditioning in Jerusalem, in Mr. Schocken's library. At Beit Aghion, one of the richest places in Jerusalem, the kitchen was in the cellar and my dad was asked to install an elevator with which they would bring the food up to the dining hall, and so he did. Today, Beit Aghion is the prime minister's house. At the Angel factory, they would put the loaves into the oven using a kitchen spoon. My dad is the one who built the burners.

From the 1920s until after the establishment of the state, my dad committed himself, of his own volition, to manufacturing weapons and ammunition, seemingly out of nothing, before there was an industry. He recognized needs, found solutions, used contacts overseas to get weapons manufacturing designs. Later, when I was chief ordnance officer in the IDF, reality dictated that we must act similarly: purchase weapons, mostly tanks, from spare parts left after World War II, which we upgraded so that they served the IDF during its first years. My dad had many conversations with people from the Haganah about weapons:

During those years, after 1929, we dealt with something very
important. There were shooting machines [machineguns that
had been smuggled into Israel], *Schwarzlose MGs, and the*
ammunition for the Schwarzlose was manufactured in 1900, and
every fifth bullet actually fired, so we decided we needed to renew
the ammunition. I built some device that would latch onto the bullet
and then release it without denting the shell. After that, I built a
device that would remove the cap so that it wasn't damaged. Then,

we removed the gunpowder from inside the bullet and cleaned and washed it, and then cleaned it with vinegar. Later, we brought gunpowder from someone who was serving in the police . . . we made caps at the basement of the physics' department at the university. In one go, we made seven copper caps . . .

The riots in the city [Arab attacks on Jews] *started in 1929. There were shooting battles with the Haganah, people were killed. At the time, I made a flame thrower out of a fire extinguisher, of which I had dozens at the university. It was the first flamethrower. After that, during the War of Independence, I developed a nozzle for the flamethrower that would squirt the lighter fluid to a distance of up to 40 meters* [about 44 yards].

I had accumulated vacation days at the university, so I had about four or five months in total. I used these days to go on vacation and go abroad. Where do you get money? I had a large lot in Tel Arza, about 1000 square meters . . . I didn't ask for money, and I went there for our business, Haganah business . . . no one had sent me. I spoke only to Yehuda Arazi [one of the leading people in the Haganah and Shai; before World War II, he went to Poland and dealt with smuggling machines for bullet manufacturing] *and received a letter from him to someone in Poland. The main thing was that I went, I sold half the lot, and I had 120 pounds . . . I was always in contact with the Haganah regarding weapons.*

Yehuda Arazi told me about a Jew who was chairman of the Maccabi organization and had a factory in Warsaw that manufactured 81 mm mortars, as well as hand grenades, everything except explosives. He gave me a letter for this man. I couldn't get anything from this Jew, but I made a friend in Warsaw who was a wealthy and influential person, a non-Jewish master craftsman I had worked with. I found him, I arrived at his house, and his wife nearly passed out when she saw me. Out of joy. I told him what I was interested in, and said: "You've fought for a country, we want to do so as well." He took me to a pub where we met two other guys

who were both master craftsmen at a factory. I entered the factory
and walked around for a week, ten days, and saw things, and was
offered things. They offered me a stencil for the casting of a French
hand grenade . . . and I received design plans for the manufacturing
of the 81mm mortar, a machinegun named Bregman . . . When I
returned and presented everything I had brought to the Haganah
headquarters, they said—a mortar? Are you crazy? Where can we
possibly create a hidden weapons storage for such a mortar? And
every shell will cost God knows how much. No. . . . They made me
sound crazy, and I went back to Jerusalem. That was at the end of
1932, and until about 1937 everything was silent.

Later, a British unit used a mortar and the Haganah people secretly
started showing interest in what they were firing. Only then did they
go back to my dad, and in 1938 the first mortar was ready to be used.

During the War of Independence, when Mount Scopus had fallen
and Jerusalem was under siege, my dad created a military industry in the
city, entirely on his own initiative. There were weapons manufacturing
workshops for land mines, incendiary bombs, grenades, and Davidkas
(homemade mortars). The connection with Jerusalem was cut off and
you couldn't count on the Israel Military Industries that was starting
up in Tel Aviv, so dad and his men needed to create all the weapons
alone:

It turned out that we didn't have anything in Jerusalem, not
materials, not people, not factories, we had nothing, we needed to
do something . . . we had a workshop that focused on aluminum
molds, and it was in the new market at Beit Israel, a few hundred
meters from Sheikh Jarrah. I had a feeling the Arabs knew that
people were working there. And anyway, shells fell in the garden,
shells from a mortar, but we didn't really notice. They were falling
all over the city and they were falling on us, too. The shells were
against people, and they would explode at the slightest touch on

the tiles of a roof. They hit the roofing tiles and didn't breach the ceiling into the classrooms, but they fell in the garden, and shrapnel injured people through the windows. Turned out that they were bombing us with 81 mm mortars, and they couldn't reach Bezalel with the mortars, so they started bombing us with Ordnance QF 25-pounders. The neighbors would yell at us, "From the moment you got here they started bombing us." But regardless, we stayed there, with the equipment of the Brandeis vocational school, where there were workshops and lathes. It was, in fact, the first equipment we used for the military industry. We carved out mechanisms, we had mines that we made out of Polish grenades instead of the mechanism with the lever. It was a mechanism with a firing pin and a cap, that was it.

During the first lull in fighting I went to Tel Aviv, and then went up on a hill in Ramat Gan to where the headquarters were, and where Ben-Gurion was. Thanks to a Jerusalemite named Nehemiah Argov, I was able to go see Ben-Gurion. Ben-Gurion asked me: "What do you want?" I told him we have nothing in Jerusalem. He sent a messenger, brought in Levi Shkolnik (later, Levi Eshkol), and he listened to what I wanted and gave me a letter. The letter said that I should be given anything I need to protect Jerusalem. I went to the IMI systems with this letter, and they gave me all sorts of things. In Jerusalem, we had been working out of 18 different, spread-out locations.

My dad's preoccupation with weapons stemmed from his belief that weapons are important for protecting the Jewish settlements as well as from his technological expertise, which was required for the development, maintenance, and manufacture of weapons. My dad and technology were intertwined at the heart and soul. I found one expression of this special connection between my dad and technology in the things he said when he was asked about how he feels about his life in hindsight:

I think I've done a lot. Why did I do a lot? Because I was part of a society of people who didn't know that explosives are a simple thing, but you must be careful with it. They didn't know that weapons were like any other technological device, a machine that does something. A machine needs to be precisely right in every aspect. There is no way you can say "this screw, no big deal, it can stay the way it is." It must be 100% functional, so that the person using it will not be in danger. That is why I looked for ways [to make it work] and I wanted to know what we would do, but the thought was always that it was a machine like any other machine. The fact that the use of this machine results in the death of people is another matter, that has nothing to do with the machine itself. Even with a regular machine, if a person falls into it and dies, it isn't the machine's fault, do you understand?

In the Palmach—When Our Paths Crossed

When I was in the Palmach, my dad knew almost nothing about me, until we started dealing with weapons, a field in which our lives were connected. This is how he wrote about it:

Amos would show up, shower, change his clothes, and leave. Yitzhak Rabin would come to headquarters and yell: "Amos." He would come, he had a tiny Austin 7 car, and short pants. They sat in Neve Ilan, sat on the way to Bayit Vegan. The guys from Harel would come. Once, he brought this guy who later died, and developed a sophisticated gurney for injured soldiers. Some guy named Shimon who dealt with bomb disposal. Then Amos would come asking for detonators, and we had a detonator factory. They were good detonators, number 8, so we would give him detonators, to Amos. I made a delay safety fuse and a blasting cord, I made flare mines and detonators, and all sorts of stuff.

Amos once came to Jerusalem and said to me: "Dad, you want to make this Davidka?" Then he said to me: "We have a Davidka in Neve Ilan, and if you send someone with me, they could sketch and check, so that you have the design plans for the Davidka."

Okay, so I sent a Jew, an engineer named Mishkowski, he was an engineer for the "Cheirut" company, the plumbers. He went with Amos in a jeep. At that time, we took one cannon out to the yard of Alliance Israélite Universelle, where blacksmiths worked, and they cut, and I got three barrels . . . We made the back lid and the mechanism and we drilled the hole for 91 mm. We did all the carving and etching at Takhush's welding workshop on Agripas Street. There was a good lathe there and we made the mechanism . . . We made five cannons, a Davidka . . . In two of them, the shell exploded inside the Davidka and killed both mortarmen at the university and Bnei Brit . . . After this happened, I changed the barrel and we found out what was in there. Turned out that the rim inside the shell wasn't right, and then we learned something even more important, that the Davidka shell is dangerous when filled with TNT gunpowder. It would light up and explode from just about anything. The Davidka shells we made after we learned what the reason for the explosion was, didn't explode prematurely any more. On the last attempt at conquering the old city, we fired over 700 shells at the old city and they all exploded just fine.

Knowing his own abilities and connections led my dad to continue serving even after the military force was properly established and the IDF was formed. When he dealt with purchasing abroad, he no longer needed to sell half of his lot. In 1948–49, he served as an emissary to the Skoda factories in Czechoslovakia to purchase Czech weapons. I have a Ruger 10/22 gun that my dad got as a present from Skoda. When we received this weapon, it was like a breath of fresh air during Operation Nahshon, which was a significant turning point of the War of Independence. What I especially remember from that operation, after so many years, is that Czech weapon. I don't know if I can convey the feeling with words—what it means to take a new gun out of a box, properly packed, properly browned, not worn out, not in parts, and not something that hadn't been used for ten years! New! Until that operation, what did we have? Not every soldier had a gun. The quantity meant that each soldier could have a gun—this was extremely important. Suddenly, we felt like things were coming together, that maybe a battalion would actually be a battalion, and a company would actually be a company, and we would have auxiliary weapons; you could fire, you could provide assistance.

My dad designed scuba-diving systems for the Navy when it was just forming and had only a naval sabotage division. Air bubbles that give away your location come out of the scuba-diving system. He developed a bubble catcher. The model he built is on display at the entrance to the Naval Museum in Haifa.

A Technologist in Civil Service

Dad dealt with the development of scientific equipment. He designed and built scientific devices that you couldn't buy here and were hard to import from abroad. He made excellent things in the medical field and other fields. That was dad, a real genius. With his exceptional skills, he solved difficult problems for the professors. A chemist, Professor Gideon Czapski, the future rector of the Hebrew University, said to me: "I owe my doctorate to your dad, because during the experiments I needed a specific catalyzer that was impossible to get. Your dad made it for me."

Two entrepreneurs founded the Teva company in Bayit Vegan in Jerusalem. My dad designed and built the required machines for them to manufacture medicine. I have certificates from the Teva company from back then. I remember that when I was a teenager they manufactured a medicine for skin treatment, a drug made from pure asphalt. Every once in a while, at the Dead Sea, a chunk of pure asphalt would rise to the surface—I'm assuming someone would notify them—and they collected it and made the medicine out of it. I used it to take care of my dog, a boxer, who suffered from skin diseases. I really loved boxers.

In His Memory

People very quickly liked my dad. He knew how to laugh, to make people happy. I went with him to the Machaneh Yehudah Market, and everyone there knew him. Elek, they called him. In 1977, when my dad was seventy-six years old, together with Yitzhak Chernyavsky, a Technion graduate, we established the Elek Sochaczewer Foundation for scholarships for Jerusalem students to study at the Technion. The foundation is active until today. In 2017, we gave out the scholarships for the fortieth consecutive year. We've given out about nineteen hundred scholarships. Over 60% of the people who benefited from the scholarships returned to Jerusalem—about one thousand engineers.

At the first scholarship awarding ceremony, my dad sketched out the essence of who he is in precise and calculated words, and among other things, he said:

> . . . *Looking back, I think natural inclination and youthful curiosity are what pushed me from the day I started to be aware, to check what something was made of, what makes it work, how can you use one thing or another, and even how can I improve and make it function more efficiently . . . I was never encouraged to do any of this, nor was I guided professionally or otherwise by my family or anyone else . . . the deep-rooted antisemitism I encountered when working with non-Jewish tradesmen and even among teachers at school who expressed their strong opinions about the parasitic Jews who can't and don't want to work in anything creative were also a strong motive for my decision—to show them that I am a Jew who can do everything well, at least as well as they could. And so, the ideas of national revival and the rehabilitation of creative Jewish*

work were combined in my mind, and in order to bring them to fruition, I made Aliya . . . I can testify about myself that I tried and searched for ways to make a childhood dream a reality—in the Gdud HaAvoda, in the Haganah, in the IDF, and in the research institutions of the Yishuv and the state. And what is the conclusion? This is not the place to judge whether or not the state that was established 20 years ago is the complete realization of the dream of national revival, or only a partial realization of it . . . but what happened to my dream of Jewish professionals, who create in their own country for self-utilization and export, products that we would be proud to mark with the symbol of "Made in Israel"?

Yigal Allon—the Man and the Loss

Yigal Allon—commander of the southern front

Washington, April 1ˢᵗ, 1956
. . . This morning, at 7 a.m., the telephone in my room in New
York rang. Imagine my aggravation at being bothered at such an
early hour, especially after I had stayed up until after midnight, but
please, try to imagine my joy at hearing the sound of Amos's voice
on the other side of the line . . . About an hour went by and we were
already sitting at breakfast in my hotel room . . .

That's what Yigal wrote to Ruth, his wife. That was the quality of our relationship, from the time he was my commander at the southern front until the day his heart stopped beating.

One day, before Operation Horev, Yigal called me, erased the name "Sochaczewer " and wrote "Horev" under it. I went to consult with Shoshana, my wife: "What do I do?" She responded, "Sochaczewer, in Russian, means dry, and Horev is also dry." So, we adopted the name. Today, there is only one man left who still calls me Sochaczewer, and not Amos, and that is Zvi Zamir. I feel that name deep in my soul, in which both names exist in harmony—Sochaczewer and Horev.

I chose to dedicate some space in my book to Yigal Allon because to me he was a friend and a mentor like none other. And maybe because he didn't get the place he deserved in the early history after the establishment of the State of Israel, when he became a part of the political system.

Yigal represented us all. You said "Yigal" and you said "Palmach." None of us was a fool. It wasn't a rabbi-and-blind-followers situation. In his personality, Yigal embodied everything we saw as representing the best of all of us. His personality was an interesting and beautiful combination of ethical and moral, a true friend with genuine sensitivity for the people he was in charge of. On the other hand, he was a leader and a commander. A man who knew how to direct and make decisions at the right moment.

I remember Yigal's way of behaving, putting a hand on your shoulder, which helped you accept from a place of understanding that something needs to be done a certain way. I remember very few incidents in which Yigal raised his voice. That being said, he could be tough as steel when necessary. He wasn't just a commander, he also had military wisdom. His senses were good and healthy, and he had exceptional intuition, which was based on a deep understanding.

I was a platoon commander in Tel Amal when my dad needed my immediate assistance at the factory where he was working on weapons systems for the Haganah. I asked to meet with Yigal, and we met in Haifa. Yigal listened, he didn't make me feel like I was under investigation, and he approved my request to leave. His interest in personal matters—not in gossip but in people as people—was what made him unique.

I remember driving to Jerusalem in his car. I was driving, and he was sleeping peacefully. I was almost proud, because he once said to me, "If I don't trust the driver, I can't fall asleep." That was the relationship between us, a relationship of trust that was very important to me—and to all of us. That was the man, Yigal as a friend, and acquaintance, the man who makes the right decision at the right time.

And so it was on the southern front in the way in which he conducted meetings between the members of the different staffs who were so completely different from one another. People were free to argue, without concern, that was his strength. The decision taken allowed all of us to accept it wholeheartedly. It wasn't a compromise, not an arbitrary decision, and not a decision taken because everyone was burnt out and exhausted, but rather a decision made in its time, and we understood the reasoning behind it. Yigal Allon was a man who always looked ahead, saw things as they were developing and forming. He was interested in actions and their future implications.

The Dismissal

In September 1949, Yigal went to England for reasons pertaining to his daughter Nurit's health. Rabin took his place for a short period of time at the southern front. Later, Yigal conducted a military tour in England and France, and visited the French army, which was stationed in Algeria. While there, in October, Ben-Gurion dismissed him from command of the southern front, and appointed Moshe Dayan in his place. Ruth, his wife, and my Shoshanah sent him a letter, and that's how he found out about the dismissal. It was a political dismissal. The main argument between them was about the borders at the end of the war. Allon claimed that you can't end a war with the borders we had at the time. When he came back, he left the army. He was only thirty-one when he was dismissed.

Yigal represented us all, and the Palmach did not take the dismissal well. Ben-Gurion understood more than anyone else how special Yigal's position was—not only as a commander but as the representative of a movement—and he was concerned.

In her book *Yigal Allon—Native Son*, Anita Shapira mentions that Allon found out about Dayan's appointment as commander of the southern front from the French officers who were hosting him. "There was a general shock." Rabin pushed him to return immediately and join the protests, but Allon refused to cut his official visit short. He also wrote to Rabin, "I will not fight despicable people," and avoided taking any action against his dismissal.

Rabin personally expressed his objections to Ben-Gurion, who pressured him not to partake in the protests that were about to take place. Rabin participated anyway. The price of his participation was an extremely long deferral of his appointment as chief of staff.

On October 14, 1948, Yitzhak Rabin, Haim Bar Lev, David Elazar, Zvi Zamir, and many others participated in a protest march in the streets of Tel Aviv against the dismantling of the Palmach, the dismissal of Yigal Allon, and—no less important—against the way in which he was dismissed. Despite Ben-Gurion's clear instructions to military personnel not to partake in the event, six thousand members of the Palmach and their families were there. I myself was busy with my position at the southern front and could not participate.

The commanders of the three Palmach brigades—"Yosef'le" Tabenkin from Harel, Shmuel Mula Cohen from Yiftach, and Nahum Sarig from Hanegev—were all dismissed. Other officers, among them battalion commanders such as Zvi Zamir and Yeshayahu Gavish, were tried, reproached, and their behavior was noted in their personal record. Many others left the IDF.

A Civilian—Not an ordinary citizen

When Yigal Allon became a politician, he united the labor movement. His relationship with the government in general, and with Ben-Gurion specifically, was very good.

His first political biography, *Yigal Allon—Native Son, A Biography* was written by Anita Shapira 14.7.2004). Zerubbabel Arbel and I corresponded with her. We disagreed with some of the things she wrote. At a convention in Eilat, Shapira said, "Amos Horev also said that when Yigal returned from his studies in England, he had lost his 'native-Israeliness.'" What I really said was that Yigal lost his natural fighting spirit and became more calculated. He didn't become a proper politician, but he did lose his military commander's charisma as the leader of the Palmach. When he was with us, he was a lot more combative. In politics, opposite Dayan, he was too gentle. That was my feeling, that he lost something.

But to the extent that leaders can see into the future, Yigal was unmatched, not even by Ben-Gurion. Ben-Gurion was a courageous leader: it requires a lot of courage to establish a state. But he didn't understand what we understood, that at the end of the War of Independence we were facing a historic opportunity that would not present itself again. During the Six-Day War, before the IDF conquered the West Bank, I met with Yigal at his apartment in Tel Aviv. He presented the outline of a feasible, long-term political plan that was later called "The Allon Plan." Its two main points were an eastern security border in the Jordan Valley and separation between us and the population of the West Bank. Even back then, Allon could identify the potential problems that would result from the conquest of lands. Yigal permitted Levinger and Rabbi Goren to hold their Pesach Seder in Hebron in 1968, and that was the beginning of the first settlement, but he was not the "father of the settlements." The initiative to build them was not his and they were not part of his territorial approach.

Yigal Allon and me—what a friendship!

My good relationship with Yigal continued and grew even stronger after the war. It was no longer a commander-soldier relationship, but a more open, smarter one, and through it I got to know Yigal in his home as well, with his family and his problems.

Politics

I didn't go with Yigal on his political journey. I watched from the side, and there were things I didn't like. Yitzhak Rabin was appointed prime minister for the first time, and Yigal was the minister of foreign affairs and not the minister of defense. We thought that Yitzhak was not doing the right thing by Yigal. This manifested in the way he would express himself regarding Yigal's suggestions, in his body language, which, from the side, appeared to be disrespectful. It pained us. We, all the friends, talked to Yitzhak about it, but it didn't help.

Yigal didn't talk to me about entering the world of politics, but he was the only one with whom I would have gone. I supported him

very much in his race to be head of his party. We had a house party
for him here in the garden. To prove to him that he had supporters
from outside the Palmach, not a single member of the Palmach was
invited. More than one hundred people showed up; Shoshana had
invited them. Yigal was surprised by the number of people. Later,
there was an article in Maariv written by Yosef Hariph, saying that I
was the one intent on being minister of commerce and industry in
his government. Yigal never spoke to me about it, but I suppose it
was a practical possibility. And then, to our dismay and pain, he died
suddenly of cardiac arrest.

To This Day

Until today when I think about Yigal in our current situation. I feel
that this man who left us could have influenced our country in the
political, security and social fields as well. A man who could have
been the leader of the Labor Party, he would have brought historical
changes in the fields of peace, war, society and education. I think of
Yigal in today's situation, he had very sharp senses, a sound man,
never shot from the hip, never said populist things, a different man,
an intelligent man. I miss him, we miss him.

At the Palmach headquarters in Gedera, we would train and run
through the vineyards. Speaking of running, he would always tell
me his life motto, "Amos, I will do everything, but I will not make
a fool of myself." If he had been given the chance, he would have
contributed a lot to the state. He has receipts to prove it.

Thank You

To the person who interviewed me, heard my life story and organized it as a basis for the book, and asked not to have his name mentioned. I am sorry for that, but I will respect his request, and I wish to thank him.

To Dror Shapiro, Dana Avidar, and my Yehiam, who read and commented on the manuscript They were a great help to me.